# JIMMY HOGAN

## The Greatest Football Coach Ever?

Ashley Hyne

electric blue publishing
2019

# Jimmy Hogan

First published 2019.

Electric Blue Publishing
Stowmarket
Suffolk, IP14 5AE

www.electric-blue.co.uk

Copyright © Ashley Hyne, 2019

The right of Ashley Hyne to be identified as the Author of the work has been asserted in accordance with the Copyrights, Designs and Patents Act 1988.

ISBN 978-0-995539-650 (paperback)

All rights reserved. No part of this book may be reprinted or reproduced or utilised in any form or by any electronic, mechanical or other means, now known or hereafter invented, including photocopying and recording, or in any information storage or retrieval system, without the permission in writing from the Publishers.

# Contents

# Contents

| | |
|---|---|
| Chapter One: 1882-1903 | 1 |
| Chapter Two: 1903-1905 | 13 |
| Chapter Three: 1905-1908 | 25 |
| Chapter Four: 1908-1913 | 37 |
| Chapter Five: 1912 | 47 |
| Chapter Six: 1914-1916 | 59 |
| Chapter Seven: 1916-1919 | 67 |
| Chapter Eight: 1919-1925 | 81 |
| Chapter Nine: 1925-26 | 99 |
| Chapter Ten: 1926-1932 | 107 |
| Chapter Eleven: 1932-1933 | 127 |
| Chapter Twelve: 1933-1934 | 139 |
| Chapter Thirteen: 1934-1935 | 147 |
| Chapter Fourteen: 1935-1936 | 157 |
| Chapter Fifteen: 1936-1939 | 165 |
| Chapter Sixteen: 1939-1945 | 183 |
| Chapter Seventeen: 1947-1948 | 189 |
| Chapter Eighteen: 1948-1950 | 195 |
| Chapter Nineteen: 1951-52 | 203 |
| Chapter Twenty: 1952-1959 | 211 |
| Chapter Twenty-one: 1960-1974 | 229 |
| Appendix | 235 |
| Bibliography | 243 |
| Index | 245 |

Jimmy Hogan

*'For Trudy and the Circle of Priority'*

Jimmy Hogan

# Acknowledgements

I wish to thank the following for their help and guidance in the production of this book. Without them this book would simply have not been possible. Firstly, to Susan Gardiner for her vision and knowledge in ensuring that this publication comes to print.

Mark Chapman, Tamas Karpati, Arie P Heijstek, Georg Gangusch, Karen Poolton, Prof. Matthew Taylor, John Lerwill, Suzanne Wheeler, Markwart Herzog, Miklos Nemeth, Roger Hull, Paul Keogh, Shirley Ashton, David Bohl, Dr. Gregory Quin, Frank Rafters, Derek Gillard, Stephanie Haeupl, Anette Fuhrmeister, Balasz Haraszti, Dr. Andreas Hafer, Dr. Wolfgang Hafer, Joanne Hetherington, Dr Denes Tamas, Christophe Chaillet, Rogan Taylor, Travis Timmons, Elisa Kuster, Garreth Cummins, Harald Igel, Erik Garin, Dan Jewell, Mat Kendrick, Bernd Mayer, Henry Wahlig, Rob Staton, David Thompson, Andrew Dabrowski, Chris Daggett, Jerome Berthold, Gunnar Persson, John Whittaker, Ray Simpson, Andy Elliott, Lawrence Gregory, Norman Fox, Keith Baker, Jane Standing, David Conn, Rory Smith, Gerard van der Houten, Veronica Simpson, Jim Hannah, David Taylor, Henrik Hegedus, Peter Szegedi, Simon Marland, Maura McColgan, Mama Sykora, Charles Beuret, Sandra Gill, Dorothy Blackett, Catherine Arnaud, Claudia Schmidtt, Brian Glanville, Keir Radnedge, Christophe Schottes, Prof. Jurgen Hermann, Dr Liam & Fenella Gavin, Andy Bayes, Phil Cunliffe, James Fanning and Paul Caine.

The cover photograph was reproduced with the kind permission of Aston Villa Football Club which owns all rights to this image.

Jimmy Hogan

# Foreword

## Foreword

Jimmy Hogan was one of those British guys who helped to implement football on the continent, maybe even one of the most important. He might have been a little bit of an adventurer on a Grand Tour which led him to Holland, Austria, Hungary, Germany, Switzerland and France although he was definitely also a serious representative and instructor of British football, and in the end he even became something of a myth in England.

No doubt, it's worth writing a biography on such a person. Thus Ashley Hyne is not the first person to have written about him. But Hyne's brilliant book, describing Hogan's life in the context of the essential development of football particularly in the first half of the twentieth century, is more than only a critical biography on Jimmy Hogan and British football, it is first of all a book on the nature of football itself, on its becoming a global game and about the development of a global discourse about how to play it best. From a continental perpective this aspect of globalisation is of special interest. It was not only a matter of football but of British sports altogether, as tennis, rugby, athletics or hockey which became a part of the living culture of the liberal, continental middle and upper classes at the beginning of the twentieth century. More than that, British sports became for a lot of them an emblem of social modernisation, of political and economic progress, setting new standards of lifestyle.

Only after the Great War football became a working class sport on the continent too. Around 1900, many young liberal Jews saw in this British style of life a kind of a model for their own emancipation. One of them was Hugo Meisl, who in the 1920s and 1930s became one of the most important football managers on the European continent then trying to develop football there to a professional mass entertainment modelled after the British. Like so many Viennese Jews, he was born in Bohemia and immigrated to Vienna at the end of the nineteenth century. He was only one year older than Jimmy Hogan, to whom he was a friend since 1912 and with whose career he stayed tied up in many aspects until his death in 1937. For a grandson of Hugo Meisl like me, this book is highly interesting, telling a lot about the relations between these two men. But, in the first place, for me as historian, Ashley Hyne's biography on Jimmy Hogan is of outstanding importance and interest since by embedding the

# Jimmy Hogan

biography of Jimmy Hogan within European football relations he tells us a lot on the development of the modern Europe too. This has to do with the "European life" of Jimmy Hogan but as well with the outstanding role football played (and is playing) within European culture.

Why was football able to play such a role? Jimmy Hogan had a very simple answer to this: "The attraction of football which is spread all over the world, is a clear proof of its popularity," he stated and from this he concluded: "There is no game or sport comparable to football."

I wish the book by Ashley Hyne a great spreading, not only in Great Britain but in whole Europe.

Andreas Hafer, 2019

# Introduction

## Introduction

"A good footballer should not only be able to kick with his right and left foot, but he must also be able to kick the ball with the inside and outside of the foot. Many players can only kick the ball with the inside of the foot; therefore the game becomes unnecessarily difficult."
Jimmy Hogan, 1929.

A few months ago a friend of mine was talking about "old-time football" and whilst talking about his dad, the great Chester and Wrexham forward Mick Metcalf, said "You know, it's like the old Hungarians. They were the first team to play proper football." That statement fascinated me because it was both true and not quite true at one and the same time. Hungary in the 1950s, the Magical Magyars as they were called, were a talented group of footballers who played a brand of football that was good enough to change British perceptions of the foreign threat to our football heritage. But that brand of football, though developed in Hungary, had its roots in football as it was played in Great Britain before the First World War and this is the story of how that brand of football was communicated to Europe and how it was returned to Britain with devastating consequences.

Jimmy Hogan was not the first football coach. He wasn't even the best football coach. But he is an important football coach in history and so deserving of study. The reason he is so important is because he did more than most to promote the *importance* of coaching throughout Europe. To do this he relied on the favourable cultural climate within which he worked. This is as much to say that Hogan's practice sessions, when he went to teach in Europe between 1910 and 1936, might not have been followed at all if the players he taught were not enthusiastic enough to follow what he was teaching. Of course not everyone followed suit, famously Puskás could not kick with his right foot, but, in the main, that willingness to be taught how to play the game distinguished the Europeans from their British counterparts. Hogan always felt that the British were "natural" footballers, demonstrating an enthusiasm for the game that had to be instilled and taught to those born overseas.

But in Britain, Hogan had to battle against a national reluctance to be taught and told. It would be obtuse to say that that reluctance is *the* reason for the indefinite angst the British endure as a result of their sporting failures, but it is certainly one of them. It was something George Raynor, who *was* the best football coach, once captured perfectly: "Young British footballers learn by example, not by tuition." Like Raynor after him, Hogan had to endure the difficulties that came about in seeking to convert the British to his way of thinking. He was more intuitive as to best ways to achieve this developing a brilliant rapport with the print media to raise his profile and elevate discussion regarding the promotion of coaching nationally.

Of the people Hogan worked with in Europe perhaps the most important was Hugo Meisl, who is seen as the leading figure in the development of Central European football. Together Hogan and Meisl, literally overnight, set out one of the very first coaching programmes for a cohort of players in Vienna in 1912. This programme saw virtue in regular exercises that ensured that players could master the basic skills required to play the game and to control the football with both feet, and other parts of the body. Before 1912 coaching did exist throughout the continent, in Prague, in Budapest, even in Stoneyhurst College up in Clitheroe, Lancashire, but a programme of coaching had not been formulated anywhere until that time. So both Meisl and Hogan, driven on by the despondency of Hogan's early pupils, set about creating a scheme of activities in which Hogan would demonstrate and the pupils would imitate. Their programme required a real, almost religious commitment on the part of Hogan's pupils to adopt the skills a competent footballer requires to play the game correctly. And religion, ironically, was no doubt at the heart of their mindset; Hogan and Meisl representatives of the two great religious movements, Catholicism and Judaism, that drove the development of football in Europe before the advent of professionalism swept across the continent and developed matters further.

And matters were developed further. After 1925, when the offside law was altered, the tactical development of the game grew exponentially. But the game remained the same. It does not matter whether the team is playing in a 2-3-5 formation, a WM-formation, a diamond formation, without wingers or with a deep-lying centre-forward one thing is definite. If you want your team to be good; if you want your defenders to head the ball harmlessly away from a busy penalty area, or for a midfielder to precisely release an inside forward onto a swift counter attack or for a forward to snatch a last minute winner then all the players need to be proficient in executing the basic skills required by any footballer. And that is why Hogan is so important. It was his input in putting together the basic

# Introduction

building blocks that enabled those technical architects to devise a game that reached the heights it did when Hungary "were the first team to play proper football."

Ashley Hyne, 2019.

KEY TO FOOTBALL GRAPHICS USED IN THE BOOK

——————— Pass
------------- Run
- — - — - - Dribble

# Jimmy Hogan

## ONE

## 1882-1903
'I had the time of my life at St Bede's...'

One of birthplaces of modern European football sits on the banks of the gillaroo-teeming River Moy in County Mayo, in the Republic of Ireland. In the nineteenth century, the residents of Ballina (pronounced Ba-ly-NAR), which even now boasts a population of only 10,000 people, were faced with three options. They could either live there forever, make their way up the estuary to one of the steamers heading out on "the northern route" across the Atlantic, or head out across Ireland for work in Belfast, Dublin or across the Irish Sea to England's industrial north. Margaret O'Donall's family took the latter of those routes, arriving in Bradford while she was a teenage girl in the 1870s.[1]

The O'Donall's impressed upon their daughter the importance of devoting her life to the Roman Catholic faith and it was of no surprise that that should have a profound effect on her first born son, Jimmy. Indeed if there is one thing that can be said about a career which lasted the best part of fifty years, it was that Jimmy Hogan demonstrated his mother's tenacity and her unwavering commitment in equal measure. From his father, James, Jimmy inherited an aspirational attitude, and also a love of sports, particularly football and even through that interest in football had gnawed away at Jimmy from a young age, it was his mother's desire that Jimmy should join the Holy Order and become a priest that predominated all other concerns in the Hogan household for a time. Therefore we can say with some certainty that when Hogan, at the tender age of seventeen, took the bold decision to explain to his mother that he was rejecting her wish and ideals to become a footballer that that would come to represent *the* key moment in Hogan's life, the implications being felt in European football, and perhaps, even in British society to this very day.

Hogan[2] was born on 8 October 1882 at 66 Victoria Street, Nelson in Lancashire. Victoria Street is a wide avenue of terraced homes which gives some clue as to the economic situation the family found themselves in: wider streets normally infer better financial straits so it was not the wrong end of town and the family were not the wrong type of people. Jimmy's father had only recently brought his family from across the Pennines to work in the cotton trade as a dryer. The Hogans at that time already

# Jimmy Hogan

comprised Jimmy's two eldest sisters, and Ellen and Sarah, like their father, soon found themselves working "in't mill" as weavers. In this regard Jimmy was fortunate in being born when he was because the new system of public education ensured that he was saved from a similar fate.

By providing for penalties against those seeking to employ children, the 1880 Elementary Education Act ensured that young Jimmy would have to stay in school until the age of thirteen[3] and this presented him with opportunities that were not afforded to his sisters. In October 1887 Hogan attended St Joseph's RC School[4] in McLeod Street, Nelson for the first time. Teaching in those days was, by and large, by rote. Children learnt by repetitive exercises, chanting "one and one is two", a methodology which was still effective and still being used in state primary schools a century later. The 1882 Mundella Code had served to increase the range of subjects taught and introduced scientific instruments to supplement a curriculum based on the three Rs. A good explanation as to the type of lessons Hogan would have encountered as a child is set out as follows:

The curriculum of 1871 (reading, writing, arithmetic and, for girls, needlework) had, by 1896, expanded greatly: the three Rs, needlework for girls, drawing (for older boys), object lessons or one class subject. In addition schools could provide (with certain restrictions) such class subjects as singing, recitation (the reading, memorisation and speaking of poetry), drawing, English, geography, science, history and domestic economy. ... Specific subjects (again within limits) included mechanics, chemistry, physics, animal physiology, agriculture, navigation, languages and shorthand. Girls could also be taught cookery, laundry and dairy work, and boys could be taught gardening. Explicit provision was also made for manual instruction, physical exercise (including swimming and gymnastics), and visits to institutions of educational value. There was much emphasis on the "object lesson", sometimes involving simple demonstrations in science, sometimes using concrete examples to convey abstractions (especially in number work), and sometimes "as a process of discrimination among colours, forms and so on." Science became more widely taught, often by peripatetic teachers.[5]

The teacher taught and the children, like parishioners at a sermon, listened and, hopefully, learned, their interest and capacity to learn founded on a simple fear of the teacher's cane. This is important for our understanding because when it came to his first stab at coaching, Hogan would have imitated what his teachers would have done which is to have demonstrated and hopefully imbued an understanding from showing rather than getting his students to "do".

After the age of thirteen, children would then have been expected to have started work and contribute to the family's income. If a child did not follow this route, there would have had to have been significant reasons as to why that was the case, because a child staying in education after that age would have meant the family foregoing income, something the vast majority of families were wont to do, especially in the case of a first-born boy whose potential income in the labour market was higher than that for girls.

By the time of the 1891 census[6] the Hogan family, which now lived at 38 Victoria Street, comprised father James, mother Margaret, daughters Ellen, Sarah and Jimmy's younger siblings Joseph, Annie and Mary Agnes, grandfather Michael and a boarder, Mary Cullin.[7] Four incomes would have kept the wolf at a reasonable distance from the door so it would be wrong to say that the family struggled inordinately during Jimmy's childhood and that led to Jimmy living and enjoying a rather carefree existence, playing in the streets and the financial situation that family found themselves in also saved him from working from a young age. After the 1891 census would come Kathleen and twins Gabriel and Josephine.[8]

Sometime after April 1891, the family moved once again, this time to 218 Padiham Road in Burnley which came about, possibly, because Hogan's father had the chance to get a better job in that larger town. As a result of the move, Hogan now attended St Mary Magdalene School, on Gannow Top in Haslam Street, half mile or so away from his home.[9] 218 Padiham Road has long since been demolished but the road in part still exists and its location is of interest to us here because it is barely two miles tramp to Turf Moor, the home of Burnley Football Club, one of the Football League's founding clubs. It would have meant a big deal for that small Lancastrian town to have had representation at the highest level within what was fast becoming the national sport and the impact of this would not have been lost on young Jimmy Hogan. Young children, like Jimmy Hogan, living in those industrial towns were becoming indoctrinated into football quite readily because it was a sport that was already played within the school system and one that received considerable publicity in the printed press. This partly explains the speed with which it overtook all other pursuits and also explains how knowledge of the game and the uptake of skills became inured inside of a generation.[10] As a result, while playing locally with his friends, Hogan became fixated by football at a fairly young age kicking "empty salmon tins, paper balls, rag balls, Aunt Sallie balls, pigs' bladders (inflated) …"[11]

Hogan did well at school by developing a handy knack in being able to pass his exams, as a result he stayed on at St Mary's after his thirteenth birthday, assuming a role as a class monitor, helping the younger pupils learn, but just before he turned fourteen, the family decided to send Jimmy to St Bede's College in Manchester as a boarder.[12] This decision gives us clues about the family's attitude to education and to their value system. The Hogans were quite willing to defer any benefit to better their children where possible and Jimmy's younger sister, Kathleen, would benefit from this approach going on to become a highly-respected teacher at St Mary's.

St Bede's College was founded to ensure a pipeline of young clergy by transitioning the Catholic youth of Manchester away from Protestant philanthropic societies, the workhouses and factories and into the Church.[13] The founder of the College, Cardinal Herbert Vaughan, set about securing a future for the Catholic Church in Manchester by funding a census of all Catholic boys within a radius of Manchester and that led to the development of a fund that saw the construction of St Bede's in 1876.

Hogan later stated that he was "extremely lucky" that his parents pushed him toward St Bede's and he believed this for a number of reasons. Firstly, it was there that he developed his own identity and there that he experienced the first sense of separation from his family and community. Therefore that journey from Burnley to Manchester was crucial in his development because it made all future journeys possible. To begin with his religious education, evidenced by him acting as an acolyte during the opening Mass for the new College chapel in 1898, was uppermost. However, other curricular interests soon caught his imagination and his primary focus saw him seek to distinguish himself from amongst his contemporaries. He joined the debating society; he became a member of the elocution club[14] but, against that, he was finding higher level academics hard, achieving only a Second Division pass in the Preliminary Oxford Local Examinations in July 1898.

Secondly, sport became a handy diversion for him and it did not take long before he realised that he could make his mark on the sports fields of the College where he was first introduced to organised games: " ... I had the time of my life at St Bede's," he wrote, "especially on those wonderful playing pitches at Whalley Range." He came second at the College sports day which required him to throw a cricket ball as far as he could, do the long jump, and then race 400 yards but these individual events ultimately held little pull for him. Cardinal Vaughan's objective to gather the young from the North West, from Manchester, Bolton, Blackburn, Preston, Liverpool[15] meant that Hogan's schoolmates represented a generation of young boys who were able to read and understand the football press and were keen to know all about the new professional class of footballers playing for the big football teams like John Cameron at Everton, Charlie Athersmith at Aston Villa, Ned Doig at Sunderland, Steve Bloomer at

Derby, and the famous Welshman, Billy Meredith of Manchester City.

The young lads at St Bede's were religious converts, but for some their religion was the ball and their chapter and verse became the gossip columns from an expanding sporting press, the *Athletic News* and the widely read provincial newspapers. Footballers apparently had an idyllic life, they were mentioned every week in the broadsheets and known across the country; their fame spread beyond England; even dignitaries from overseas now attended the Cup Final.[16] The swirl of this fame and fortune would not have been lost on Hogan. Hogan's classmates had a life mapped out in front of them but a life of adherence to the Church, sequestered away from the bluster, noise and excitement generated by the clamour of football did not attract Hogan. While some young minds were directed toward their studies, focused firmly on the quiet passion of a life of dedication, Hogan's mind led him down a path in which he started recklessly believing in a career in which he could ape his heroes; in which he too could play for the "big clubs" and for his family, his small town to see his name in the papers. All of a sudden he was playing football on a bed of soft grass with real boots, real footballs and encountering players of a standard decent enough to consign him to the second XI.[17] Hogan suddenly became focused not on his religious studies but on getting into the first XI. That was where the acclaim and the interest of his school pals lay and, as a result, he was becoming more and more fixated on the game and less and less on his education. He wrote, later: ".... even at [St Bede's], I always had the feeling that one fine day I would become a professional player with the big clubs. I studied very little; I lived football; I talked football; I just breathed football."[18]

Finally, the impact of another aspect of his stay at St Bede's cannot be underestimated. Prior to going to St Bede's he had been under the strict domination of his parents and now, with this first taste of independence, he was impetuously making decisions for himself for the school served as a place where his individuality was cast. His enthusiasm on the football field had taken him to the captaincy of the first XI and when he was on leave from school all those tales of him and his friends running about on muddy fields and chasing the devil's hindmost must have come as something of a shock in the Hogan household. On those term-break visits to Burnley he would have entered into discussion with his family and listened as his mother's position on the matter of his education was made clear but from his point of view her wish to see him dog-collared to the Church was heading right out the window. She may have been dismayed by the way he was organising his priorities but that would hardly have compared to the fall out when Hogan took the decision, sometime around the summer of

# Jimmy Hogan

1899, to leave St Bede's.[19] St Bede's is important because his decision not to pursue his studies brought him into direct conflict with his mother and was the real trigger for his future career in football. When he left the school at the end of the summer term in 1899, he wrote that his parents did not talk to him for two weeks. His mother's sense of deep public shame and anger borne of the despair in knowing that her high aspirations for her son to become a priest were already at an end, would have been difficult to hide. As a result of this Hogan precociously resolved that he had no option but to fully commit to a career in professional football. It was that single dispute that drove him on to a career in football and to achieve what he ultimately achieved.

The tone of the conversations after he returned home having vacated college life in order to find a lowly paid job with a local accountancy firm in Burnley would have been pointed because a career as an office actuary would in her eyes have been but nothing compared to the kudos of a life devoted to the close pursuit of God, yet his mind, turned by the games on those fields at the College, had now become resolved. He sought freedom from a position where plans would be mapped out for him but freedom is a moveable concept and, whereas the office desk gave him more control than being indentured to the factory floor, his sense of liberation drew him toward Saturday rather than the working week, for Saturday was still a work day for some but for him it was a football day. His mother's bitterness because he had forsaken the cloth would hardly have been assuaged by young Jimmy committing himself to the local church side: St Mary's, a church that used to sit on Yorkshire Street in Burnley,[20] but it was as a footballer rather than a parishioner that his involvement mainly rested.

Very soon Hogan found that work was getting in the way of his football not the other way around. Saturday was not a rest day from work, so Hogan was constantly arranging leave just in order to go off and play for *gratis* for the church side. Just how long Hogan stuck with this arrangement of playing for St Mary's is not known but it is possible that it lasted for a season and a half. Hogan's quality, at that low level, understandably shone through. He was of a standard which was better than those he was playing with and against and consequently, Hogan states that he was "quickly spotted"[21] by one of the more prominent amateur sides in the area: Burnley Belvedere.[22] However, this is open to conjecture because Jimmy Hogan only appears to have come to prominence as a Belvedere player after turning nineteen in October 1902.[23]

Perhaps out of deference to his family, Hogan seemed to stick with the accountancy job for longer than he wanted. This was obviously not a lucrative period in his life and there must have been some relief when

Belvedere came along and introduced him to senior local football and it is ironic, given that Belvedere were an amateur club, that Hogan should receive his first pay packet in football from them because the wealthier players and directors subsidised him travel and "team money". This meant that he could keep his weekly shilling savings and from that moment on his engagement with the game would only ever be on a commercial footing. Hogan later argued that he was playing at a high standard with Belvedere: "They were members of the Lancashire Amateur League," he wrote, "[it] was a very strong combination in those days."[24] but on occasions those standards were shockingly poor. In January 1902, against Great Harwood, a call had to go out to the small crowd to secure the services of someone to keep goal.[25] However, one thing is certain and that is that Belvedere, being a club that represented an educated group of players, had the administrative resources to send match reports to the *Lancashire Evening Press* and this raised Hogan's value in the local market place. This becomes another signpost in Hogan's life, that in relation to his relationship with the press. His first attraction to football came as a result of the press and now he was, for the first time, seeing how the power of the football press could have an impact on his own livelihood. He was a young inside-right running into form while Belvedere enjoyed a fine January, winning three times, twice against Blackburn Etrurians and Great Harwood, indeed the club's form was such that there rose the argument that Belvedere should form the Burnley reserve side for the 1902-03 season.[26] The Burnley reserve side was got rid of at the end of the 1901-02 season. Belvedere would have represented an attraction given their monied members. On 31 October 1903 it was announced that they "paid their way" [when playing at Turf Moor] by "as much as £150"[27] and, as if to add weight to this suggestion, in February 1902, Hogan found himself selected for Burnley reserves against Stockport.[28] Of that game, the *Lancashire Evening Press* reported "[it was] undoubtedly the best [performance the reserve] team had given [this season]. There was a remarkable freshness in all that they did ..." Hogan "[not only showed] a good turn of speed but [displayed] a tenacity in front of goal which was quite out of common amongst the reserve players."[29]

Despite raising his profile while playing for Belvedere, the Amateur League was not as demanding as Hogan would have hoped. It was, after all, a nine-team League and even then the Police Athletic Club had difficulties fulfilling their fixtures, prevaricating before finally agreeing to fulfil their commitments. He had reached an early *impasse* and because his heart was not in the accountancy position he took the huge decision to throw his lot in with the controversial Nelson club in the autumn of 1902. Nelson had a dreadful reputation at that time, having been expelled by the Lancashire

# Jimmy Hogan

FA after their fans rioted at an FA Cup match in October 1898 and suffered further censure when their secretary lost his cool in a committee meeting at the offices of the Lancashire Football Association that winter. Notwithstanding all that, he was invited to play in a friendly match in which he impressed[30] and, following the game, nineteen-year-old Jimmy Hogan sat down to talk money with the club's directors. Hogan had not discussed any of this with his family and it says something about his self confidence that he represented himself in negotiations despite the fact that his friends did not support the move to Nelson. But this was the great fork in Jimmy Hogan's life; he felt compelled to sign a professional contract, no matter how modest it would appear in retrospect. Nelson's people offered 10s. He wanted 12s 6d and did not get it. In addition, he knew that Nelson would only agree to weekly terms, meaning that if he played poorly, the balloon would go up, he would be dropped and not be able to play or get paid, but Jimmy Hogan was fated to sign those forms because if he was to be a professional footballer he would need to find a paid position to play football; a step he needed to take if he was to graduate and he would have to graduate into the ranks of the professional football community to prove his doubting mother wrong.

When Hogan went home and informed the family the news was received in shocked disbelief. His father stopped speaking to him for a fortnight "but, it had to be," wrote Hogan, "I knew I was made for the game."[31] Thankfully, his father did not hold his grudge for long, in early October 1902, he took Jimmy along to Turf Moor to watch the match against Manchester City, starring the famous outside-right Welshman, Meredith.[32] Later, dad helped Jimmy in an unsuccessful attempt to improve his speed and fitness by constructing a static push-bike which, if true, provides evidence only that Hogan saw his dad in a supportive light. Others, though, were less forgiving: his boss at the accountants summarily dismissed him.

Hogan began his professional career playing for a club that might have been non-league but had a very commercial mind-set. Hogan got a start because three players had been dropped: "...the committee not best pleased with the form of some of the players"[33] and, given the pressure he was under, it is understandable that his early form was shaky to say the least. Against Heywood, in November, he missed a penalty and an open goal as Nelson crashed to a 2-0 defeat[34] but for all that Hogan began to star. By the spring of 1903, his right-wing pairing with Johnson led the *Lancashire Evening Post* to declare "[they are] always the best wing of the Nelson team"[35] and so Hogan served his apprenticeship in short order and, as a result, Nelson were now willing to double his wages but Hogan precociously declared to them that it wasn't enough. Rochdale Town were offering 15s and the captaincy, so Hogan went there.[36] This served merely as a hiatus however, because by the October of 1903 Jimmy Hogan was already being associated with Burnley.[37]

The money Rochdale were offering was confirmation to himself that his decision to pursue his dreams was justified, but the standard of football and the conditions within which it was played overshadowed his early joy. In early September,[38] Rochdale's new captain of the club lost the toss against Bryn Central and had to kick off "uphill". Surmounting the cliff face, Hogan scored in the first half but Bryn took full advantage of favourable conditions in the second half, ran down the hill with the ball and won 5-2. The following month, "before a small attendance," Hogan helped Rochdale beat Clitheroe Central 3-2.[39] That match had some interesting footnotes to it. Clitheroe were playing "the one back game" to ensure that Rochdale kept being found to be offside, Hogan himself had a goal chalked off for being offside in the first half. As a result of Clitheroe's dubious tactics the Rochdale faithful started to get wound up and pretty soon words were being exchanged between the supporters and a big old punch up was only averted when the referee, J. T. Howcroft of Bolton, a person we shall meet again, issued a request for calm, warning all the Rochdale supporters "in regard to their conduct".[40] The reality of this football life was not marrying up to Hogan's childish expectations. All of a sudden however, Jimmy Hogan received contact from the local professional club.[41] This was his big moment; the vindication of his stance against a life in the Church. This was when he would properly convince his doubting mother; in October 1903 he signed for Burnley.[42]

# Jimmy Hogan

## Notes

1 The spelling of her family name is in dispute given the inconsistencies in the records.
2 His registered name, for the purposes of the birth certificate on 20 November 1882 was James Hogon. Thanks to Shirley Ashton at Burnley Central Library and Jane Standing at Lancashire Central Libraries for the information regarding the family.
3 Acknowledgement to Derek Gillard.
4 Jimmy's mother was active in raising funds for the construction of St Joseph's Church.
5 http://www.educationengland.org.uk/history/chapter06.html
6 Conducted on the evening of 5 April 1891.
7 Hogan's parents, James and Margaret (b. 1854) were married in Bradford in the summer of 1876. Their daughter, Ellen, was born in Bradford, and was already a weaver by the time of the 1891 census. She married Peter Melia in Burnley in 1911. Sarah was born in Bradford in 1879, another weaver. She married Fred Guilfoyle in 1906 in Burnley. Brother Joseph, b. Colne, Lancashire 1885, Annie, b. Colne, 1888. She married Bert Melton in Burnley in 1919. Mary Agnes, b. Colne, 1890, died as an infant. Hogan's grandfather Michael, b. 1823. Mary Cullin, a laundress, b. 1854.]
8 Kathleen was born in 1892 in Burnley' she never married and died in 1983. Gabriel and Josephine (twins) were born in 1895; Gabriel died in infancy.]
9 The M65 now covers the foundations of the demolished school: a beacon of the future flattened by the march of progress.
10 Walvin, *The People's Game*, (1994), 58.
11 *Sport*, vol. 16, no. 315.
12 Information from Lawrence R Gregory, the Salford Diocesan Archivist. Hogan's admission to St Bede's was registered on 7 September 1896.
13 Information regarding St Bede's was provided by Sharon Wheeler, Development Officer at the College.
14 Lawrence Gregory research.
15 *Sport*, vol. 16, no. 316.
16 *Cup Final Extra*, 52.
17 Brian Glanville, *The Footballers' Companion* (Billing and Sons, 1962), p. 457. He also later wrote "I am a product of Burnley rec football. If you can control a ball wearing clogs you can really play the game." *Burnley: A Complete Record*, (Breedon Books Sport, 1991), p. 97.
18 *Sport*, vol. 16. He later wrote that "the only training we did at school was 'shooting-in' ". Letter to *Athletic News*, 29 April 1929.
19 *Sport*, vol. 16, no. 316.
20 When she died in May 1936, his mother's funeral service would take place at the church.
21 Glanville, *Companion*, p.458.
22 A club which was peopled by the offspring of the cotton manufacturers living around Burnley.
23 Fox states that Hogan signed as a semi-professional shortly before his eighteenth birthday, October 1900. I have found no records to verify this.
24 Glanville, *Companion*, p. 458.
25 *Burnley Express*, 11 January 1902.
26 *Lancashire Evening Press*, 19 February 1902.
27 *Lancashire Evening Post*, 31 October 1903.
28 Mitchell, his club mate, was also included in the line-up.
29 *Lancashire Evening Press*, 17 February 1902. The game finished 0-0 and Southport's goalkeeper that day was Arthur Wharton. This is likely the reserve match, referred to by Fox, upon which Hogan based his application on joining Burnley. The date would make sense, given Mangnall's arrival as manager. It was public knowledge that Burnley's finances were heading south since Harry Bradshaw had walked away. On 1 September 1902, the *Athletic News*

announced that despite attracting £1,785 in fees, the club owed £2,400 to all creditors. Of interest is that Cornelius Hogan, no relation, was re-signed by the club that month.
30 They beat Blackburn Rovers' reserves 1-0 in August or September 1902 [date unknown].
31 Glanville, *Companion*, p 460.
32 Both inside-rights (the position Hogan now occupied) would score goals in a 1-1 draw. *Gloucestershire Echo*, 19 February 1937.
33 *Burnley Gazette*, 18 October 1902.
34 *Lancashire Evening Press*, 8 November 1902.
35 *Ibid.*, 11 April 1903.
36 He signed for Rochdale on 17 August 1903 *Lancashire Evening Post*.
37 In the *Lancashire Evening Press* account of the fixture against Clitheroe Central, it is stated "Craven (of Blackpool) scored twice for Rochdale, and Hogan (Burnley) once."
38 7 September 1903.
39 *Lancashire Evening Post*, 3 October 1903.
40 *Lancashire Evening Post*, 5 October 1903.
41 The *Northern Daily Telegraph* reported [23 October 1903] "It seems that after all the Burnley club got hold of him."
42 22 October 1903, reported in *Burnley Gazette*, Saturday 24 October. It would be interesting to discover just what the terms were when playing for Burnley in that first season.

## Jimmy Hogan

## TWO

## 1903-1905

'The Scots believed in starting at the foundations by making their players able craftsmen, masters of the ball...'

Since Hogan made his Football League debut in the autumn of 1903 this is a good juncture with which to take a step back to place Hogan and the game that was being played at the time in context. By a matter of almost divine alignment, Hogan's life mirrored the development and growth of the game itself. In 1882, that being the year of Hogan's birth, football was a pastime run, controlled and dominated by amateur sides in the South of England and up to that year no professional side had ever won the FA Cup. By 1900, when he turned eighteen, professional football had become legalised, a Football League had been created and the game had engulfed the North West, the Midlands and was infiltrating London. By 1910, at the end of his playing career, the game had expanded globally and there was now a federation of international associations.

Contrary to the accepted notion, the game was also well advanced in terms of tactics and technique by 1900. This advancement owed a great deal to the Scottish players; skilled professionals who had been attracted to the clubs in Lancashire, Yorkshire and Warwickshire. They had helped develop the game by importing an idiosyncratic style into the English game.[1] This was the style that came to be most commonly associated with Jimmy Hogan but one needs to tread carefully when uniting the style with the man.

When Hogan was born, the English game was all about "individualism, inventiveness, experimenting"[2] but by 1903, when he made his League debut, the game everywhere had yielded "in the public estimation to the necessities of general combination"[3] and the most popular form of combination came to be "the Scottish style". The Scottish style, as it was played initially, was neither quick nor relatively effective and it formed only one aspect of the general combination play in which the game was played. The style had become popular because it was a style which formed the basis of the success of the famous Queen's Park side from Glasgow in the early years of the game. Other clubs soon started incorporating the style into the way they played and this led to players teaching themselves the rudiments of the Scottish style as though it was fundamental to the way the game should be played. Queen's Park's dominance came to an end because they did not alter their style and other clubs, not restricted by the amateur code, could attract players who were at a higher level of footballing ability. As these Scots migrated to English professional clubs so they took with them the Scottish style and the style became the pre-eminent one within the game in England. It was not only to England that the style was exported: one of the Scottish clubs, Celtic, formed in 1887, were invited to tour central Europe in 1904 and one of their number was the inside right John Madden, who accepted an offer to coach the players of Prague soon after and therefore introduced the Scottish style to the Continent.

At its heart, the Scottish style was an attacking formation made up of three players: "The half-back, the inside-forward and the outside-forward working in unison by short passing to one another on the move."[4] Bernard Joy wrote: "… the wing-halves pressed up-field to provide the base of a triangular movement which carried the ball forward with dainty inter-passing. Final touch was usually left to the winger who did not attempt to cut in, but lobbed the ball into the middle from the neighbourhood of the corner flag."[5]

Joy wrote: "the Scots were not concerned with [the centre-forward's lack of] contribution to the approach to the penalty area, but regarded him as the scorer-in-chief."[6] To be proficient in the Scottish style, players would need to develop a familiarity with their colleagues such that when passing first time they knew that their team mate would be running into position to receive the pass and that knowledge could only be borne via continuous practice, immaculate ball control and players who had the physical ability to pass and then jog quickly into space to meet a return pass. It should also be noted that the final stage of the play i.e. crossing the ball from the corner flag required a precision from the outside forward that again could only come from many hours of practice in landing the ball precisely for the centre-forward to volley, head or drive home. Therefore two aspects stand out for us. Firstly, the fact that to play in that way requires practice outside of a match situation as the familiarity is borne and instilled between team-mates and secondly that practice can only come about using a football.

The Scottish style was not necessarily effective but it was used commonly because, before the change in the offside law in June 1925, it was far easier to play attacking players offside than it was after the change. The old Law saw to it that for a player to remain onside he would either have to be behind the line of the ball or behind the third last defender when the ball was played. As a result, short, interlinking passes were favoured because there was less chance of a player being found offside when advancing as part of a close passing unit.[7] In addition to the Scottish style was the long, raking pass that was sent out from the half back or centre-half to the outside forwards but the Scottish style was favoured over that form of attack because if three players advanced on the opposition defence in unison then they had greater numbers than the defensive partnership of the full back and the wing half. This created a situation in which there were more attackers than defenders, reduced the opportunity for offside and allowed the attack to exploit the spaces created. Bernard Joy, later, described the style as being: "neat and tidy. The Scots believed in starting at the foundations by making their players able craftsmen, masters of the ball and highly skilled at dribbling and passing. They could 'kill' the ball at their feet in a trice, and pass it stylishly along the ground to a colleague. Attacks were methodically, *even sedately*,[8] built up on the wings."[9]

Joy went onto write: "It was a bit staid, and perhaps lacked imagination, but it was polished, correct and attractive to watch. ... The Scottish crowds ... appreciated the finer points of skilful footwork, and positional play, on which the dramatic highlights depended."[10]

The Scottish style had proved successful and so was followed but its overall popularity had more to do with the notion that there was no other way to play the game. In 1960, Arthur Rowe, the Spurs' coach during their famous push and run years, said: "... the more I think about it the more I am inclined to feel that this triangular game was a fashion. It was a [style] that dominated peoples' thoughts, so that they accepted it blindly without any thought. And they played that way because they had always played that way."[11]

Perhaps the enduring popularity of the style also came about because the fundamental aspects of the Scottish style, mastery of the ball, control, passing, positional play are elements which are vital to success in football regardless of the tactical formation or age. As such the Scottish style, founded on that bedrock of sound technical ability, became a mainstay within the game until the middle of the 1920s and still has relevance today but its application has long been lost as the game has continued to speed up. And this is where the association with Hogan comes from. Although

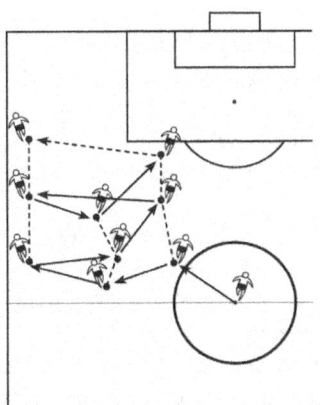

Fig. 1

# Jimmy Hogan

the Scottish style was tactically weak, in that defences could organise themselves as the attack slowly formed itself, the technical standards required by the players was high and when Hogan was first employed as a coach he was asked to deliver training so that the players could become expert in the type of ball control required by players who sought to replicate the Scottish style which meant repetitive exercises and practice in trapping, gently passing and jogging into position after delivering the pass.

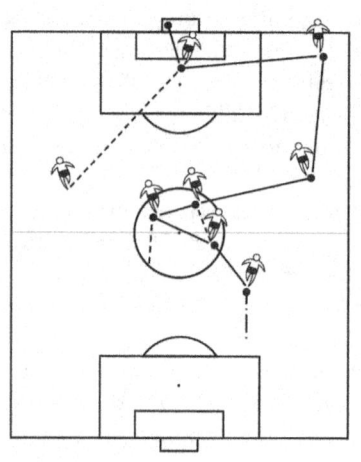

Fig. 2
*1927 Scotland goal in 2nd minute against England.*

This (fig. 2) goal shows a variation of "the Scottish style" following the advent of the change in the offside law in 1925 and is one of the most famous goals in history. In this attack, McMullan, the Scottish captain and right back retrieved a rebound off the post, dribbled the ball and passed short to Alex James, the deep lying inside right for Scotland. James then inter-linked with his inside left partner, Jimmy Dunn, before playing the ball out to Alan Morton. Morton took the ball to the corner flag and crossed deep into the English goal area where Alec Jackson, the outside left, heading Scotland into the lead. The speed of the attack negated the need for McMullan to kick the ball long to Morton and therefore reduced the risk of the Scots losing possession. Note that whereas the inside right and outside right are engaged, James' vision to pick out Dunn to springboard the attack from a defensive position negates the need for the right half to be used.

## Centre-half and half backs

A corollary to the development of the Scottish style, was the introduction of the centre-half, the so-called "third half-back". Alcock wrote in the late 1890s that "his appearance was a fresh revelation in football tactics", because this introduction presaged the development of combined teamwork. The centre-half and his two wing colleagues, the wing halves, undertook two primary functions. The wing-halves were there to defend against the outside forwards, just as the full-backs were there to defend against the inside forwards. The centre-half was there to help out in defence when required but his fundamental role was to start attacks, send out short passes to his inside forwards or raking passes to the outside forwards depending on which player was in space to receive a pass. Each of the halves could advance up field with the ball, knowing that the backs would support any counter-attack thrust. The centre-half back role was a demanding position on the field of play for the halves were continually moving backwards and forwards like waiters in a busy restaurant. In 1901 Ernest Needham, the greatest half in the kingdom wrote:

> "To be a success the half-back must be sound and strong, as he will be on the go from start to finish. He must be prepared to defend and attack, as both duties will fall to his share. When his side is being pressed he must fight like a 'back' and when his forwards are advancing he must both feed and help them. Often he will have as much chance of scoring as a forward, and then must seize the opportunity."[12]

Needham was the apex half[13] and his style of play was profoundly influential. If he was saying that the only defensive duties of the half were when "his side [was] being pressed" then so be it and gives us clues as to the key point of his role, that of being a creative force within the team. When Hogan was playing, the half-back was the fulcrum of the side and helped triangulate attacking play. Needham's description of what a half back did was the style of play that predominated in Britain until the 1925 law change when the great fracture took place and Britain, influenced by Chapman's Arsenal, went one way and decided to do away with the old style attacking centre-half, such as Needham and introduce a "stopper" centre-half in his place. In Europe, even after 1925, there was still the need and appetite for there to be an attacking centre-half. Jimmy Hogan's part in upholding the traditional role of the half-back is, in part the subject of this book because in "feeding and helping" his forwards, the centre-half was required to adopt the Scottish style of shot passing and quick movement into position.

## Hogan's professional career, 1903-1905

There are two main strands that stand out when assessing Jimmy Hogan's professional playing career as a footballer. Firstly, he was honest enough to admit that he was just "a very ordinary League player."[14] That later served Hogan very well for none of his contracts were sinecures, he moved quite regularly from club to club and found opportunities to play at the highest level hard to come by. Therefore he was required to prove his place in the first team and work hard in training and practice and in building relationships with his colleagues to get a start. Secondly, although many link him to the Scottish style of play it was only for a very short time that he got to play alongside Scottish players who were of a level that he felt qualified them as worthy of recall and even then there are doubts as to what influence they actually had on his playing style.

His first professional club was Burnley Football Club. At the time they were managed by Spence Whittaker who had made changes to the club after taking over from Harry Bradshaw. Under Bradshaw, Burnley had acquired a reputation for being a "Scottish" club, selecting a great many Scots to play for them. But Whittaker had undertaken a purge of those players and by the time Hogan made his debut in 1903-04,[15] there were only two Scots on the Burnley playing staff, one of whom was Hogan's inside wing partner, Jimmy Crawford. Things were not too great when Hogan started, and in his opening two first team games[16] Burnley shipped twelve goals but soon righted themselves and finished a very respectable fifth in the Second Division. Hogan's part in that could not been gainsaid for he was a member of the team that went on a thirteen game run which saw only one loss to set a new club record.[17]

Although his influence on the club's history is as important as Bradshaw's, "Spen" Whittaker has not been served well by history which is possibly due to Hogan himself. When Hogan came to write his life story, serialised in *Sport* magazine in 1954, he reminisced about an incident when he asked "a trainer" at Burnley for some advice after miskicking a shot. Hogan does not name the trainer however, the response, according to Hogan, was depressing and dismissive. Some have come to the conclusion that that trainer was Whittaker. As a result of the incident, Hogan wrote: "So from that day I began to fathom things out for myself. I coupled this with seeking advice from the truly great players. It was through my constant delving into matters that I became a coach in later life. It seemed the obvious thing, for I had coached myself as a young professional. It was not easy."[18]

We don't know when the incident took place or who Hogan actually spoke to.[19] The strange thing about that incident was the response not of the staff member at Turf Moor but Hogan himself. In those days, the training of players was the concern of the players themselves. Secretary-managers simply put the players on the park, a role not very much different to how the position became shaped in Europe all those decades later where the manager would interact with the Board to release funds to purchase a suitable player upon discussion with a technical coach and the coach would fit that player into the system he preferred the team to play. With no "coach" to speak of, Victorian and Edwardian players were very much left to their own devices when it came to figuring things out for themselves so Hogan's comment, which highlights his own inexperience or lack of self-belief in actuality, needs to be put into context. *If* Hogan received the withering retort at all, it would not have been ignorance nor dismissal on the part of the Burnley staff member, just a reflection of the *laissez faire* attitude which dominated thinking in clubs at that time, i.e. "if *you* have a problem, *you* go fix it." This attitude was in keeping with the star quality the better paid players brought to the big matches. Steve Bloomer[20] and Ernest Needham could and did have licence to alter tactics in the course of games they played and would have been stunned at the mere suggestion that they should labour under tactical instruction during games and the same went for advice about training. In essence, the players were their own boss. For instance, reference is made to Ernest Needham's famous on-field tactical decisions. Of the March 1899 FA Cup semi-final between Sheffield United and Liverpool, Needham wrote "... in our great Cup tie against Liverpool at Bolton,[21] when *my* team was two goals to the bad, and only eight minutes to play, *I* took the chance of having only one back, one half back, and thus eight forwards."[22] [my italics]

Needham would do the same thing in the Final, when he exploited the gap unnecessarily created by Derby when the Rams switched their inside-left, Billy MacDonald, to left half, in a game which Sheffield United won 4-1. Players could take advice from fellow professionals but, in the main, they would not be inclined to take advice from the Manager. The very idea would have been offensive to players in Victorian clubs because, after all, they were paid to play because they knew what they were doing. Of course, there are always exceptions to the rule and one such case was Preston North End of whom it was written in the 1880s: "The conflux of so many expert players led [Preston] to pioneer new methods and approaches. Off the field Major Sudell, a man who could well cope with soccer's tactical side and Nick Ross, introduced the blackboard to the North End dressing room. They also began to plot moves utilising chess pieces on a billiard table to demonstrate possibilities ..."[23]

As you can see, however, that decision to share tactical ideas was driven not by the manager but by agreement from those "expert players" themselves but this leads us to another point, that with regard to how training was conducted within the professional game.

When the professional game took root a lot of players played football to supplement their income as full time workers. For instance, when Steve Bloomer first signed on for Derby County he was a striker in Ley's foundry sited near to Shaftesbury Avenue. As professional football wages

# Jimmy Hogan

increased so the first full time professional players started to predominate but this created a problem. Players who were reliant on their football income to top up their pay, were inclined to better themselves and make sure that their spot in the team was secured. However, as the professional movement and League football structure developed so more and more players were inclined to do less and less; having signed the yearly contract they were assured income barring injury and illness. Therefore, players found themselves paid regardless of their interest in training and practising. Players lacking motivation but receiving pay regardless adhered to the mundane schedules that most clubs accepted to be adequate. The player's fitness rather than his skill level became the pre-eminent issue and as in any workspace, the majority, when required to undertake some form of voluntary continuous professional development, elected for the easy route and did nothing. The lax players, happy to take the cash and not over tax themselves, easily outnumbered the thinkers and doers. William Bassett, when a director of West Brom, pined for his day in the 1880s and early 1890s when players, otherwise employed, maintained an enthusiasm for the game that professional players, i.e. ones who did not need to work, lacked: "... you must not tell me that the man who practically lives on a football ground is going to enjoy his football, or look to it with such keenness as the men of old did."[24]

Bassett set out the typical schedule that clubs followed in 1906. This involved going for a brisk walk on the Tuesday, skipping or boxing in the afternoon; running and sprint exercises, and ball practice ("once a week, and once a week only, the men have ball practice."[25]). But, Bassett then went on to state: "I cannot see that [limited practice with a football] is beneficial ... Personally, I would much rather see sides formed. ... It would be infinitely more interesting and infinitely better practice than the stereotyped methods now in vogue. My own opinion is that men get nothing like as much actual work with the ball as they need."[26]

The ideology that Bassett was advocating was clearly supported by those who had invested in publishing *The Book of Football* for he was given ample opportunity to reiterate his key message:

> "... a man does not get sufficient match practice in the course of a season to turn him from a moderate player into a high-class one. This is quite apart from training, and it ought to be sufficient to draw attention to the matter, and leave each footballer to work out his own improvement. I am afraid that some of them think they have nothing to learn, in which case they will learn nothing. But they are not all like that, and the rest would do well to lose no single opportunity they may obtain of perfecting themselves in all the methods which go to make up the sound footballer."[27]

However, his message, when it came to the rank and file full time professionals, fell on deaf ears. Bassett, to them, was just some old duffer with a point of view. There was no legislation obliging any player to remain on the training ground, or to sneak a football out of the cupboard and practice kicking corners until it got dark and as older players progressed into management or became trainers so their ideas and methods became entrenched and training became a system of mainly keeping fit and building stamina. As Hogan's interaction showed if players wanted to practice then that was left to their own inventiveness, inspiration or indoctrination. So there is no period after the introduction of full-time professionalism when there was not a crevice, a *disconnect*, between those willing to apply themselves and those who shared the predominant attitude of laxity that increasingly characterised the majority of players. Of course some of the players did not share the outlook and mentality of the herd. The rise of the modern manager was forged during the period between 1900 and 1914 and involved those who felt dislocated by the prevailing malaise. Players like Clem Stephenson, George Jobey, Frank Buckley and Charlie Roberts were out of kilter with their age. The older brigade Billy Meredith, Steve Bloomer, Bassett and Needham were not backward in coming forward. All bar Needham became coach-managers.[28] But as time went on so the situation moved not a jot until the early 1920s when players of a certain standard were becoming full internationals when previously they would not have passed consideration for the trial matches. This statement is vindicated by the fact that in 1923 Norman Bullock[29] became an England international on the back of a natural curiosity as to what a centre-forward's role could be. This led to him trialling a few ideas in practice, playing a certain way at Gigg Lane and gaining three England caps.[30] A question which arises amidst all this discussion is as follows: was Hogan one of the practitioners or one of the lazy ones getting by with what he could? We're actually never going to know the true answer to that question but one question does arise, if Jimmy Hogan was so committed to perfecting his art during his career, then why did he play for so many clubs?

So that brings us back to why Hogan would have bad-mouthed Burnley in the first place? This is a difficult question to answer, but the fact remains that, like Nelson and Rochdale beforehand, Hogan's stay at Burnley was accompanied by another pay dispute. Fox, lifting a reference from Hogan's serialised life story, states that Whittaker refused to offer Hogan £4 a week.[31] He also refers to Hogan's tale that one of the Burnley directors put Hogan in touch with a local ironmonger, so that he could top up his income through his work as the company accountant but Hogan did not

# Jimmy Hogan

want to do that. The evidence points to Hogan, even at that early stage in his career, agitating for more and more cash since he was money-driven and this new professional occupation was his vehicle. What motivation Hogan had for being that way inclined is open to conjecture. One could refer back to the cleft caused by his decision to leave the seminary, to prove his circumspect mother wrong over his choice of career, or one could simply argue that as a typical young Northern lad he had been imbued by his dad with the understanding that "money was the thing". And when he didn't get what he thought he was owed, he was not averse to holding a grudge for years and using the press to ridicule those who he felt had sleighted him. Whittaker, or the "trainer" was the one at Burnley. But, as we shall see, it says more about Hogan than the person being sleighted in the long-run.

The lack of a pay rise should not come as a surprise. In that second season[32] Hogan scored fewer goals, and the club finished eleventh. In addition, as early as September 1904, Hogan suffered a leg injury at Chesterfield[33] which would plague him for the rest of his career[34] and in January he was dropped after missing a sitter in the replayed Cup tie at Lincoln City. The club was reliant for the revenue that the Cup run could amass so the loss to fellow strugglers Lincoln City was galling. At the end of that season, with the club in eleventh place, and no Cup run to speak of, Hogan went to speak to Whittaker about a pay rise and got short shrift. The club couldn't afford it, there had been no increase in the gate, and the idea of promotion was quite fanciful. But Hogan was insistent, he knew his worth and wanted his penny and when the fee he had in mind was not forthcoming he determined that he best up sticks and find a better deal. It would be a key feature of his life from that point on. Hogan started to look around for another contract and the club he went to was his old club, Nelson.[35] If Nelson were willing to pay enough for his services then he was quite happy to turn out against League reserve teams.[36] He hacked it for two short months but it was at that stage that his mind was turned by Fulham Football Club in the Southern Football League.

# 1903-1905

## Notes

1 Charles Alcock attributed the rise in prominence of the Scots to the victories that Scotland had over England in their annual international matches and the number of tours from clubs on both sides of the border: Marriott & Alcock, *Association Football* (Routledge, 1903), 77.

2 Meisl, *Soccer Revolution*, 50.

3 *Association Football*, 77.

4 *Association Football* (1960), vol. 4, 16.

5 Joy, *Soccer Tactics*, 93.

6 *Soccer Tactics*, 94.

7 As the, earlier, example of Clitheroe shows, if a non-League side were using that tactic you can be confident that the use of a single defender was used in the professional game in 1903.

8 This should be noted by those who argue that the Scottish style was a quick passing movement.

9 *Soccer Tactics*, (1955), 91.

10 *Soccer Tactics*, 94.

11 *Association Football* (1960), vol. 1, 104.

12 Needham, *Association Football*, 29.

13 As well as being capped by England, under his captaincy, Sheffield United won the League title in 1897, the FA Cup final in 1898, and the FA Cup in 1902.

14 *Athletic News*, 3 March 1930.

15 Possibly a reflection of depressed economic circumstances at the club; the previous season they had been re-elected to the League. The Scots had left in numbers.

16 His first team debut coming on 7 November 1903 at Bristol City's Ashton Gate.

17 He played 25 games and scored five goals that season.

18 *Sport*, vol. 16, no. 317.

19 *Ibid.*

20 Refer yourself to Bloomer's late goal in the 1901 clash with Scotland when – out of the game's dying embers and the Scots ahead by a nose – he picked up a loose ball in the heavy mud of the Palace field, ignored his team-mates, strode through the defence and beat the 'keeper to face-save King and Country.

21 Played in March 1899.

22 *Association Football*, 41.

23 *One Hundred Years at Deepdale*, 22. As a direct result of that mentality, Bob Holmes, Preston's left-back of Invincible days coached at Stoneyhurst College in Clitheroe for fifteen years and for a couple of years at Ampleforth College in York. But Holmes was the first and in the early days, the only player who took that path. See also *Men Famous in Football*, 1905, p 187.

24 *The Book of Football*, 110.

25 *The Book of Football*, 111.

26 *Ibid.*, 111.

27 *Ibid.*, 113.

28 Meredith and Roberts became joint managers of Manchester Central FC in the late 1920s.

29 Charles Buchan wrote of Bullock, "He was a studious type of leader, not a battering-ram but beating defenders by positional play." *A Lifetime in Football*, 78.

30 Yet, *that* germ of an idea formed the basis of George Raynor's tactical ideas of *G-men*, "false 9s" and the great Swedish national sides of the late 1940s and 1950s and subsequent developments. See Hyne, *George Raynor* (2014).

31 At the time the highest paid players were earning around £5 a week.

32 Once again Fox highlights a clear ignorance of the facts referring to Hogan's "four

successful years" (p 34). Two years going backwards in the Second Division hardly a successful four-year stay makes.

33  5 September 1904, Burnley won 2-0 against Chesterfield. The *Sheffield Daily Telegraph*, 6 September 1904, reports that he had to be taken off the field.

34  He undertook a spell in the reserves while he was trying to get back into the first team – 15 October 1904 against Nelson. (*Lancashire Evening Post*).

35  He was signed on 13 September 1905. (*Lancashire Evening Post*).

36  On the 30 September 1905 he played against Blackburn Rovers' reserves – *Burnley Gazette*, 4 October 1905.

## THREE

## 1905-1908
## 'I have yet to be impressed with the football of Hogan.'

Just as George Raynor required Norman Bullock so Jimmy Hogan's big break came as a result of him meeting Harry Bradshaw.[1] Bradshaw had been one of the founding fathers of Burnley Football Club but Hogan did not meet him at Turf Moor.[2] Bradshaw's work with Burnley, however, does give us some clues as to the person he was and the influence we can assume he had on Hogan's later career.

When Burnley first came into being they were a "local" club for local players but because results seemed to go against the club Bradshaw proposed that the club would be best served employing Scots[3] and so, to do this, Bradshaw entered into the shady practice of paying players. For Bradshaw, though a proud Lancastrian and Burnley man, saw the coming of the future: with all the best will in the world, local players could not do what foreigners could and, as a result, Bradshaw was instrumental in making the club an imitation of their "betters by procuring talent which was not altogether local." By December 1884, Burnley had fourteen Scots on their books and those numbers continued to rise exponentially as did the club's income. The impact of having Scots at the club was a "no-brainer", Preston North End were put to the sword in November 1884 ("no mean achievement in that season"[4]) and Blackburn Rovers were flattened 5-0 the following spring, between which, Burnley had been banned by the Football Association, faced extinction but were then resurrected Phoenix-like by the prevailing wind of change when professionalism was legalised.[5]

In 1899, Bradshaw had only just taken Burnley to their highest ever League position when he surprisingly left Burnley to join Woolwich Arsenal, a decision that left many scratching their heads because the key metrics at Woolwich, the finances, crowd numbers and staff turnover, were all heading south. The Boer War had meant that munition production was increased which had a detrimental effect at the turnstiles and to add further woes Arsenal, being a Football League rather than Southern League club, were having to shell out a small fortune to pay for their team to undertake away fixtures to far flung places in Lancashire and Yorkshire. In short, times were hard and the club was going out of business so the decision to attract and then capture Bradshaw saved Arsenal. As Bernard

Joy later stated: "Arsenal were fortunate to secure Harry Bradshaw as manager. He proved the best manager before Herbert Chapman."[6] From Arsenal's perspective; it was the last throw of the dice; but the gamble paid off because Bradshaw knew what he was about, and proved his worth immediately when quickly securing two defenders. One just happened to be Jimmy Ashcroft, a Gravesend-born goalkeeper, who was fated to become one of the Edwardian greats but it was the next purchase that should really capture our imagination because Bradshaw strengthened the side by convincing Newcastle's Jimmy Jackson, a precocious Scots-Australian to come to Woolwich.[7] Jackson, who assumed both the left-back position and role of club captain, had just helped Newcastle gain promotion from the Second Division and, in doing so, had received a fair old grounding in the wonders of the classical "Scottish" style. Together the manager and the player were a positive boon to the London club. Joy wrote of Jackson and Bradshaw "[they] brought to Arsenal the old Scottish style of short, accurate passing and moving into position."[8]

Of Jackson's tactical nous there could be no question, one of his innovative ideas was to advocate "double-cover", which meant that when the left-back advanced, *or vice versa*, the right-back would file across on the diagonal to provide cover for the space vacated, backing up the advancing player. In doing so the team would naturally revolve cog-like so that the respective wing-half would fall back into a defensive role and everyone would move one position around the centre-half. In other words, players started to undertake roles other than what their primary function required of them. Halves became forwards, forwards halves and halves full backs. Furthermore, when the occasion demanded it, Jackson would persuade centre-half, Percy Sands, to act as a defensive "third back"[9] to consolidate the defence. Of course the use of the third back in England was as old as the professional game, teams intent on holding a lead were inclined to put an attacking half-back in defence as early as the 1890s. What made Jackson's move innovative was that he was bringing Sands back

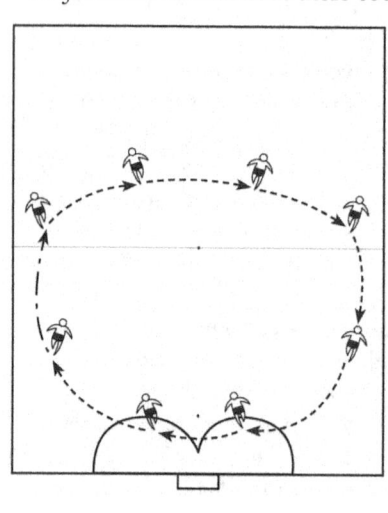

Fig. 3

purely as a third defender, Jackson's genius realising that Sands' defensive qualities would enable the attacking thrust to spring from the wing halves. Jackson's impact in Hogan's story may be indirect, it is likely they never actually met, but it should not be underestimated in that, given that the role he performed at Woolwich, Jackson would have influenced Bradshaw's thinking as to the type of player he was sought when managing football teams. Jackson's inventive manner would have definitely impacted on Bradshaw's mentality, bringing to his attention the type of player who had that sense of creativity, so telling in League matches, and which we have well and truly lost as a nation. Of interest to us is that whereas Jackson may have developed his tactical inventiveness, briefly at Glasgow Rangers and on Tyneside, there was also the influence that he brought with him from Australia where he played Australian Rules football. In writing about field positions on the Aussie Rules' field, Montague Shearman, in April 1887, wrote:

> "[As well as the 15 players on each side] who have places to which they must in the main adhere, the four who are called 'followers' stand up to the field umpire when he bounces the ball, and *follow it in its wanderings* over the field. They ought never to be very far from it. The rover is an individual chosen for his quickness and readiness to go wherever he is wanted. He observes the turn of the game, and follows when he sees his own followers being over-weighted by their adversaries, leaves them if he finds they can hold their own, and stations himself wherever he thinks that extra work may be required."[10]

One could argue that Jimmy Jackson brought that enlightened Aussie sporting liberalism with him to conservative Britain in which field positions were set and players, like soldiers, did as they were told. Perhaps Jimmy Jackson, the young Aussie Rules player turned footballer, is one of football's great random elements at a focal point in time: a player who married the technical excellence of the Scots with that archetypal Australian inventiveness and disregard for the unquestioned order of things that, refined over time and regulated onto the football field, became the "whirl" and later led to the development of "Total Football." Bradshaw and Jackson oversaw the survival of Arsenal. In 1900-01 the side finished seventh in the Second Division, the next season they finished fourth and 14,000 turned up at the Manor Ground to witness the Cup visit of Newcastle United. A summer 1902 archery tournament helped pay for a new forward line and in 1903-04 a zip-zip draw with Port Vale ensured that the Gunners went up with Preston North End to the First Division for the very first time. But Bradshaw saw promotion not as personal vindication but simply as a means to up his market worth and leverage another pay day, this time with Southern League Fulham.

Being a Southern League club, Fulham were not hamstrung by any silly notion of a maximum wage cap that held back the Football League, and Bradshaw immediately took advantage of the favourable financial climate at Craven Cottage by setting out on a shopping spree to attract the best talent from wherever to get Fulham elected into the Football League. Bradshaw's job was made easier when the club purchased Jack Fryer, the goalkeeper, from Derby, whose display in the 1903 Cup final may have been a disaster[11] but he had given sterling service to the Rams over a number of successful seasons and eleven[12] clean sheets in his first season in London vindicated the outlay. Bradshaw then set about streamlining the business, cutting waste and Fulham reaped the returns. Whereas seven players had played only once in 1903-04 and nine others had played less than ten games by the following year, seven players played over 25 games and in the Cup run, Fulham lost 5-0 at Villa Park in the Third Round, eight players had played in all eight ties. As the quality of the football improved so did the size of the gate: 7,615 in 1903-04 increased to an average of 9,641 the following season.[13] What made this all possible was that, in his first few months, Bradshaw signed seven new players; six of whom were Scots. They were right-back Harry Ross (born in Brechin; the former Burnley player who had come to the big smoke with trainer Jack Stuttard); Jimmy Sharp from Jordanstone, a former Dundee left back and Scottish international full-back, the outstanding Fulham player of this era, and rated by his contemporaries as the finest back in the country;[14] Bob Haworth, a right-half from Blackburn Rovers; Willie Wardrope a centre or inside left from Third Lanark, Wishaw born; Bob Graham, an inside forward from Glasgow, another Third Lanark player; Mark Bell, from Edinburgh, an outside left, formerly with Hearts and Willie Morrison, born in West Benbar, a centre-half from St Bernards.

At Fulham they joined a left wing-half whose name was Willie Goldie a "dour, defensive" Glaswegian[15] whose accent was so strong that, when he was before the FA on a charge of breaking contract at Liverpool the committee needed the services of a translator to understand him.[16]

A lot of writers have linked Goldie with Jimmy Hogan's "working knowledge" of the Scottish style for, despite all the other Scots on the books at Craven Cottage, Goldie is the one who Hogan apparently befriended.[17] Given the fact that there were so many Scots at Fulham one is left to wonder as to whether the fact of Goldie's League Championship medal from his Liverpool days had anything to do with Hogan's sycophancy. Furthermore in all the time that I have been researching Jimmy

Hogan I have found nothing whatsoever to link him to Goldie and cannot say for certain whether Hogan befriended Goldie at all. However that being said, if there is one Glaswegian Hogan *did* relate to at Fulham it was the Robert C. Hamilton with whom he shared a curious friendship. Hogan and Hamilton's friendship came about for a couple of reasons and the primary one was that, like Hogan, Hamilton had difficulty convincing Bradshaw that he was not surplus to requirements.[18] Secondly, Hamilton had aspirations beyond his football career, later becoming the Provost of Elgin, and this caught the attention of Hogan, conscious that things in professional football were not transpiring as one would have hoped. The two discussed a great many things and Hamilton even encouraged his young friend down the line of taking his civil service entrance exam but Hogan, not for the first time, baulked at the prospective imprisonment of office life and never actually sat the exam.[19] But we are getting ahead of ourselves, so let us go back to how Jimmy Hogan found himself at the Cottage in the first place.

Hogan signed for Fulham from Burnley, for £200, not because they were offering to improve his game but because he could earn more money there than he could get at Turf Moor. Hogan clearly had no compunction about leaving a first team role with a Football League team to become a reserve player with Fulham in the Southern Football League. However, he did not only go to the club because they were offering favourable terms. He went there because Bradshaw was a Burnley man and would therefore be favourable to Hogan. Be that as it may, it is fair to say that a lot of what I have read about Hogan's stay at Fulham is utter tripe and is misleading.[20] In his biography, Norman Fox wrote: "Bradshaw saw his job as organiser of the club and team selector, experimenting continuously. ... Hogan thought his style of management neglected the need for coaching. On the other hand he agreed with him over the importance of giving the Scottish players their heads since they played in the way he admired."[21]

This is wrong in various ways. Firstly, there was not much experimenting going on because Bradshaw knew exactly what he was doing. Indeed, ridding the club of the chaos of the previous seasons was the very reason why Fulham progressed as they did under Bradshaw. Secondly, implying that there was any more or any less "coaching" going on at Fulham, as opposed to any other club, shows a serious lack of knowledge as to the way the game was organised at that time. And thirdly, as a reserve team player, Hogan had no say in how Fulham played so stating that there was some agreement with Bradshaw, implied or explicit, is way off the mark. Reserve players don't tell the manager or coach how things should be, they didn't in 1906, still don't now and never will.[22] And that was the point, when Hogan first appeared for Fulham, during the 1905-06 season, he

# Jimmy Hogan

was the third inside right the club had tried that season, but even then, he did not impress enough to hold down a first team place. But, curiously, that did not stop him from appearing in the Lancashire newspapers. In November 1905 an article was printed in the *Burnley Express*. Hogan had just made his first team start against Reading who beat Fulham 1-0 but of Hogan a "correspondent" stated: "Hogan played very well indeed at inside-left. He is full of dash and fire and doesn't forget to shoot. It would not be surprising to see him take Wardrope's [the inside-left's] place until the muddy season commences."[23]

That peculiar news item, highlighting the play of a Burnley old boy in a match played in London, was a key moment for him because he had a hand in the production of the story. We know this because the item which is written anonymously, contains some glaring errors and has minimal relevance to Burnley readers. The source of the story could not have been a local Fulham news reporter because they would have known that Wardrope and Hogan did not play in the same position after all, both were playing that day for Fulham. They would also have known that Hogan was in the team at inside-right, not inside-left and that Wardrope, being a first team player, was unlikely to have been at risk of being dropped. Also the *Burnley Express* would hardly have dispatched a writer to travel all the way south to report on Fulham v Reading. So who wrote that piece? My suspicion lies in Hogan having a hand in that match report somehow or some way.

His relationship with the press, which was fostered within those reports featuring Belvedere, thereafter became one of enduring significance. Hogan was the first modern coach. Not on account of his tactical awareness or of the way he taught his players, but on account of his relationship with the press, and how he managed his news and how he managed the information that was presented by and about him. He knew from an early time, far earlier than his contemporaries, how important it was to control your publicity. Modern writers analysing Jimmy Hogan overlook just how much Hogan controlled information about his life, in fact, a lot of what we read about him, even now, can be sourced directly back to him. He later dominated the dissemination of his own publicity, creating a profile that positively represented the persona he wished to promote. When the British read of Continental football in the 1930s, a good proportion of that information came from Jimmy Hogan himself. Hogan was the great Continental coach because Hogan told his friends in the provincial press that he was and they, in turn, accepted that without question and communicated that fact to Britain. Ask yourself why don't we know much about Teddy Duckworth, the collaborative architect of Switzerland's astonishing Olympic silver in 1924, or Johnny Dick, one of Bradshaw's old boys who went on to teach and coach Prague before the Great War? Why did it take so many years before the work of William Garbutt, in Italy, came to light? Why is Raynor still misunderstood and overlooked? Is it to do with the fact that in none of those cases were those individuals intent on constantly communicating to Britain what they were doing while overseas? For it is in that regard that Hogan is principally distinguished. Yet, ironically, there was very little at Fulham and at that time, to write about when it came to Hogan. In the next game (against Watford) the *Sportsman* described the Fulham forward line as "disappointing" and Hogan was recalled for only three other games that season which was galling for him because the inside right position, Hogan's preferred position on the field, was not one that Fulham had a natural choice for throughout that season. In other words, as far as Bradshaw was concerned, Hogan was not quite up to the mark. That would explain the "modest contribution" that he made to Fulham during what was a successful period in the club's history.[24] The following season was a repeat of the first. Hogan could not secure a first team place, being selected to play only nine times, and when he did he was tried in the inside left position. In two years Hogan had appeared in just fourteen first team games, and yet the team had twice won the Southern League and had now been elected to the Football League.

Meanwhile, in 1907 Hamilton returned to Glasgow and Hogan was left to languish in the reserves as Fulham entered their first season in the Football League,[25] a season for him which was yet another personal disappointment. He received a call up for the first team in October 1907 but when he played there were significant concerns about his ability at this higher level. Of his return to the first XI, the *London Daily News* reporter was particularly scathing after a game against Oldham Athletic when he wrote: "Hogan and Dalrymple, the right wingers, were practically passengers throughout, and I have yet to be impressed with the football of Hogan. He has appeared in four matches but in no single instance has he been at all successful, and Dalrymple requires a better partner."[26]

He had to wait for his next outing, a leg injury serving to add to his absence from the first team,[27] but his return would signal yet another disaster. In the February, Threlfall was injured in the match at Leeds and a space became available for Hogan, at outside right, to play in the semi-final of the FA Cup where Fulham were matched up against mighty Newcastle United, the strongest Cup team in the kingdom at that time. Fulham were a goal down but still very much in the game when Appleyard kicked Fulham's keeper, Skene, deliberately on the ankle before tapping in the second. The Geordies took full advantage of that, knocking in four further goals to record a 6-0 victory. As for Hogan, he was dismissed by the reporter as being "quite weak"[28] and could make no head room against that better class of opponent he faced that day. And on that note Hogan's career at Fulham came to an abrupt end. Bradshaw later summoned Hogan to his office and after apparently telling him that "he had been a good footballer and very clever with his head but that season had seemed to lose his art"[29] gave him the news that he best seek alternative accommodation.

So here we have a dichotomy: Hogan's personal disappointments and the club's impressive run of form and here is a question: was Fulham's success used, later, by Hogan to give himself some type of credibility by association? We talk of this great cultural phenomenon of Central European football in the 1930s as being the apex form of artistic football, of Hogan at the vanguard dictating the aesthetic style so loved by the Viennese and yet Hogan's *actual* experience of "the Scottish style" of play was only ever from afar or second hand. But when he went to Vienna in 1914, Meisl was engaging someone who, apparently, had played with all "the great Scottish players", and was asking his new coach to coach his players in the style exhibited on those famous Continental tours by

Jimmy Hogan in 1908.

# 1905-1908

Everton, Chelsea, Spurs and Rangers, teams Hogan could only ever dream of playing against and so the great aesthetic movement was founded on nothing more than the notion that Hogan knew what he was talking about. An empire built on sand.

So Hogan found himself on the tramp once again and got work, finally, at the County Ground at Swindon Town thanks to their secretary-manager, Sam Allen. Allen, like Bradshaw, was aided by the absence of a wage ceiling in the Southern League. For once, Hogan's natural luck escaped him for when he signed forms with Swindon as inside right, for at the same time Allen was offering papers to two others: Jock Wallace a tough tackling left back from Glasgow Rangers, now lost to history, and another inside right who just happened to be the genius that was Harold Fleming, destined to become one of the greatest inside rights of the all time.[30] As a result, even accounting for the fact that Hogan's time at Swindon started with a bang it would soon end with a whimper. He only played nine times, started as a centre forward, scored seven in two matches in his conventional inside right position before Fleming's abilities relegated Hogan to the sidelines. "Someone" made sure that news of Hogan's early success at the club was broadcast far and wide however, for in the *Athletic News* of 12 October 1908 a column appeared which was nothing short of an advertisement for Jimmy Hogan. Who would have written such a thing? That's right! Jimmy Hogan would have been the "Swindon correspondent" writing one of his regular letters to J. A. H. Catton to ensure that maximum publicity was presented to the Northern clubs as Hogan sought to return to his roots and get back to

> **SWINDON'S MARKSMEN.**
>
> My attention has been called by a Swindon correspondent to the fact that in summarising the results of the games played in the Southern League in September, I erroneously stated that Hogan had scored six goals. As a matter of fact, Hogan netted the ball on seven occasions, and should have been bracketed with Hughes, the Southampton centre, while Harold Fleming, also of Swindon, was equal with Jefferies, of Southampton, he having scored six times. I hasten to make the correction, for James Hogan has earned the distinction of being the top-scorer in the Southern League up to Saturday, the 3rd inst. Twenty-five years ago Hogan was born at Nelson. Originally intended for the clerical profession, he seized the earliest opportunity of deserting it for the vocation of a professional footballer. He served a couple of seasons with Nelson and a similar period with Burnley ere the South attracted him, and he joined Fulham as understudy to Kingaby. Although intended for the outside-right position, Hogan did very useful service at inside left in season 1906-7. In fact, his smartness was largely responsible for Fulham's success in winning the championship for the second time. Last season an injury prevented him showing his best form, but the result of his work at Swindon has shown that when physically fit he is a great force in the line of attack. He is a well-educated youth, and, with the assistance of E. C. Hamilton, when at Fulham, he studied for the Civil Service, but did not sit for examination.

# Jimmy Hogan

his childhood sweetheart, Evelyn. The press release did the trick, by the third week in October he had only added two more to his tally but his early flourish, and the accompanying press release, was enough to secure a move to Bolton Wanderers, with whom he made his debut on the 14 November 1908 in a 2-0 win over Chesterfield. His time at Swindon, though, identifies a worrying trend in Hogan's life. Hogan never seemed to be able to hold down a job for any length of time, concerns in regard to his form and ability militated against his retention. Returning to the North West would have seemed a signpost to his retirement, but Hogan's move to Burnden Park would provide him with a gateway to a long-term future he could have not dreamed about.

Swindon Town Football Club, 1908/09.

# 1905-1908

## Notes

1 (1853-1924). Manager of Burnley 1894-1899, Woolwich Arsenal 1899-1904, Fulham 1904-1909.

2 Catton, *The Rise of the Leaguers* (Sporting Chronicle, 1897). J. A. H. Catton wrote of Harry Bradshaw, "Burnley owe their existence to a few enthusiasts, and not one of the number has been so zealous, so staunch, and so tactful as Mr Harry Bradshaw." When he left Turf Moor (to join Woolwich Arsenal in 1899) Burnley had League status, a ground and a top four finish in the First Division for the first time in their history. Bradshaw was majorly responsible for all of that.

3 "We began to be the busiest amongst those clubs who took a great fancy to amateurs of Scottish parentage and birth."

4 *The Rise of the Leaguers*, 46.

5 Such was the culture change in opinion that we find that what was immoral in January 1885 was by October 1886 so acceptable that Prince Albert Victor graced the charity match between the professional players of Burnley and Bolton Wanderers Football Clubs with his presence. Little wonder then that Burnley would be invited to a place at the top table when the Football League was formed in September 1888.

6 Joy, *Forward Arsenal* (1952) 16.

7 Born in Rutherglen, he migrated with his family to Australia at the age of two, returned to the UK, alone, in his teens to forge a career as a professional footballer with Glasgow Rangers. He was a relative of Archie Jackson, the Keats of Australian Cricket. Magical genetics in that family.

8 *Forward Arsenal*, 16.

9 *Ibid.*, 16.

10 Shearman, *Athletics and Football* (1894), 422-423.

11 Bury beat Derby County 6-0 to record the highest score in Cup final history although Jack Fryer was not in the best condition to participate in any type of game, let alone one of such importance.

12 Turner, *Fulham: the Complete Record* (Breedon Books, 1984), p. 232 – the club had fourteen that season; Fryer was not present for all.

13 *Ibid.*, 232-235.

14 *Ibid.*, 11.

15 *Ibid.*, p 103.

16 Gibson, *Association Football and the Men Who Made It*, vol. III, p. 75. Goldie had already won the League title with Liverpool and at Fulham had helped form a left-wing triangle along with Wardrope (inside left) and Bell (at outside left). Between them they have scored 25 goals in Bradshaw's first season, a sizeable return (when contrasted with the fact that the rest of the players only added a further 21 goals that year) which gives some clue as to how the team operated tactically and which characters predominated.

17 It is a point Turner and White refer to in their complete history of Fulham (see above).

18 They appeared on a number of occasions for the club, at one time against "The Rest of the Southern League' (*Sporting Life*, 18 September 1906) but Hamilton had difficulty winning over the fans and would only stay in London for one year before heading back to Glasgow.

19 *Athletic News*, 12 October 1908.

20 Fox writes: "[Hogan's] own skill was fundamental to Fulham's winning of two Southern League Championships" (!) and further "... because of [Hogan's] contribution, Fulham reached the semi-final of the 1908 FA Cup." That being the FA Cup in which he played in only one match: the semi-final.

21 Fox, *Prophet or Traitor: The Jimmy Hogan Story* (2003), p. 36-7.

22 Acknowledgement to Dave Brammer, ex-pro with Millwall: "You know nothing about football if you think players can go and openly chat with the manager. It doesn't work like

that."

23 *Burnley Express*, 5 November 1905. One must ask if an inside right is so good why would he be best positioned to replace a first team regular at inside left?

24 Turner, *Fulham: the Complete Record*, p. 170.

25 Fulham were elected to the Football League on 1 June 1907. (*Burnley Express*.)

26 21 October 1907.

27 He reputedly suffered a leg injury at Fulham before his transfer to Swindon, as reported in the *Burnley Express*, 28 November 1953.

28 *Athletic News*, 30 March 1908.

29 *Burnley Express*, 4 August 1934.

30 Fleming was the greatest player in Swindon's history, bar none. As the splendid Swindon Town website declares: 'Between 1908 and 1914, Swindon won the Southern League title twice, finished as runners-up three times, and reached the semi-finals of the FA Cup twice - as well as winning the Dubonnet Cup' all during the time of Fleming.

## FOUR

## 1908-1913
### 'This upward and outward surge of the game'

When Hogan went to Burnden Park in the late autumn of 1908[1] it was at a time of considerable strife at the club. Never the wealthiest of clubs, Bolton had yo-yoed their way through the Edwardian years and now, relegated to the Second Division, early season form was such that the directors decided to get rid of four first team players. Three of them were low-cost sales but in the case of Albert Shepherd, a star England international, the decision was founded on two things. Firstly, his sale could fund the purchase of new players and, secondly, he had started to display an "attitude", or as Percy Young states "he was too selfish." Shepherd quickly attracted a £1,650 bid from Newcastle[2] and that cash opened the door for four new players at Bolton: three Billys, centre-half Robinson, centre-forward Hughes, outside left Hunter, and Jimmy Hogan.[3] It would have been a case of *déjà vu* for Hogan. Bolton, like Fulham beforehand, had no regular inside right but unlike his time at Craven Cottage the impact of that season would be felt far and wide for years to come.

In the immediate term, the four new players had a dramatic effect on the fortunes of the club because up to their arrival, the club's performances that season had been awful. "On 7 November," wrote Young, "defeat by Bradford brought civil commotion."[4] but, miraculously, by the following spring of 1909, the club had righted themselves and it was at that moment, on 13 February, that Herbert Baverstock, the club captain, issued a simple, direct statement to the players: "they must not lose at home" and, bar one loss to fellow title-challengers Spurs, nor did they.[5] The crowd, which had dropped to 8,000, now numbered 30,000 as Bolton played Hogan's old club, Fulham, in their final fixture, Billy Hughes scored the winner and Bolton Wanderers returned to the First Division as Second Division Champions.

That meant that as one of the form teams of the season the club could accept an invitation from the Football Association to tour Holland in the summer of 1909. This practice of representing the FA overseas had been undertaken for a few seasons. In May 1905, the "combined" Central European tour of Everton and Spurs[6] was financed to the tune of £600 by the FA and therefore undermines the general view that the Football Association's insularity retarded the development of the game abroad.

Indeed, it should be stated, that no country did more to promote the game, internationally, than Britain and no National Association did more to export coaches around the world than the Football Association. As Geoffrey Green wrote: " ... the [Football] Association, by sending out teams and English coaches to various parts of the world, helped to play a vital part in this upward and outward surge of the game."[7]

The Association were keen to expand the game regardless of venue and opponent and the Bolton tour, itself, was a case in point. The FA happily ceding to a Dutch request made that spring to repair relations that had been soured by the Boer War between the two countries.[8] Prior to Bolton's tour, it was Chelsea's tour of 1907 that really opened the eyes of the Dutch to the sporting opportunities that football offered. During the Pensioners' tour they played Haarlem,[9] who played Dirk Lotsy, a Dordrecht player as a "guest". Lotsy, later, wrote of Chelsea's astonishing performance: "How could such excellent combination come as a result of practice and exercise?"[10] The following summer Everton and Chelsea both visited Haarlem and played an exhibition match. Everton's 4-0 victory[11] and the performance of both sets of players confirmed to all in attendance that the Dutch *must* have British coaches. Within a short space of time the FA was in receipt of requests from Haarlem for British players to come and coach in Holland and, as a result, Fred Coles, formerly one of Bradshaw's men at Woolwich Arsenal, the ex-Leeds' left back Jack White both went to Haarlem and Edgar Chadwick took over the Dutch national team post.

Meanwhile Dordrecht, title runners-up in 1905, formerly one of the great movers in the Dutch game had noticed how such developments in other parts of the country were starting to overtake them. In 1907, they avoided relegation by the squeakiest of margins[12] and the players and secretary found themselves in dispute with the owners. Dirk Lotsy and Tonny Staal, player and secretary of the club, insisted that a British coach was needed but Nico Bouvy, another player, was not so enthusiastic because the club could hardly afford the asking price so, by way of compromise, they settled on offering to host a British touring team. In 1909 that touring team was Bolton.

Bolton did well: they played five, won five and Hogan scored four times in the match at Zwaluwen, a club that had been bolstered with some Dutch internationals, but it was the game between Bolton Wanderers and Dordrecht played on 1 June 1909 that is so significant for us. Bolton won 10-1[13] and Hogan recalled an incident involving McEwan[14] during that game that was quite light-hearted and gives some reflection as to how little Bolton were being stretched that day. The typical narrative hereafter holds that Hogan, by some virtuous altruism, resolved to go teach the Dordrecht players "proper football" but that's just nonsense.

The reality is this. Dordrecht had lost their position in the game in the Netherlands and wanted to recover that position. Things had been on the slide for a few seasons and since 1905 they had finished every season in mid-table. Bolton's 10-1 win emphasised that if Dordrecht wanted to push on then they would need some outside influence. This was not popularly accepted at Dordrecht because although they were amateur (and had wealthy patrons) they were not in the business of simply throwing money away; after all, a foreign coach does not necessarily guarantee success. However, once the club had settled their internal disputes, they contacted the Dutch FA and they in turn communicated with James Howcroft, the referee, to seek to find a suitable candidate for the role of club coach. Howcroft did a side line in acting as an intermediary between Football League clubs and foreign Associations, a role he had assumed after refereeing a number of spring-time internationals between Belgium and Holland and was therefore familiar to the Dutch FA's hierarchy.[15]

Howcroft lived in Bolton[16] and it reveals something about the characteristics of Hogan and himself that Howcroft should offer himself as a scout for coaches to the Dutch FA and that Hogan should present himself to a Football League referee to find him a new job. Howcroft and Hogan may have known each other for years[17] but it was only during the 1909-10 season that a conversation about coaching overseas had ever come about. The reason the conversation arose in the first place had everything to do with the way Bolton's season was going during 1909-10 season; a season which Young notes "was a sequence of disaster" at Bolton Wanderers. With a toxic brew of limited finances, a small complement of players and the onset of illness and accident the club, once again, found themselves beset by the choppy waters of relegation from the First Division. Notts County came from three goals down to win 4-3 on New Years' Day 1910 and in February a spectator was evicted from the

# Jimmy Hogan

main stand for "using disgusting language" no doubt frustrated by the club's reckless performances on the pitch.[18] Deputies brought in to shore up the loss of first team regulars "were insecure and the team was rarely able to function in unity."[19] Hogan was not exempt from the ill-fortune surrounding the club, he was dropped, injured, played just fourteen times and scored two goals.[20] Fox tells us that at the end of that season, a season in which the club lost ten home matches and finished bottom, "all of the players had their wages cut."[21] So, in the circumstances, it makes sense that he should present himself to Howcroft in order to fashion an exit away from Burnden Park.

However, that does not answer the question as to whether Howcroft or Hogan proposed the Dordrecht coaching role first. Did Hogan first say to Howcroft that he fancied taking on the role because it paid more than he would get at Bolton? From Hogan's perspective, heading over to Holland seemed a good idea for a number of reasons, firstly, because his injury was hindering his chances to play first team football, secondly, because it would bring in cash which he needed knowing that it was likely that Evelyn would soon agree to marry him and thirdly, because it was a fixed term contract and if it did not work out he would be back at Bolton the next year anyway. Lastly, and perhaps a minor thought was that this might lead to something else and keep him away from the drudgery of some confined office job which might have been on his mind as a career following football.

De Bolton Wanderers, welke eenige wedstrijden in ons land zullen spelen en begonnen met H. B. S. met 4—1 te slaan.

Or did Howcroft, unsolicited, ask if Hogan was interested in taking the role? It's a bit of a chicken and egg puzzle that has never been questioned by historians writing about Hogan and yet the circumstances surrounding that chat are everything, because if that conversation did not take place then who knows how things would have turned out? In the end, it served both Bolton and Hogan well for him to take the 1910-11 season off, in that it freed them from paying him a wage, further to which Howcroft got his finder's fee and Hogan got a coaching fee, possibly in excess of what Bolton were offering anyway. So all told it was convenient for all parties and is therefore nonsense when Fox states that, at that time "increasingly, Hogan was becoming aware that 'training' in Britain was failing to improve the natural abilities of the players."[22]

In all truth, Jimmy Hogan couldn't give a monkeys' about the failures of training in Britain because he did nothing about coaching footballers in Britain for at least two decades after hanging up his boots and when he finally did so it was only because someone was willing to pay him.

Later, Hogan wrote: "I was young and foolish enough to go abroad ..."[23] but he was now neither young, nobody's fool when it came to money and certainly not backward in informing all and sundry as to his big adventure. On 30 May 1910 the *Athletic News* reported the news that Hogan would be heading across the North Sea to go work in Holland. When he arrived, Hogan quickly identified that what was causing Dordrecht's slide down the League table. It was the attitude of the players who, idly rich and effortlessly wealthy, were simply not performing. "They were fond of the pleasures of life," wrote Hogan, later, "such as smoking and drinking," but one thing Holland did expose him to was a class of educated, professional men who wanted to learn how to play football and brought thinking into what they were doing. As a result of this and for the first time, Hogan encountered training which required the use of footballs and players who wanted to listen, watch and learn what they were being taught. Holland therefore first introduced to Hogan the concept that would be seemed so alien in Britain. Footballers at Dordrecht did not feel belittled by being coached to play football and saw the logic in having footballs to train with. The appointment came at the right time for Hogan. Ever since Fulham he had been over-thinking as to why his career was now on the skids. He stated, later, that he had been preoccupied during those final months at Bolton with thoughts of the conversation that he had had with Harry Bradshaw at Fulham, forcing him to wrack his brains as to why he had lost his form. Holland crystallised to him what the problem had been all along it was: "because he had been starved of the ball in training."[24] Which, as a side line, raises a question as to why he considered his time at Craven Cottage as being so seminal to his later career when he admitted himself that ball practice was a scarcity, notwithstanding the apparent "training ethos" of all those old Scottish professionals he once played against.

Once again luck was on Hogan's side when he took up his appointment. The light-heartedness with which the Dordrecht players brought to the

# Jimmy Hogan

game enabled him settling in time when a coarse, demanding audience may have hurried him back from where he came once they took consideration of his limited coaching skills for even when he went to Austria a few years later, after honing his teaching craft in Holland over the course of the 1909-10 season, he recalled: "I could see everybody was disappointed, but what could I do? I had to show them what I showed people at home."[25]

The question is raised that if that was how bad he was in Austria in 1912, heaven knows what a mess his lessons were in Holland in 1910! In light of that, however, it should be noted that we have no evidence as to what those initial coaching sessions consisted of. We are led to believe, only by implication that he could give instruction in technical matters, like heading, like passing, like shooting, but something he was lacking in was the understanding as to how to get a side to combine. It was an issue that would dog him throughout his coaching career; he was great in demonstrating high technical ability but lacking when it came to evidencing tactical nous and, in those early days, deficient in tactfulness for after one performance Hogan found himself press-ganged into broadcasting his thoughts about the ability of each of the players for the benefit of the Dordrecht club magazine:

> The members of the DFC asked me to write some comments about games and players for the magazine weekly. Before I do that, I must state that I wish no one to break down or to flatter my articles and I trust the players to receive it in the spirit in which they are written solely in their own interest. As for the game Sunday against Haarlem, I must confess that I was quite disappointed, although we won. There were no combinations and no assistance was provided. I strongly believe that the Harlem team ... was much better. As for the players themselves, I begin with the goalkeeper Van Driel. He was very confident and his game suits me best. The back-players were strong, and F. Koopman is a useful player in each position, A. Klein justified all that I have of him ... he is an excellent player behind, [passing] the ball just in time and is powerful. C. Klein is a good right-middle player, but I wished that he played more on the [inside forward].
>
> Lotsy played a good game, here there and everywhere, he had certainly a remarkable energy. He should pay a little more attention to the midfield. H. Koopman was too slow and was very tired, I would like to see that he practiced some more. As for the forward line, I [would] speak about Van der Hoeven but [have] no opinion, because he was sick; it was a miracle that he was playing at all. C. Heck was very good and he will be even better, if his knee is stronger. His goal was a nice effort, the result of the exercise in headers. Sunderman was not fast enough, he should be faster and shoot more. He is an excellent shooter and I expect this season many [goals] from him. Fruijn was poor, he seemed to forget that he had a player beside him on the wing and in the center. He [held onto] the ball instead of passing and that had caused the [game to slow]. N. Bouvy was by turns good and bad.

> If the ball was taken from him, he did attempt to regain ... it; but, as I said, he had a weak player [beside him]. I wish all players [brought more energy] into the game and the middle players supported more when applied to this pressure. I am convinced that they will play better next week, and that I will see a new victory for DFC.[26]

And that tells us all we need to know about Hogan in Holland in 1910. The goal comes as a result of an exercise in headers but in totality there is no combination and no evidence of the skills gained with all those "wonderful Scottish footballers" at Fulham, the half backs haven't been drilled to support the forwards and if we accept that then where would be a good place for the buck to stop?

Notwithstanding this, later that same month, the Dutch FA asked Chadwick to step aside and appointed Hogan to coach the Dutch national side in their match in Kleve against Germany. Under Chadwick's guidance, Holland had beaten everyone and scored abundantly, against all bar the English, so just how it came to pass that Hogan should be handed the reins for the first match in Germany is a historical curiosity. In any event, Hogan was given a challenge to resolve prior to the game and, once again, we see that element of his individual coaching influence but not of his ability to gel the team. He was told by Dutch FA officials, or interfering representatives of the clubs concerned, that Nol van Berckel, Quick Nijmegen's inside right, must make his debut in the game but that the more experienced Guus Lutjens, Den Haag's inside right, must also play. So it was decided that Van Berckel must play as the outside left!

Hogan was therefore set the task of leading individual coaching sessions with van Berckel in order to convert him to play on the other side of the field to the one he was used to. Miraculously, van Berckel half-volleyed

The Dutch national team that beat Germany in Kleve, 16 October 1910.

the winner after a quarter of an hour[27] and won the tie for Holland but, otherwise, the Dutch team struggled to dominate their opponents, as Chadwick's teams had done, and Hogan, always the technician but not the tactician, had not the whit to answer some of the questions the Germans asked of his team and, accordingly, he was never again asked to lead the national side.

In the same way, Hogan's impact at Dordrecht also showed limitations. He developed a quick line in memorable expressions: "It's an old Scotch game," he was supposed to have said, "you play together with intelligence with the ball on the ground."[28] but catchy sayings were not enough to win League title and Dordrecht, labouring to another sixth place finish decided not to proceed with the second-year of Hogan's contract, allowing him to quietly return to Bolton in the spring of 1911 before replacing him with Billy Hunter.

Upon his return to Bolton,[29] Hogan married his old-school sweetheart, Evelyn Coates, up on the Blackpool coast, in Fylde near to her family's home. While he was working in Holland she had been living with her father in the Dragoon pub in Blackpool. Given that he was marrying a publican's daughter and was now laid up with an injury on reduced wages, one might have thought that the marriage would not have been welcomed in the Hogan household at 43 Todmorden Road in Littleborough, Rochdale[30] but nothing could be further from the truth. The Coates were a devoutly religious family which assuaged any concerns that his mother might have had on reflecting that at one time Jimmy was ordained to become a priest of high social standing but now he was nearing retirement in his chosen career.

The simple fact was of course that although he had returned to play at Bolton there was no place in the first XI at Burnden for him. In Hogan's absence, Harold Hilton had taken over his duties at inside right and done remarkably well, indeed in 1910-11 season, while Hogan was in Holland, Bolton had been undefeated at home and finished second in the Second Division. A key reason for the rise in the fortunes of the club had been the arrival of Joe Smith and Ted Vizard on the left wing. Smith, "all resolute and determined" and Vizard, "an artist", shared an instant, uncanny understanding that led to 69 goals being scored that season and would serve the club well into the 1920s. As a result, when Hogan did return to playing duties he was considered good enough only for a friendly fixture against Blackburn Rovers, a game that was so ill-conceived that Angus Makant, the Club President's son and on leave from Cambridge University, turned out for the side.

His first team recall in the end did come but only after a tortuous process when Harold Hilton sustained ligament damage at Notts County.[31] The club went through five different players before finally, almost reluctantly, choosing Hogan but when they did he saw out the rest of a season that had seemed a lost cause but ended with the club achieving their highest finish since 1896.

His playing career, hampered by that leg injury, was clearly on borrowed time. Could Hogan return to Holland? Unfortunately, that door appeared to be closed, but Howcroft was able to come up with another assignment following a match he refereed in the May of 1912.

# Jimmy Hogan

## Notes

1 Transferred on 26 October 1908. *Burnley Express*, 28 October 1908.

2 The curious side-note about Shepherd is in his "selfish" style of play; in some ways out of place with his period. Rather than subscribe to the slow, deliberation of the Scottish style, Shepherd had what could be called a modern mind for goal. Soon after his arrival at Newcastle on 23 January 1909 he scored four goals against Notts County "using his speed and strength to burst through the thinly-held [defence]." Joy, 48.

3 Who cost £600. *Burnley Express*, 28 November 1953.

4 Young, *Bolton Wanderers* (Stanley Paul, 1961), p. 87. The *Athletic News* reported "at one period [Bolton] were playing so bad that the shareholders held condemnatory meetings, which proved beneficial, even if they created ill-feeling at the time." 3 May 1909.

5 They also beat Fulham at Craven Cottage. Hogan joyfully scoring the winner.

6 The terms of the tour were confirmed in the January of that year.

7 Green, *The History of the Football Association* (Naldrett, 1953), p. 260.

8 That being the first overseas tour sanctioned for a FA representative side.

9 The match was played in May 1907; Chelsea won 7-3.

10 Acknowledgement to Elisa Kuster, erstwhile redoubtable Secretary of Dordrecht FC.

11 3 May 1908 – note that rsssf.com states that Everton won 3-0.

12 They beat Concordia Delft to stay up.

13 Marland, *Bolton Wanderers: the Complete Record* (DB Publishing, 2011), p. 550; Dordrecht hold that the game was actually played on 31 May – acknowledgement to Elisa Kuster. Also Arie Heijstek and Frans van den Nieuwenhof, club historians at Dordrecht.

14 Once again reported (in Fox, p. 45) but lifted straight from the life story.

15 You do come across "busy" referees from time to time and Howcroft seemed particularly so, putting down the whistle and picking up the pen as soon as his career was over. Hogan and Howcroft seemed very suited to one another, strange but telling that Hogan should make but passing reference to such an important person in his life.

16 17 Fold Street, Bolton. (*Men Famous in Football*, 1904 edition.)

17 See the reference to the Belvedere match in Chapter 1.

18 Young, *Bolton Wanderers (1961*, p. 89.

19 *Ibid.*, 89.

20 Simon Marland reported that Hogan sustained his only notable injury at the club that season in the game at Spurs on 11 December. The match ended 1-1.

21 Fox 45, again lifted from Hogan's life story. We aren't to know for sure but since Hogan upped-sticks at the end of that season there is probably some truth in the story.

22 Fox, 47.

23 Another lift by Fox p. 52; he signed a two-year contract in August 1910 but was only retained for one of them.

24 *Burnley Express*, 24 August 1934.

25 Glanville, *Soccer Nemesis*, p. 69. Strange that he mentions "home" since it is not recorded that he undertook any coaching in England before that time.

26 *De Dordrechtsche Courant*, 1 October 1910. We also read in the paper that the board of DFC, selflessly made Mr Hogan available at the service of the Dutch team.

27 Game played on 16 October 1910 in Kleve. The information (reported first by Glanville (in 1955) and copied but never checked by Fox that von Merckel's goal came in the last ten minutes is wrong.

28 Acknowledgement to Elisa Kuster.

29 In April 1911, reported in *Athletic News*, 10 April 1911.

30 Shirley Ashton research, Nelson Library.

31 9 December 1911 at Notts County. Bolton lost 2-3. Acknowledgement to Simon Marland for checking the club's archives for that information.

# 1912

## FIVE

## 1912
### 'I simply went on the field and worked with them.'

On the 5 May of 1912, James Howcroft refereed the 1-1 draw between Austria and Hungary in Vienna. For the previous two seasons, Austria had put their arch-rivals to the sword, but now, with the Stockholm Olympics just two months away, they scraped out a lucky draw thanks to a goal two minutes from time by Adolf Fischera. Coaches and managers are not usually inclined to seek the opinion of referees as to whether their team performed well or not, but Hugo Meisl, the Austrian coach that day, was not a usual coach. History tells us that he sought the opinion of Howcroft following the game and Howcroft proposed that the best way forward would be for Meisl to engage the services of Jimmy Hogan. That Howcroft proposed Hogan to Meisl and that Meisl accepted and followed up the proposal represented a huge leap of faith on the part of both men. In 1910, the Dordrecht club had signed Hogan on a two-year contract and at the end of that first year had decided to terminate that contract and ask Howcroft to find them another coach.[1] Now less than two years later, James Howcroft was overlooking that poor reference and proposing Hogan to another appointment and, as a result, for six weeks starting in the May of 1912, Jimmy Hogan took up a contract with the Austrian Football Association in Vienna and Stockholm.

Hugo Meisl.

It is worthwhile to take stock here and review how it came to be that Meisl needed a coach in the first place but first let's look at Meisl and what the key drivers were that went to make up the man. Hugo Meisl played a fundamental role in the development of Austrian and Central European football. The game always held fascination for him and in the very early days, when continental interest in the sport was "only lukewarm",[2] Meisl was already to be seen kicking the ball about with his school chums. Hogan and Meisl became long-term friends, possibly because they both shared certain characteristics. Like Hogan, Meisl had a fairly comfortable upbringing since his father's trade in textiles gave him the luxury to choose a career path for himself and, accordingly, Hugo first meandered into becoming an accountant at his dad's company but when that went bust, plumped strategically for a subordinate position with the Österreichische Länderbank. Meisl had no truck with the idea of being chained to a desk and saw greater opportunities to expand his influence through sport rather than through working within an office which he found tiresome. But the bank role served several purposes. Firstly, it paid the bills, but importantly it did not over-tax him enough to sufficiently draw him from his evolving interest in football.[3] Meisl's brother, the author Willy, later described Hugo's impact on Austrian football in the following way: "[he] ... organised [the] visits of British sides not only for Vienna, but also for Prague, Budapest and also for German, Swiss and Italian clubs and associations. He managed to get rid of a small fortune in the process of fostering Austrian soccer."[4]

These "visits" by touring teams proved to be profitable to Meisl, who, though a football fan foremost, was not blind to the understanding that he needed to cover his outlay and so whereas the principle objective behind bringing teams over was to develop football in Austria Meisl also needed to attract a paying audience. Historians have leaned too far one way in their analysis of Meisl. Of course, he had an interest in developing Austrian football to be of a high standard, certainly to be better than Hungary, but just what that standard amounted to depended on what appealed to the largest number of spectators, after all who cares about great art if no one wants to see it?

Therefore, Hugo spent money to bring teams over to Austria, but rather than generate a profit, Meisl seemed more driven by the desire to create an environment in which football could become a sustainable sport in Vienna. We are not here, however, to explore the mentality and drivers of Hugo Meisl, interesting though they are. Suffice it to say that Meisl had to be cognisant as to what the viewing public wanted. Those who had sponsored the games in which the English teams played after all, needed a return to cover the cost of hiring the grounds where the matches were played, on officials, security, administrators, to accommodate the paying audience, and publicity. What the paying crowd wanted the paying crowd got and what was popular obviously had an impact on the type of football that Hugo was inclined toward promoting and delivering. That would have been a key motivator to Hugo Meisl and was key in shaping the development of Austrian football under Meisl. British football won over the Viennese not because it was "better quality" football necessarily but because it was exciting. And "exciting" was football played manfully with hard-tackling. 1905 was to be a high point in relation to the Continental tours undertaken by British clubs because in the space of a couple of weeks, thanks to Hugo's administrations, the Viennese were to be witness to some of the best players in British football history but this was no window-shopping exercise. The objective was to sell this game bells and whistles to the Viennese and the plan was to attract crowds in large numbers.

As to which of the teams the Austrians moulded their style on in seeking to reach "high standards" in those early years is still open to doubt and one of the reasons for that is that Hugo's brother, Willy, was the historian who charted the early history of Austrian football, not Hugo himself. And this means that we are hamstrung in having to rely on secondhand knowledge as to what motivations drove Hugo. Willy stated that Rangers were the team upon "...whose style the Austrians were to mould their game,"[5] but given that that is just hearsay one should be cautious before accepting Jonathan Wilson's assertion that: "... *everything* [Meisl] did tactically could be traced back to a nostalgic attempt to recreate the style of the Rangers tourists of 1905;[6] he insisted on the pattern-weaving mode of passing, ignored the coming of the third back, and retained a sense that a centre-forward should be a physical totem ..."[7]

The simple fact is that we don't know and possibly never will know what team Hugo Meisl wanted to mould his Austrian national team on and that has implications as to what instructions he gave to Hogan when he came to Vienna and has implications as to our whole understanding of how things became shaped as they came to be. For instance, Willy Meisl may have suggested that the Rangers' team was the template that Hugo followed but it is telling that Willy makes more reference to the combined tour undertaken by both Everton and Spurs in May 1905.[8] Everton had just been deprived of the title by a point after Newcastle snatched a victory over Middlesbrough on the final day of the season and Spurs, the famous Cup winners of 1901, who were led by John Cameron, were a principal club in the Southern League.[9] Of this encounter, Willy, wrote: "... on 7 May 1905 Hugo staged an exhibition game between Everton and Tottenham. The two teams fought as if it were a Cup tie. Never before had the 10,000 spectators – the crowd record was doubled by this sensational encounter – seen such tackling."[10]

The great turning point was reached when Everton and Spurs met in Vienna. From that time onwards, progress was made to continually raise the standard of football in Vienna, and to keep attracting crowds in sufficient numbers to justify investment in the game. But that development came far too quickly. Instead of concentrating on quality, clubs entered into a frenzy of matches, a plan which was designed to ensure that money, no matter how much, would still be coming through the turnstiles. Unfortunately this was leading to lots of matches being played in front of sparse audiences so in October 1911 Dr Ignaz Abeles of FK Austria introduced an English-style points system and a Championship was formed with the hope that one outcome would be that there would be less but higher quality matches and second that a more successful national side would be brought about but, as mentioned, the March 1912 draw against the Hungarians militated against such an understanding. And so the call went out for Jimmy Hogan!

When Jimmy, Evelyn and their first born, Joseph, arrived in Vienna in May 1912 they would have been astonished. Even to the locals of the day Vienna was a place of wonder, gentility, culture and art and would have been a world away from what the Hogan's knew and had grown used to. "To leave … dark, gloomy industrial Lancashire for Gay Vienna was just like stepping into paradise," Hogan later wrote.[11] As the inaugural Championship came to a close, Hogan was set to work travelling between the key Viennese clubs to "coach" and also assess the players who had been selected for the Austrian Olympic squad. His remit may have been confined by the city limits but it was an exacting schedule, made so by the fact that representatives from the Vienna club asked that they too should be involved in the scheme. The players were strictly amateur in those days and so to fit around their work Hogan's day started with the dawn chorus before heading to the Vienna club for a 5.30 a.m. start, conduct a two-hour session before all showered and headed off for their coffee, pastries and the day job. Meanwhile, during the working day he trained the Olympic XI who were, initially, less than enamoured with his training "scheme." You can be sure that, since Hogan wrote his version of events, where he does refer to criticism of his work it was probably worse than he made out; it would be quite natural if that were the case. Previously in Dordrecht he had been indulged by those friendly Dutch players but here in Vienna he encountered a different work ethic and one that was married to concerns the Austrians had regarding their form going into the Olympics. These new attitudes and demands provided something of a culture shock to Hogan who had set out in his early sessions, his training "regime" for others to follow. The sessions were not popularly received: "I could see everybody was disappointed, but what could I do? I had to show them what I showed people at home."[12] Just what "home" Hogan was referring to is a matter for debate, for he had certainly never coached in England. What he said he did was offered "the usual British training methods for the day, and finished with a team game,[13]

… but does not elaborate further as to what these methods were. What we do know is what he said he did in Holland: "I simply went on the field and worked with them. Then it was a case of thinking out little ideas and exercises in shooting, ball control, trapping, heading, combination stunts, and afterwards playing in side games with them."[14]

Willy Meisl later wrote: "It was in Vienna that [Hogan] discovered how primitive British training methods were …"[15] but this seems to divert attention away from the truth of it. It wasn't that British training methods were primitive; it was that the training methodology Hogan brought with him to Vienna was founded on nothing more than a series of exercises that he had concocted either as a player or while he was in Holland. In essence, when he took the coaching job in Vienna, Jimmy Hogan did not have any idea as to how to coach others. To him coaching meant letting others watch you undertake a few exercises. Coaching in his mind would have been akin to teaching and teaching, as we have seen, amounted to a person at the front of the class explaining and showing, not letting the class run amok with some Bunsen burners, or in this case, with some footballs. But demonstrating an exercise that you're adept at doing to others who aren't skilled in doing that exercise misses the whole point of what a coach is supposed to do. As a coach you must transfer your skill verbally or visually then get your students to demonstrate their understanding and then analyse where your students are failing and correct that through further analysis and exercise. Hogan was good at demonstrating the skill of controlling a football because that is what he saw as being prerequisite to being a professional footballer, but that did not make him a natural coach of others. But this is where the relationship between Hugo Meisl and Jimmy Hogan became so important.

Hogan was always blessed with that charmed Irish luck and in Vienna in 1912 this was seen in two ways. In Meisl he had a manager who did not panic but smoothed any strained relations without fuss or fanfare and became the perfect foil for Hogan by becoming a sort of bridge helping to overcome the language barrier and get his message across to players, encouraging them to persevere with the exercises and to wait and see. The effect of this was immediately noticed by Hogan: "What pleased me most was that my judgment was acknowledged and highly respected. There was no interference in my plans of campaign."[16] However, whereas Meisl *publicly* backed Hogan with the players he did so only because he had no other option. When it came to his attention that there had been concerns raised about Hogan's teaching methodology, that led to what we might now term a crisis meeting between him and Meisl and this led Hogan "to study [coaching] even more intently."[17] In combination, as Willy Meisl later wrote, the two "worked out a more satisfactory scheme, probably the first modern training schedule in soccer."[18] This was the moment in the coaching history of European football.

So in came nights of fretting and broken sleep and chewing over ideas as to best forms of practice and planned activities and Hogan became transformed into the most diligent teacher. Activities were trialled and re-tested and through constant repetition Hogan became adept at the discrete skills that his pupils now demanded of him. No doubt there were occasions in those early days when Hogan, like all teachers, would have been posed a question or challenged on his knowledge and not come up to the mark. This is natural within all teaching disciplines for not all consequences within the learning environment can be foreseen. It is the fear to avoid these situations that leads to self-testing the exercises to be taught which is exactly what Hogan started to do over and over again in order to master the skill he requested of his players and as he repeated the skill so he may have slowed it down, reduced each to its component parts in order to best demonstrate to the players. This might sound obvious but in practice it is an easy mistake to supplant speed for skill. I have a personal example of that.

I once went to a training session at a Football League club to see a coach train some of young female players. The coach set out cones and asked that the girls approach the cones by dribbling and then, using a step over, move around and past the cone with the ball. Now, stepping over the ball with a leading right leg requires the right leg to circle the ball [1] be planted on the ground [2] have body weight placed on it [3] before the left foot can flick the football away from the opponent [4]. Slowing the process down to constituent parts enables the learner to time the movement rather than simply run at the opponent and hope for the best when you get there. I couldn't count the amount of times one of the girls kept hitting the ball with the cone on that cold Sunday while her shivering parents looking on expectantly. In essence, she was learning nothing because the coach did not have the ability to segment the lesson into bite sized chunks and did not bother enough to identify where there was a failing and address it. That is where Hogan, following the meeting with Meisl, became distinguished over time. Hogan was not a strategist but he was obviously committed enough to learn how to analyse what he was doing and distil the essential part to others. He became first, foremost and at the end someone who inculcated a range of basic footballing skills. Whether he could transfer that knowledge sufficiently well for others to do as he did is a matter of ongoing debate with everyone stating he could and me on my little soapbox stating that I am still to be convinced. One thing is certain; in those early days Hogan would not have been an effective coach because he would have been preoccupied in identifying which were the most effective activities to practice and demonstrate to his pupils. What made the difference in those early days was Meisl. It took Meisl to bring the players around to what Hogan was demonstrating but it also took the arrival of British touring teams to embed the philosophy of constructive football into the minds of the Austrians. Without this Hogan's coaching career would have come to a shuddering halt. The fact remains, however, that all the time he was in Vienna in those six weeks in 1912, Hogan was being fed information from Meisl regarding games, players and different patterns of play Meisl had seen on his travels and this would have slowly become distilled in Hogan's mind as he developed his practice..

The patience Meisl showed Hogan, however, was not a characteristic that Hogan extended to others and this concerned the second stroke of fortune. Glanville later gifted Hogan an acknowledgement he barely deserved when he wrote that "so quickly did the Austrians improve, during the six weeks that [Hogan] was in Vienna, that they defeated Tottenham Hotspur ..."[19] but it would be foolish to give Hogan credit for this. To begin with things looked bleak when, in late May 1912, Hogan's Viennese-trained players lost heavily to Woolwich Arsenal.[20] Partly as a result of that loss, a few days later, the Olympic squad was bolstered when five players from Deutscher FC Prag,[21] coached by Johnny Dick, who was another of Bradshaw's men from Woolwich Arsenal, arrived from Bohemia.[22] In early June, the new revitalised "Olympic" team beat Tottenham 3-0. Spurs had already drawn and then narrowly defeated the Hungarian Olympic side[23] but even when aided by the new Prague players, Hogan still sought to ram home whatever advantage he could get. Although they found themselves two-nil down, the Spurs players had been anxious to kick off the second half immediately, since they were clearly getting back into the game when the referee blew up for half-time. They sought Hogan's agreement but he point blankly refused because he knew if his side could hold on for the win that it would boost his credentials with his Austrian pay masters and would be reported back in England. And, as luck would have it, Tottenham were not able to recover their momentum and so their players limped to the finish line, conceded another goal, and ended the game with ten men. If Hogan was trying to build a reputation for himself, it was an effective but shoddy way to do it.

Before the Austrian team left for Stockholm there were disputes to be resolved and, as it always seemed to be the case with Hogan, the dispute involved money. The Austrian FA didn't have enough money to cover Hogan's fees and expenses and so Meisl had to curry favours with the clubs, cap in hand, to ensure that Hogan remained a part of the touring party.

# Jimmy Hogan

Hogan would go; the sole coaching representative for the squad.

### 1912 Olympic Games

The official Olympic report author was scathing in his criticism of Hogan's Austria in what was his first Olympic Games. The author's view on the Austrian team was that they were over-enthusiastic, boorish and unnecessarily physical: "Both Denmark and Holland had a fairly confirmed British style, both these teams relying more on science, combination and agility than on speed and hard rushes, especially as regards the play of the forwards. The opposite was the case with ... Austria [and] Hungary (in the case of the latter, less, perhaps)."[24] The theme would reach its natural conclusion in the Consolation Final when Austria and Hungary belted seven bells out of each other at the Råsunda where skill was demonstrated momentarily and the overriding impression was summed up quite dramatically: "... a rougher game has never been played in Sweden."[25] However, it was only natural that this should be the case since the mutual animosity between then Austrians and Hungarians typically got the better of them: "... scarcely anything else was to be expected. Hard knocks were given and taken without a word, and there were one or two little accidents, but there is nothing to be said, for football is not what it is, unless physical advantages were allowed to be advantages."[26]

This all highlighted the attitude that both countries brought to the game for in those days anything which brought the two into conflict was an excuse for excess. Victory, no matter how it was achieved, overcame all other considerations and so rather than condition themselves to retain a cool detachment both the Hungarians and Austrians forsook all sense of level-headedness in order to get ahead. Earlier in the competition, the Hungarians had fought fantastically against the Great Britain team but did not have the composure to convert the chances they created and ended up losing 7-0. Against this the Austrians peppered each game with a smattering of combination but the games were normally an excuse for throwing themselves blindly into the fray.

The lack of composure was obvious from the first match against Germany. The right-wing combination for Austria of Ludwig Hussak and his inside partner, Robert Merz (one of Dick's men at Prague) was notable, "but the forwards fell asleep with the ball when they came near the goal."[27] In the second half, "[the forward's] rushes came with lightning rapidity and with lots of power behind them, and during the course of one of these attacks (from which Müller scored) the German goal-keeper [Weber] was hurt pretty badly."[28]

Austria's prize in the second round would be a game against Chadwick's Dutch side which presented Hogan with an opportunity to meet up with his old friends from Dordrecht, Nico Bouvy and Karel Lotsy, but the tactical naivety of the Austrians, married to the supremacy of the Dutch left him bitter for years afterwards. "The front five of the Hollanders soon found out how to trick the Austrian defence, which everywhere went in for hard, rushing tactics."[29] After ten Cate's tap in made it 2-0 to Holland, Austria "began to play with all the energy of despair," wrote the Olympic reporter.[30] "Despair" and yet just twelve minutes had elapsed since the start of the game! Hogan would later write that the skill demonstrated by the Dutch, who won 4-3, was not a reflection on their long-term coach, Chadwick, but in actual fact on himself; Holland, he wrote, were better because "they had the benefit of my coaching in the years before I started work in Austria."[31] It was a bizarre, rancorous announcement made forty years after the event, his bare credentials, taking Dordrecht to a mid-table finish and beating the Germans by the odd goal in three in a friendly, being airbrushed by him for his unsuspecting readership.

The Austrians now travelled to Traneberg where they would begin the Consolation Tournament with a win against Norway. The Austrians "had no lack of opportunities ... but every chance was thrown away."[32] The forwards finally corrected their flaws against the Italians in the semi-final when they "did the best piece of work of all of their performances during the Olympic competition ..."[33]

So to the game with Hungary, where both sides were at full strength. Austria's defence was re-organised for the third game on the trot but Wiener's Hussak came back to lead the side alongside Cimera at left half, the only player to appear in all matches, and Merz moved to the centre-forward spot where he would play alongside Alois Müller. The match was played in a beastly manner throughout: "On one occasion Mr Willing (the referee) was obliged to call the teams together and admonish them to play a more gentlemanly game."[34] The referee's lecture led to "the best play of the match ... the Austrian forwards combined better than those of Hungary, but the latter's backs, Rumbold especially, played brilliantly."[35] This was more than could be said for the Austrian defence, which was pulled here and there by the sweeping wing-play of the Hungarians. Despite repeated evidence, Hogan's team had simply failed to address what had been a recurring theme throughout the competition. From yet another breakaway, a goal made by Ferencváros, Pataki increasing the Hungarian's lead, the cross coming from Borbás on the left: "The Hungarians began to force the game, sending the ball from wing to wing, with the result that Borbás, after a brilliant individual attack, gave Hungary its third and finest goal."[36]

Hogan returned to Bolton for the last time as a professional player. His knee was now a permanent source of pain and, as a result, in 1912-13 he was recalled for only three more first team games. It would have been, bar an odd footnote, a mundane way to end his playing career but the footnote came during the German and Austrian tour of 1913. Hogan may well have been a reserve in his final season but he was invited to attend the tour in the May of that year which saw him turn out for the Lilywhites in a match in Berlin before the side travelled to Vienna to participate in a four team event.[37] It would prove to be his last match as a Bolton player and it was somewhat apt that his final game should be on foreign soil.

# 1912

Notes

1 Billy Hughes, Hogan's Bolton teammate took over the coaching of the club.
2 Capel-Kirby & Carter, *The Mighty Kick* (1933), Foreword.
3 Acknowledgement to Dr Andreas Hafer, Meisl's grandson for his input.
4 Willy Meisl, *Soccer Revolution* (1956), p. 57.
5 *Ibid.*, 57.
6 Wilson means the tourists of 1904, there was no Rangers' tour in 1905; acknowledgement to Jim Hannah at Glasgow Rangers FC.
7 Wilson, *Inverting the Pyramid* (2009), p. 61.
8 Newcastle, the Civil Service and the London Casuals had also toured central Europe in the May of that year.
9 Some of the players the Viennese would have seen in those few weeks in 1905 would have included Peter McWilliam, Billy McCracken, Colin Veitch, Jimmy Lawrence (from Newcastle), Jimmy Settle, Harold Hardman and John Sharp at Everton but we do know that Vivien Woodward was definitely there, as was John Cameron and Jack Kirwan from Spurs.
10 *Soccer Revolution*, 57.
11 *Sport*, vol. 16, no. 319, p. 6.
12 *Soccer Nemesis*, 69.
13 *Sport*, vol. 16, no. 319, p. 6.
14 *Sport*, vol. 16.
15 *Soccer Revolution*, 58.
16 *Sport*, vol. 16, no. 321, p.6.
17 *Sport*, vol. 16, no. 320, p. 5.
18 *Soccer Revolution*, 58.
19 *Soccer Nemesis*, 70.
20 http://www.rsssf.com/tablesb/brit-ier-tours-prewwii.html#r
21 The goalkeeper Noll, a half-back Cimera, the defender Graubart, the veteran Kurpiel and the inside forward Merz.
22 http://scottishcomedyfc.com/scottish-footballs-coaching-pioneers-2-john-dick/
23 Match played on Sunday, 2 June 1912 at WAC-Platz, Vienna. Austria Olympic Team: Otto Noll (DFC Prague) – Bernhard Graubart (DFC Prague), Jakob Swatosh I (1st Simmeringer SC) – Franz Weber (Vienna), Karl Braunsteiner (Wr.), Karl Tekusch II 'Dr Karl' (Wr. Association FC) – Ludwig Hussak (Wr Amateur SV), Robert Merz (DFC Prague), Johann Studnicka 'Jan' (Wiener AC), Leopold Neubauer (Wr. Sports Club), Alois Muller II (Wr.).
24 1912 Olympic Report, 501.
25 *Ibid.*, 499.
26 *Ibid.*, 502.
27 *Ibid.*, 485.
28 *Ibid.*
29 *Ibid.*, 490.
30 *Ibid.*]
31 *Sport*, vol. 16, no. 321.
32 Olympic Report, 496.
33 *Ibid*, 498.
34 *Ibid*, 499.
35 *Ibid.*
36 *Ibid.*
37 15 May 1913 v Sports Club Rapid – *Neues Wiener Abendblatt*, 25/4/13.

Jimmy Hogan

1914-1916

SIX

## 1914-1916
'A strange light began immediately to fall and grow on the map of Europe...'

Hogan's failure to secure a new contract with Bolton for the 1913-14 season and the fact that his young family now numbered four meant that he was coming awfully close to having to do a normal job for a living so it came as a blessing when he received a letter inviting him to the Adelphi Hotel in Liverpool for a coaching job in Berlin. In preparation for the 1916 Olympics, the Germans had sent agents to England and invitations had been sent out to a number of players who wished to be considered for coaching roles in Germany. When Hogan arrived at the hotel he was awestruck by whom he saw. Bloomer, Brearley, Pentland were there. "As I gazed around the room, and noted the prominent players in attendance, I almost 'gave up the ghost.' "[1] Hogan was the last to be interviewed and, partly on account of the fact that he could speak a smattering of German, was given the impression that the job would most likely be his and, being asked for a reference, told the interviewer to contact Hugo Meisl.[2]

When Meisl heard from the Norddeutscher Fussball-Verband, the first thing that would have struck him was that two years out, the Germans were already preparing for the Olympics. By comparison, in 1912, the Austrians had engaged Hogan barely a month prior to the Games. The second thing that would have struck Meisl was that Hogan was seeking employment and following this, Meisl made enquiries of the clubs in Vienna, and then wrote to Hogan, inviting him and his young family to Vienna for a second time. As things transpired it was to be, in football terms at least, another short stay, the sudden onset of the War bringing his work to an abrupt end. Seen from our eyes one would have thought the impending war would have given cause for concern for anyone seeking employment in Central Europe but there were no grounds for fear when Hogan arrived early that summer to take up his contract. Churchill remarked that, in the spring and summer of 1914, Europe had been marked by "an exceptional tranquillity." None were to foresee what was to happen.

Hogan arrived in Vienna in the May of 1914[3] with Evelyn, three-year-old Joseph and Mary. The family had already had what might be termed a taster for the finer parts of Viennese life when Hogan first worked in Austria but

# Jimmy Hogan

now they quickly acclimatised themselves to a lifestyle that they must have imagined would be theirs for the foreseeable future. Vienna in that summer of 1914, would have represented an experience of utter good fortune for the young family. He would have been pinching himself at the very idea that here he was getting paid to undertake a role that would have paid a pittance in England and it was a role that opened the door to a lifestyle that would have been incomprehensible to the Hogan's friends and relatives. In the evenings, after his training exercises had been done for the day, Meisl would invite Evelyn and Jimmy to the Prater for *al fresco* dinners before an orchestra competed with the evensong of the park's residents in the comfortable warmth of the Viennese evening. Long gone from his mind as he sat there in his evening suit eating bread for starters was the archetypal image that English clubs had of their "trainers" swinging a bucket of freezing water, while they raced across a rain-soaked mud bath of a pitch with a dirty rag to wipe blood from a gashed knee.

And all the while the startling exposure that Hogan was experiencing of "Dear Old Vienna" was impressing on him the distinctive civilities and cultures one would witness in the streets, sights and sounds of the fine city of Vienna that "bow and sweep of the hat" that came to shape Austrian football: "I have often compared Austrian football with the Viennese waltz, in that it is so light and easy."[4] The Austrian love of the waltz was apparent within those footballers he was teaching who would finally dispense with the disinclination to play the physically confrontational type of game that Hogan had grown used to over his playing career and adopt a far more aesthetic form of the game. It was not that the players had a distaste for the physical side of the game, it was just that over time it came to their minds that that did not represent them and their way of doing things. Instead they wanted to play in a distinctive manner, especial to the Viennese, one that would distinguish them from their local rivals. Whether Hogan had time enough to inculcate this understanding within the short window that he coached in 1914 is an interesting point but there is no reason to assume that it would not have had a bearing on him when he had thought things through in the round over time because to coach the Austrian way one had to live and work with the Viennese.

His previous experience had also given him more confidence. The meetings with Meisl and his understanding of the Viennese taste for things, and their way of doing things, had enabled him an insight into what he was doing and the effect of the type of coaching that he was now developing. The development of the training schedule that Willy Meisl later referred to now started to come into its own: "What I said was 'law' and my ideas were known as 'The Hogan School of Football' throughout the length and

# 1914-1916

breadth of the land."[5]

He was set a programme of work by Meisl, visiting each of the principal clubs in Vienna, including FK Amateure Vienna and First Vienna Football Club and reacquainted himself with players he had encountered in 1912, assessing the potential of those who would one day make up the Berlin Olympic squad. His training regime, first set out with Meisl in 1912, had become formulated into "continuous ball practice, followed by side games. In the latter, positional play, movements, covering-up [marking], tactics and everything appertaining to the game, was drilled into my pupils."[6] What was becoming obvious to Hogan was that whereas British footballers were "naturals" at the game, in that they either did not need to be taught or, as George Raynor later came to realise, did not actually want to be taught but naturally felt inclined toward the game, their European cousins were already demonstrating appetite for instruction and reflection.

Hogan had been in Austria for barely a month when startling news reached Vienna of the assassination of the Archduke in Sarajevo. In far off London, Winston Churchill, on overhearing Sir Edward Grey reading Austria's ultimatum to Serbia, found himself experiencing a reverie of horror, "a strange light began immediately to fall and grow on the map of Europe," he later wrote.[7] And so July 1914 became a month of encircling doom, disputes arose but were left unresolved, conciliatory talks were cancelled and everyone, Hogan included, suddenly came to grasp an awareness of things not previously thought out. On the 2 August 1914, conscious as to where all this discord was heading, Hogan sent a letter to his father at 43 Todmorden Road, Burnley encouraging the chin to remain in an upward direction in spite of all the worrying signs. It would be the last time he would be able to write to his family that year. The same day, Hogan presented himself to the British Embassy in Vienna. "The [British] Counsel [officer] assured me that there was no immediate danger and advised me to carry on with my work. Within forty-eight hours of that interview war was declared."[8] On 4 August 1914, the British, now an alien presence in a hostile city, were all summarily arrested, including Hogan and his family who were roused out of bed and held. Conditions, at first, were restrictive rather than oppressive. He was held at the Police Prison on Elisabethpromenade which sat on the banks of the Donaukanal, near the centre of the city[9] but Evelyn and the children were granted a token of liberty being subject to a loose form of house-arrest. As the arrest had been effected so quickly, Hogan was unable to take anything with him so that he looked much the worse for wear when Evelyn was finally granted visitation rights later that week. He became lost in the system as the authorities struggled to work out how best to deal with him and his fellow British prisoners, one of whom just happened to be Gordon Walker, owner of a tobacco business in Liverpool. The immediacy of the war had meant that no contingencies had been determined for the foreign prisoners and there was a considerable delay as alternative plans were put in place for their continued incarceration: "For the next 2-3 months I lived in a cellar, and in consequence of the damp and exposure I contracted rheumatism, and losing my strength through this and hunger became so weak that I could not get up."[10] Meanwhile, the two-year contract he had signed with the Austrian FA had been terminated. Given that Hogan was now a prisoner it made sense that the contract was null and void but this didn't alleviate the circumstance now facing his wife and children. Hogan's incarceration entitled him to be given food, Evelyn on the other hand now found herself in a real bind because she had recently discovered she was pregnant and had responsibility for Joe and Mary in a foreign city where the locals barely spoke English and so was forced to present herself to the authorities in order to beg for rations. From August 1914 until March 1915 she was largely left to her own devices, a fact that angered him for some considerable time. She was finally saved from a state of constant hunger because, following extensive negotiations between the authorities and the neutral American Counsel, she and the children were finally granted leave from Vienna and allowed to travel back to England in March 1915.[11] They weren't the only foreigners permitted to leave Austria. In September 1914, Dutch prisoners, upon returning home, got a message through to England in order to tell Hogan's family that Jimmy was doing OK. The whole situation ensured that Hogan felt great anger against the Austrian FA for years afterwards, enough to drive him to make public his dispute in the spring of 1919 when he got back to England. When he returned to England he wrote an open letter to the newspapers: "The Austrian FA broke my contract and left [my family and me] to starve."[12] Of course whereas Hogan could convince the ignorant British public as to his dire circumstances the same was not true of the Austrians. As early as the spring of 1919 the *Illustriertes Sportblatt* caught wind of Hogan's account of his treatment in Vienna and issued a withering retort. Hogan's stories, his alleged ill-treatment by the Austrians were, they wrote, "untrue, partly disfigured and exaggerated." In addition Hogan was going to have "a hard time" convincing the Football Association to recover money he felt he was owed from the Austrian Football Association[13] for breaking his contract at a time of war between the two countries. Further to this, as late as December 1919, after having tried unsuccessfully to get the FA to resolve the matter on his behalf, he wrote an open letter to the *Wiener Sporttagblatt* that he expected to be published indicating that he felt that no English footballer should work for Austrian football until the dispute was resolved.[14] The editorial response to this letter was dismissive after all, they asked, who, exactly, was going to pay the £500 that Hogan said he was owed?

This bitterness partly explains why it is that between August 1914 and December 1932 Jimmy Hogan would have nothing to do with Austrian football and completely torpedoes the belief that his ideas gave fundamental foundation to the *Wunderteam*. In truth, it should be said that of all the footballers who went to Europe in 1914, Hogan's experience was hardly the worst. The majority of those who went actually served their country and of these some died, others were disfigured and left wholly traumatised by their experiences in the Footballer's Batallion, others were held at Ruhleben POW camp for the duration of the conflict. And that is where Hogan's experience differs from them because Hogan was not held indefinitely at the Police Station as we shall see. Yet even so Hogan would be the only one who so much as raised a complaint about his situation.[15]

He would have remained in prison for the duration of the war had it not been for the generosity of some English emigrés called the Blythe family.[16] Fox wrote, later, that "the Blythes donated £1,000 to the Austrian Red Cross" to ensure Hogan's release from the police prison and into house arrest. Just what chicanery had to have been overcome to have saved Jimmy Hogan from a labour camp is not known but an instinct of his for chummying up close to those with influence saw him make good from a dire situation. Ernst Herbert Blythe and his father, Picton Jonathan, had lived in Vienna since the 1870s and had amassed a reasonable fortune from selling clothes there. By the start of the Great War they had established themselves within high Viennese society, trading out of a store at Praterstrasse 17 in the heart of the Jewish business district of Leopoldstrasse. The intervention of the Blythe's left a lasting legacy, within their care Hogan started learning German and this helped him get work in Europe after the war in the Swiss German city of Berne.[17] He was taken by the brothers to live with Ernst and his young family at Ghelengasse 4 in the 13th district of Vienna.[18] It was a large house, which still remains, with a swimming pool in the back garden out in leafy suburbia. There seemed little reason for Hogan to venture outside into the local neighbourhood but Hogan, was, in any event, placed under special restrictions, obliged to report to the authorities every few hours and not allowed out after 3 pm.[19] "I found a good home and shelter with the Blythes and their good ladies," wrote Hogan, "I gave the children lessons in English [and] was their tutor and sports master."[20]

So while the other male prisoners were no doubt engaged in hard labour for a couple of years and others were being blown to smithereens on the Western Front, Jimmy Hogan was spending a year and a half teaching young, polite children how to perfect the overhead smash. That gentle image should always be remembered when we consider the character of Jimmy Hogan demanding that Sir Frederick Wall sever ties with the Austrian Football Association on his behalf in 1919.

> *What strenuous singles we played after tea,*
> *We in the tournament — you against me!*
> *Love-thirty, love-forty, oh! weakness of joy,*
> *The speed of a swallow, the grace of a boy...*
> [The Subaltern's Love Song.]

# 1914-1916

## Notes

1 *Sport*, vol. 16, no. 320, p.5.
2 He wrote that the job finally went to Bloomer, which, if true, would raise considerable doubt as to whether Hogan was favoured over the most famous footballer in the world at that time.
3 *Burnley News*, 16 December 1914.
4 *Sport*, vol. 16, no. 321, p. 6.
5 *Ibid.*
6 *Ibid.*
7 Churchill & Gilbert, *The World Crisis 1911-1918* (2007), p. 95.]
8 *Sport*, vol. 16, no. 321, p 6.
9 The street was renamed Rossauer Lände after the end of the war.
10 *Sport*, vol. 16, no. 321, p. 6.
11 *Sheffield Independent*, 12 March 1919.
12 *Ibid.*
13 29 March 1919.
14 9 December 1919.
15 One had to feel sympathy with Steve Bloomer who lost one of his daughters while he was living in the POW camp during the Great War.
16 Fox just accepts what Hogan states in 1954 when referring to the "Blythe brothers who owned a department store in Vienna" and everyone has followed his lead. Further research reveals that Ernst was born in 1878 (his birth registered at the British Consulate) and that Picton Jonathan was his father. In 1913 Ernst lived at Ghelengasse 4 in the 13th district and his father at the considerably more modest Waisenhausgasse 4 in the 9th district. In June 1916 they opened a new store in Kaerntnerstrasse – "the most elegant avenue in the entire empire." Acknowledgement to Matthias Marschik, University of Vienna.
17 *Topical Times*, 11 March 1933.
18 In March 1919, it was reported that he owed his favours to "one dependent English friend." *Illustriertes Sportblatt*, 29 March 1919.
19 *Burnley News*, 1 March 1919.
20 *Sport*, vol. 16, no. 321, p. 6.

Jimmy Hogan

## SEVEN

## 1916-1919
'He has shown that the football game can also be an art which is an aesthetic pleasure.'

Hogan may have been sequestered from public scrutiny during his prolonged house arrest in Vienna, but he had also become the subject of protracted discussions to release him. Indeed, a private tug of war had ensued between two well-connected businessmen in Hungary and the authorities in Austria.

When he was released, the people responsible for him were two Jewish businessmen in Budapest, Baron Gedeon Dirsztay and Arpad Brüll who were, respectively, vice-President and President of Magyar Testgyakorlók Köre, or as we know it, the MTK Football Club.[1] The Baron plays a role in not one but two stories as to how Hogan was able to go from his palatial house arrest in Vienna to a paid role coaching footballers at MTK and both stories are most likely interrelated. The first is that Dirsztay knew the Blythes and used political connections to get Hogan to Hungary. Hogan wrote "... Dirsztay [who had used] a great amount of influence to get me to Budapest, where there was a job awaiting me."[2] The second that Dr Arpad Brüll, the millionaire, acted as an emissary for the Austrian Red Cross throughout the Austro-Hungarian Empire during the War, and engineered his transfer to Budapest.[3] Hogan may have harboured ideas of being Irish but he owed his birth nationality to finally being saved, for Brüll's well-known anglophilia was the reason for his rescue. In December 1918, W. A. Berry, a sculler, writing in the *London Evening News*,[4] introduced British readers to Brüll, explaining that he went out of his way to help any Englishmen caught up in the diplomatic mess of the War. "No Englishman was ever allowed to go short of food if [Brüll] knew it and it was my mission to find out any hard cases amongst my fellow countrymen and report to him." Whichever of the two were ultimately responsible and whatever the competing reasons, their altruism had ulterior motives, the principle objective being to fill the vacant position of coach for their team, Budapest's pre-eminent Jewish football club. Hogan wrote in the spring of 1919 "... it took four months [to get me out of Vienna]"[5] and, later, that his release was effected "towards the end of 1916."[6] And so, Hogan went to Budapest to be housed and fed and coach footballers.

# Jimmy Hogan

To define MTK as being a "Jewish" club is clumsy, for the club, though presided over by Brüll since 1905, came to represent a reaction against sporting clubs in the city that were the sole preserve of the Christian population. Brüll wanted his club to be based on sound, sporting principles; reflective of an attitude that deliberately challenged the notion that the club was peopled by the less schooled and uncivilised and so the battle lines against their chief cross-city rivals, Ferencváros, were drawn. "[Brüll] believed in talent, in fair play, not in racial or material differences,"[7] and though they were laudable aims they did not stop him from investing heavily in creating as strong a club as he could. Players attracted to play for MTK might have believed in his high principles but the real selling point was his offer of better terms for better quality players. As a result the principal football stars in the country flocked to the club and the club started, slowly and then more rapidly, to grow in importance and prestige. How MTK came to consolidate resources and predominate in the national league was to have lasting implications. In the 1950s Honved, the Army club, were provided with the resources to do the exact same thing, operating as a national side within the domestic league. I discussed the matter with Rogan Taylor, who had written about Puskás, explaining that the concept must have had a practical basis somewhere rather than via the mind of some Communist bureaucrat in postwar Budapest but Rogan, though not well-versed on where the concept arose, did accept that it seemed anti-Communistic to over-laden resources in one pot rather than spread them throughout. The idea would not stop just with Honved. When Ron Greenwood first saw the principle in action when Hungary defeated England 6-3 in 1953, he thought highly enough of it to repeat it when he coached England for the first time against Switzerland[8] in 1977, picking as many as six Liverpool players as he sought to institute a club team mentality into the England set up. But the idea did not curry favour and because of the 0-0 draw, it was never repeated.

To lead his all-stars at MTK, Brüll brought Jacky Tait Robertson over to Budapest in 1911. This proved to be Brüll's masterstroke and left an enduring legacy at the club. Robertson, a Glasgow Rangers and Scottish international centre-half, knew everything there was to know about the auld Scottish style of football and if Brüll wanted a person to lay down the technical and tactical primer for the club then he could have done far worse than employ Robertson. Everything about Robertson was perfect: he played his football as a key player in a key position at a key club during a key time and if there is one person for whom we should trace the *Wunderteam* and the Magical Magyars back to it would be him; the Tesla to Hogan's Edison. A British figure who was a long-term employee of MTK, Edward Shires, who played a major role in sourcing British coaches for MTK, wrote: "The Hungarians learned more in two years [from Robertson], than from anyone else in ten years."[9] When Robertson suddenly left the club, the owners struggled to find a replacement and for a time continually turned to Britain to do so, a move that was not altogether popular. A star player for the club, Kálmán Konrád, later said. "I don't suffer from Anglomania, but I can wholeheartedly testify that Robertson laid the foundations for the future triumphs of MTK."[10] That is as much to say that, regardless of who later came to coach, and that includes Hogan, the style that the club played had already been decided by Robertson and the others merely followed his lead. Accordingly, it would be imperative for us to get an idea as to who Robertson was and, more importantly, to gain some understanding as to what "style" of play he brought to MTK.

Robertson had been a member of Rangers' astonishing Invincible side of 1898-99 season, in which they had won every single League match they had played, and had been one of the Rangers' tourists on their trip to Central Europe in 1904. Within a year of the tour, Robertson had been poached by Gus Mears, owner of Chelsea, London's newest professional club, who saw Robertson as the perfect candidate to help find players in time for their inaugural 1905-06 League season.[11] In 1906, as part of the *Book of Football* serialisation, Robertson was asked by the editors to explain how he was setting out his team at Stamford Bridge. Robertson's essay in that book gives us an excellent piece of historical evidence as to the way he felt that football should be played. At centre-half for Chelsea, Robertson informs us that he played George Key[12] who acted "as a sixth forward and then assist[ed] the defence, and generally ma[de] himself exceedingly inconvenient to opponents."[13]

"The forwards", wrote Robertson, "... can play the three inside game or indulge in those long, swinging passes out to the wings that are more effective against some teams"[14] (see Fig. 2 above and Fig. 4 below). Three things therefore jump out at us: mobility, structure and indulgence. The description of Key's mobility is interesting because Robertson saw the centre-halves' role, alternatively, as having equal responsibility backward and forwards, this contrasts with Needham's idea in relation to this. Secondly, the structure of "the three inside game" brings us to the notion of an alternative version of the Scottish style of play with inside forwards inter-changing passes between each other rather than an outside forward. However what is most interesting is Robertson's use of the verb "indulge" when he writes that the players can "indulge in those long, swinging passes out to the wings". Let's dwell on this for a minute or two for that one verb gives a very clear clue as to how Robertson wanted his teams to behave.

# Jimmy Hogan

Indulgence comes about, as in most situations, when you have the comfort to so act. In football, possibly in all sports, you only indulge if you're in a comfortable position. Yet, in England, the long, raking passes out to the wings had almost become a feature of the centre-halves' play regardless of the state of the game. Pozzo said that Charlie Roberts was known for swinging passes out to the wide men at Old Trafford and that move was still a feature of the game when, in the late 1930s, T. G. Jones was playing for Everton. However, some in the game felt that sending out a long pass to the wing slowed the attack down as the ball would be played to winger who undertook all that embroidery while the defence waited for the cross to come over.

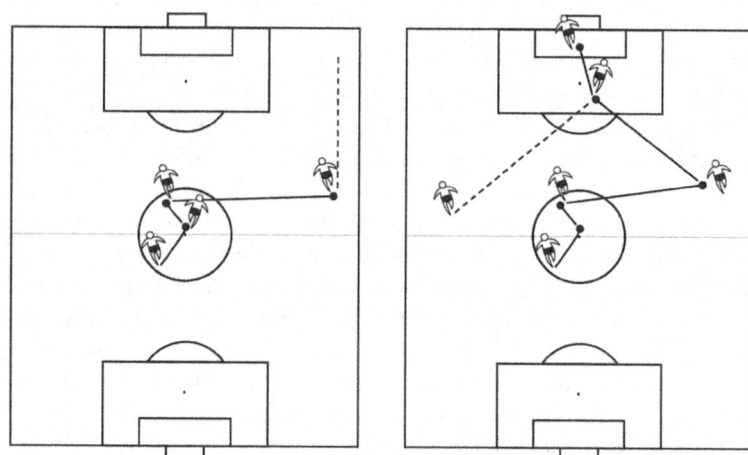

Fig. 4

So Robertson's view was that an over-reliance on "wing play" should be tempered. By all means use it if the circumstances demanded it to be used, but, in the main the onus should be on "the three inside game." This led to a quicker form of attack and if the ball did go out to the wing, Robertson favoured having the ball passed almost immediately back into the centre of the field (fig. 4). Perhaps within the use of that one verb, Robertson identified himself as being the first modern coach: moving away from the sedate, gentlemanly leisure of that great Glaswegian tradition in favour of the speed of drama; the speed of transfer from defence to attack. That played right into the mind-set of the central Europeans, whose crowds, schooled in horse racing and wrestling, demanded excitement and dramatic art in their football. That is what appealed to the crowds who had witnessed the 1905 tours in Vienna: "never had they seen such tackling" and that is what drove the money wheel and money, for Meisl and Brüll, was where it was at. Fewer paying customers meant less cash available to attract the stars, to build their stadiums, to raise their profile and so the dramatic culture, reflective of the hot-blooded temperament of their customers, became embedded and that culture instituted.

To get an idea as to what this "speed of transfer" amounts it pays to have a look at two goals. The first was scored by John Cameron, a contemporary of Robertson, when playing for Spurs in the 1901 FA Cup final replay against Sheffield United (fig. 6). The style in which Cameron organised Spurs was designed to be fast and accurate. This goal was all about passing into space and having players running onto the ball. There was little requirement to control the pass, it was all about one-touch movement. Ron Greenwood once said that the purpose of passing was to enable the person receiving the ball to play it first time. It is a very difficult skill to put into practice but you can see almost 70 years prior to that comment, the benefit of having players who passed with that aim in mind.

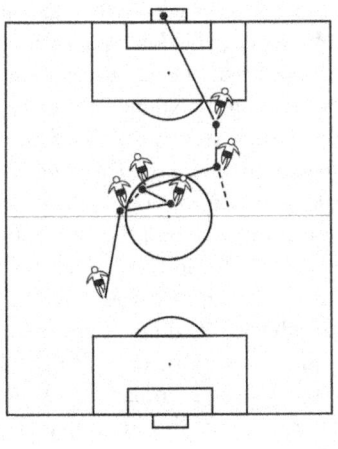

The second goal was scored by the Ferencváros player György Sárosi in the 1938 World Cup Final in Paris. This goal, with twenty minutes remaining brought Hungary back to within a goal of Italy at two goals to three. In this move, we see an echo of Robertson's "wing-play." Újpest's Zsengellér is the deep lying centre-forward. He plays the ball into space out to the wing but there's no delay when the ball is being played by Hungária's Pál Titkos, who is now in a wide inside forward position, back into the centre of the field. Titkos returns the ball into space behind the retreating defence for Sárosi to score with a first time shot.

Fig. 5

We can of course argue that there is too much distance between Robertson in 1911 and the 1938 World Cup Final for there to be a connection between the two, there was, for instance, the offside law change in 1925 which certainly sped up the game but the fact remains that the style Robertson brought to Budapest, is manifest within this goal and there is reason to assume that Robertson's style in evidence when MTK won all those League titles in the 1910s and 1920s could quite easily have remained as a legacy for the national side into the 1930s. There's also another aspect at play within both goals; an element that became a key feature of the post-examination of Hungary's defeat of England in 1953 in which the Hungarian team demonstrated the benefit of "third man theory" in which players automatically ran onto passes in game situations. We will discuss this theory later in this book but we can see evidence of it in both of the goals, with Sárosi knowing that a first time cross will be played across to the far post before the ball is sent wide and Cameron moving into position to receive an inside forward pass, the inter-play on the left side drawing the attention of the defence before the transfer to the vacant space for the goal-scorer to run into.

If Robertson had steered clear of the booze and had remained at MTK, it is most likely that Hogan would have stayed "imprisoned" in Vienna and, possibly, that would have been the last we ever heard of Jimmy Hogan but he was blessed with good fortune throughout; his break from prison, his diversion from a stay in a labour camp. So landing on his feet and securing paid work to coach football in Budapest merely confirmed that.[15] After Robertson, MTK had gone through a fast churn of coaches because for one reason or another the club never could seem to hold onto any of them for any length of time. First came Harry Ranson, formerly with Robertson at Chelsea,[16] next was Ernie Street, then Barney Gannon, a London-born physical training instructor and the title-winning coach from Ferencváros[17] but his mantra was geared toward developing running skills rather than footballing ones and the club adopted a brutal kick and rush game as a result.[18] Brüll and Dirsztay clearly had no issue when it came to robbing the stores of their cross-town rivals but transfers between rival clubs never run smoothly and Gannon was not able to further establish himself at MTK. Gannon was followed by Bob Holmes, the Old Invincible from Preston, who had been schooled in the chalk and blackboard tactics imported by the Scottish contingent at that club.[19] Holmes had experience of meeting MTK while working as a coach with Blackburn Rovers. In June 1911, a little before Robertson arrived, Blackburn Rovers played MTK and toyed with their hosts to the tune of 4-0. In May 1913, after Robertson had left MTK, the same Blackburn Rovers, but now League Champions' were beaten 2-1. Holmes was signed up by MTK at the beginning of 1914, leading them to their first League title, a season which they finished undefeated.[20] He even led them to a smarting 4-1 victory over Ferencváros[21] but Holmes was spooked by the turn of events in Sarajevo and by July 1914 he was heading across the Irish Sea to manage Cliftonville.[22] But the war made no odds to Brüll who pumped more and more money into the club. As Willy

## 1916-1919

Meisl wrote, "With Brüll as President, MTK could afford to be amateurs."[23] In 1911, he financed the development of a grand new stadium on land adjacent to a rail line on the edge of the city; a marginalised plot of land which symbolised how the Jews were treated in Budapest at the time. Indeed, that stadium would come to reflect the plight of the Hungarian Jews themselves, practically obliterated in the Second World War, a mere fragment remains of what was once such grand splendour and Brüll, who strove constantly to finance it all, would go the same way, being tricked into returning to Budapest in 1944, and then swept up in one of those hideous purges as the native German population sought to rid themselves of Brüll and his ilk; carted off to be murdered just because they were Jewish.

And so in 1916 Brüll and Dirsztay turned to Hogan, his incarceration being a boon to a club who had been without a coach since the departure of Holmes. Unlike his predecessors, Hogan couldn't leave MTK because he had to serve a loose form of "house arrest" for the duration of his stay and was therefore found digs within the new stadium. That led to an enduring affinity between the players and Hogan. As a foreigner in a foreign land, whose family was absent and whose communication with his fellow men was mainly conducted in pidgin tongue and through football, Hogan started to develop a familial bond with those around him, especially the younger players whom he adopted as "his boys" and to whom he became a revered figure, or in their words, "Bacsi" or Uncle. In 1954 he wrote "My boys were good, hard-working and quick learning students and accepted each of my instructions enthusiastically."[24] In his avuncular position at the club, he was able to improve relationships between the big egos[25] and this became utterly vital as Brüll set about constructing an all-star XI. In that light it was possibly the most talented side Hogan was ever to coach. Kalman Konrád's inside colleagues included the great centre-forward Alfred "Spéci" Schaffer and Vilmos ("Vili") Kertész. Schaffer would find fame, later, with Nuremburg and Wacker München in the early 1920s where the Germans would call him Fussballkönig, "the Football King," and he was more than happy to strut around town and on the football field with that image in mind. Two footed, Schaffer packed an extra helping of jalapeños in each shot whenever in sight of goal; but he would not be the first MTK player of the time to suffer from an excess of ego. György Orth would be another who developed a wonderfully high opinion about himself, as we shall see later. But the brightest star of all was Imre Schlosser who joined the club from Ferencváros in 1916.

Schlosser was already a five-time League champion with Ferencváros, and had been the leading scorer in the League for every season from 1908-09 before Hogan's arrival.[26] Norman Barrett later wrote of Schlosser:

# Jimmy Hogan

"... the first Hungarian player to attain fame throughout Europe. He was primarily a left-footed player, but he controlled the ball magnificently and always constituted a lethal threat in front of goal."[27] He joined MTK in 1916 because Brüll offered him a fictional well-paid job to go with his football,[28] and although Ferencváros had got eleven good years out of him they were seething at his departure, publically accusing him of being a professional and refused to participate in the Military Cup against MTK during the same year.[29] The Hungarian FA summoned Schlosser to appear before them to answer the charge that he was being paid and such was his obnoxious attitude at that hearing that he got banned for a fortnight. The transfer caused rancour that endured throughout that season. In the spring of 1917, due to the Schlosser case, both Ferencváros and MAC refused to play at MTK, so MTK won the championship by default.[30] The debacle brought about a change in the regulations which held that should a team default they would be summarily banned thereafter. Schlosser's transfer also brought about internal changes at MTK where Hogan was forced to alter the shape of the team to accommodate him. "Willy" Kertész being moved to the right half position from inside right which proved to be a stroke of genius on Hogan's part, for Kertész, happy to retain, dribble and pick out the forward pass with aplomb strengthened both the defence and attack in that position. Hogan was to demonstrate similar tinkering throughout his managerial, as opposed to his coaching career, in positioning young players so that they would not be exposed and "found out." He was to do the same, much later, with the teenage Peter McParland at Aston Villa and did the same thing at MTK with a young player named György Orth who became Hogan's first real star and was the subject of a peculiar story that Hogan spun for his readers and one in which he happily took unmerited credit for.

Hogan's greatest coup came about as a result of him "finding" György Orth and József "Csibi" Braun while walking through Angol Park in the city centre one day when he came across them both, having a kick about. The way he told it, you might have been forgiven for thinking that both were primitif, and only Hogan's expert eye could decipher the artistry inherent within them, spotting a couple of gems within an unbroken rock, suddenly the heavens start shining and a most wondrous light illuminated the scene. But it is all nonsense. When Hogan first saw Orth and Braun they had already made a name for themselves in Budapest football. Orth, who had just turned sixteen, was already a highly regarded player at the youth club ILK and that very year had broken into the first team at Vasas SC, one of the big nine clubs within Budapest. He was precocious. At the age of fifteen he went to Pisa in Northern Italy to ply his footballing trade there but in those early days his character was as his appearance. He was skinny, pale and seemed undernourished but bringing him over to MTK led to a complete change in character becoming just as over-blown at his own self-worth as Schlosser and Schaffer. It was hardly surprising that this should be for he attracted great acclaim from a young age.

"Orth is not a player like many others, he is a real artist in his field. He has shown that the football game can also be an art which is an aesthetic pleasure."[31]

When Orth made his first appearances for MTK, Hogan placed him in the full back role, allowing him to strike up a great partnership alongside Gyula Feldmann, who himself came from Ferencváros in 1917. It was only much later, after Hogan's return to the UK, that Orth would be switched to play successfully in the inside forward role, following Schaffer's decision to leave the side.

Orth's playing partner in Angol Park was Braun, a squat, heavily muscled right winger, adept at providing the most pin-pointed of crosses. He was slightly older than Orth but, like his friend, had already made a name for himself, having played for VAC Budapest's youth side before Hogan spotted him. You did not have to be an insightful genius to spot talented players who already played for other clubs in the city but that didn't stop Hogan creating the myth for English readers that he discovered them: "I pounced on them," wrote Hogan, later, "and said 'they are mine, my very own.'"[32] It was true, they were Hogan's, but they had been someone else's before him and in the end he only captured them because he had Brüll's money to entice both of them over to the club. "They were both very intelligent lads ... Every day after school I had them on the field, instructing them in the art of the game ... they quickly moved into the MTK first team."[33] Within short order both were appearing for MTK *and* within two seasons both were full Hungarian internationals. The reason for Hogan's ecstasy was that he had found two perfect students for the game who were insatiably hungry to learn anything that would benefit them in making a name for themselves in Budapest. As it turned out, their enthusiasm to undertake Hogan's exercises was a strange case of all three using each other for the purposes of self-promotion, football becoming almost incidental to the main issue but their "discovery" was an absolute boon for Hogan for the value of both Orth and Braun to him was that they influenced the other players to follow his teachings and in this way the respect the others at the club had for Hogan shot up. He later made special mention to them both.

"The list of great names would be incomplete if you were not thinking of György Orth and Csibi Braun, two of my greatest players. I discovered them one day in the afternoon when they were playing football after school in a small city wood. Under my care they acquired international glory in the international match between Hungary and Austria. They were only seventeen years old when they first played in the Hungarian national team. They played for Hungary forty times at least. Orth was the most intelligent player I have ever taught, and similar was Braun."[34] In Vienna, Hogan's practices had had to be force fed to the 1912 Austrian Olympic team by Meisl but in Hungary, Orth and Braun lapped up his ideas and since it was plain that both were developing into superb footballers so Hogan was able to use that evidence to exert influence and ensure compliance from the others. "The more one observes Orth, the more pleasure and joy he gives," wrote a reporter in the *Wiener Sporttagblatt*. "Not only is he a magnificent footballer but he uses his head as well."[35] Under Hogan, both Orth and Braun were to be found daily on the training field, their talent brought on by Hogan's "humble [ways], his diligence" and patience, of the type one could only associate with "thousands of Indian Ambassadors in England.' " It gave Hogan the opportunity to develop his coaching ethos in a respectful environment and that atmosphere would serve the club on their long journey of success.

Hogan's friendly approach would serve as a positive legacy for the club. After Hogan's departure, Herbert Burgess took over the reins at MTK and it is noticeable that in August 1921, he wrote a letter to the *Athletic News* in which he stated "never was a trainer treated with more respect, and it is a real pleasure to train [the MTK players]."[36] But it was in the way that MTK's and other Budapest players transmigrated across Europe, as the Hungarian football historian Peter Szegedi noted, into Italy, France and particularly into Austria that Hogan's influence and that of those early British coaches was able to be promulgated. This was not just as a result of training methods but also of the reverent mood and character of the players who had passed through Hogan's hands. Hugo Meisl, writing in 1924, said of the impact of the two Konrad's, Kálmán and Jeno: "They are like an oasis. Amateurs and absolute correct gentlemen in the true meaning of the word. ... They are responsible for the present high standard of Viennese football."[37]

Between the end of 1916 and the end of 1918, MTK's star-studded team were, by and large, streets ahead of most teams.[38] They would lose the odd game here, Torekves being their bogey team, but it says something about their dominance that a 4-0 score line would hardly register a smile on the lips of their supporters. So dominant was the attack that in 1917-18, the club scored 147 goals and conceded just ten and handed out some hilarious hidings during those seasons, seven times scoring double-figures but the

1917-18 season was the high point, for they remained undefeated and put everyone (bar one) to the sword in spectacular style. Rudolfshügel (the famous old Austrian side) were beaten 9-0 in a friendly; they beat MAV Gepgyar 17-0, III Kerületi TVE 8-0, that being Orth's debut, and thrashed MAC 18-1. During that season their great rivals Ferencváros succumbed 3-0 and 5-0.

Hogan's work at MTK proved that if teams are to successfully achieve the style of play that Robertson promoted they must do so with total control over the ball. In truth what Hogan did at Budapest was what he had done in Vienna.[39] Constant practice led to an improved technical ability and if you practice controlling, passing and movement enough times you become adept at knowing to whom the ball is to be passed to before it comes to you which was Raynor's life-long mantra. In other words, the whole unnatural process of receiving a bouncing round object and stopping it and moving it with your foot becomes second nature, allowing your mind to consider the position of your team mates. So Hogan's later technique married and suited Robertson's earlier style of play but whether Hogan developed Hungarian football beyond the tactical primer set down by Robertson is doubtful. To him fell the honour of coaching a collection of

Kálmán Konrád with the Hungarian national team at the game in Austria, which Hungary won 2-0 on 2 June 1918: from left to right: "Jimmy" Hogan (English co-trainer), Károly Zsák, Kálmán Konrád, Vilmos Kertész, Péter Szabó, Gyula Feldmann, György Orth, Imre Schlosser, Sándor Nemes, József Ging, Károly Fogl, Alfréd Schaffer.

star players, probably the greatest collection of players in MTK's long and colourful history and ensuring a conveyor belt of success.

They won their third Hungarian title in 1918 and the club were on their way to their third straight title in 1918-19 when Hogan, suddenly freed with the lifting of the bar on foreign nationals travelling now that the war had ended, left to return to England in January 1919. Towards the end of 1918 his position at MTK seemed assured. In December 1918, W. A. Berry wrote "Hogan still retains the job [at MTK] and shows no anxiety to quit it." But quit it he did.

The decision may have been hastened by the passing of both his father and sister, Josephine, in short order in the June and July of 1918 but if it was he was held back by the delays of diplomacy.[40] When the Armistice was announced it did not immediately mean that British nationals were entitled to free movement back to the UK which meant Hogan having to endure another Christmas in Budapest. But as soon as the green light was given, Hogan set about ending his contract with MTK returning home from Budapest with 300 fellow British nationals on 23 January 1919.[41] The journey was arduous and he was only repatriated a week later, on 1 February, returning to live at 35 Colne Road in Burnley with Evelyn, Joseph, Mary and three-year-old Frank who Hogan now saw for the first time. Although understandable, it was a financial risk for Hogan to return to an England still labouring under the debilitating effects of the First World War. He was without work and, despite the good fortunes of Budapest, still retained considerable bitterness toward the Austrian Football Association. He was owed money and set about ways to get it back.

# 1916-1919

## Notes

1 Acknowledgement to Dr Tamas Denes for correct spelling and fact-checking in this chapter and also one of the great BIM technicians, Balazs Haraszti, for generously offering time and money to purchase books and translate.
2 *Sport*, vol. 16, no. 321, p. 6.
3 This involvement with the Red Cross might explain Fox's statement that Hogan's release was due to payment being made to that organisation.
4 *Yorkshire Evening News*, 30 December 1918.
5 *Burnley News*, 1 March 1919.
6 *Sport*, vol. 16, no. 321, p. 6.
7 Mulik Rajtam, Arpad Brüll - Uncle Frédi, the President.
8 England's proper international rivals, a nation that has always caused us difficulties on the football field.
9 NS 1933. III. 15. With acknowledgement to Balazs Haraszti.
10 https://www.theblizzard.co.uk/article/exile. Unknown source.
11 Finding players had led to hilarious consequences. Robertson recalled: "I received [one application] from a man who said he was a splendid centre-forward but if that position was not vacant he could manipulate a turnstile. Another wrote: 'You will be astonished to see me skip down the touch-line like a deer.' A third was willing to 'be linesman, goal-keep, or mind the coats.' " (*Book of Football*, 73.)
12 Formerly with Heart of Midlothian.
13 *Book of Football*, 73.
14 *Ibid.*
15 21 March 1916 was his start date with the club.
16 *Burnley Express*, 3 June 1914.
17 Of Gannon's training methods: "Every day the FTC players are running and they are centering, kicking and kicking." Gannon came to MTK in the summer of 1914. http://www.tempofradi.hu/barney-gannon
18 With acknowledgement to Balazs Haraszti, translated from Peter Szegedi article.
19 Technically minded, when he retired he was to be found coaching football at Stonyhurst College, in Clitheroe. He then went on to help Bradford City, coaching them to the Second Division title in 1908 before going on to coach Blackburn Rovers when they were led by Bob Middleton. In 1912, Rovers won the title but their form could not be maintained and Holmes left the club, sensationally, in late October 1913.
20 Signed by the club as coach on 15 January 1914, he had gone to Ferencváros from London in August 1912.
21 *Scottish Referee*, 2 March 1914.
22 *Star Green 'Un*, 14 July 1914.
23 *Soccer Revolution*, 75.
24 *Die ungarische Fussballschule*, 7. Acknowledgement to Dr Andreas Hafer.
25 Laszlo Rejto, *Kilenc Klub Kronikaja*, pp. 53-4. Acknowledgement to Balazs Haraszti.
26 In 129 games for Ferencváros between 1906 and 1915, Schlosser scored 215 goals.
27 *World Soccer from A-Z*, p. 228.
28 By 1916, when Schlosser was transferred, he was 27.
29 Gustav Sebes, *A Magyar Labdarugas* (1955). Acknowledgement to Balazs Haraszti.
30 *Ibid.* MTK played only nineteen Leagues games that season and lost just once.]
31 *Illustrated Sports Sheet*, 19 June 1925.
32 *Sport*, vol. 16.
33 *Sport*, vol. 16.
34 *Die ungarische fussballschule*, p. 7. Acknowledgement Dr Andreas Hafer.
35 19 October 1920.

36  8 August 1921.
37  From an article by Peter Szegedi, translated by Balazs Haraszti.
38  They drew once – a 2-2 draw – away at Torekves on 3 March 1918.
39  To argue differently would be to argue that the presentation given in Dresden in 1926 was something that Hogan made up on the spot. He didn't. He went through a routine that he had practised innumerable times in the decade between 1916 and 1926.
40  His father died at the age of 66 on 19 June 1918 and his sister died at Todmorden Road, at the age of just 23 on 5 July 1918. (Shirley Ashton, Burnley Libraries; *Burnley News*, 29 June 1918 & 17 July 1918).
41  *Burnley News*, 1 March 1919.

## EIGHT

## 1919-1925
### 'Of a system there was hardly any.'

When Jimmy Hogan returned to England in January 1919 he was 36 years of age and, apparently, fed up with football. He had left perhaps the best football job in the world at that time in Hungary where he was being paid to coach a bunch of star footballers but now he was unemployed. He had gone to Europe with the intention to earn money for his young family and when he finally got back to England he had no job and a deep harbouring resentment against the Austrians who he felt owed him money.

When he eventually found work[1] it was neither in Burnley nor in football but with Walker's Tobacco Company Limited[2] on "Scotty" Road in Liverpool[3] as a store-man[4] either Hogan's penchant for elaboration was evidence in later, grandly, referring to the job as being "in commerce" or he was just using the typical parlance used by those seeking to massage their social status. Either way, he would stay "in commerce" until the spring of 1922 and there a curiosity lies because, for those not familiar with Liverpool's road network, Scotland Road, or the A59 as is, is the road which climbs from Liverpool's city centre, built as it is at the base of a hill, toward the areas of Everton, Anfield and Stanley Park. In other words, for three years Jimmy Hogan was working at "football central", within walking distance of Liverpool and Everton Football Clubs and yet, throughout this entire period, he made no move toward any club in the city to see whether they had an opening for him as a coach. It is peculiar to consider that Hogan, this great messianic football trainer, did not seek employment within football in post-War Britain when the opportunity would have been there for the taking. There he was armed with all that experience in Holland, Austria and Hungary, at a time when there was an exponential increase in the number of Football League clubs[5] and yet he made no attempt to get back into the game. But Hogan, ever chasing the money, thought better of trying to work as a football coach in England. The reason is not too difficult to find. In December 1920, James Catton published a letter from Charlie Bunyan in the *Athletic News* ...[6] Bunyan, who served in the war alongside his sons, had spent the majority of his journeyman career as a reserve goalkeeper but in 1905 left for Belgium to take up a coaching appointment there. Bunyan wrote: "those who have control of the big

# Jimmy Hogan

clubs [in England] do not realise the value of coaching ... it would not be possible to obtain a living wage in England for such work."[7]

Hogan could not bring himself to discuss such matters in such a way, instead he engineered a story that has come to represent a central element in our understanding of him and one that historians have hooked their hats on ever since. It is telling that he never makes mention of this incident at the time of it happening, but when he came around to doing so, the chief target of Hogan's ire was long dead and not able to defend himself.

The story starts like this. Within a month of his arrival back in the UK, Hogan had met with Dan Irving, his local MP, and had presented himself at the offices of the *Burnley Express* to voice his anger at how the Austrians had treated him and his wife whilst he was overseas. On the 12 March 1919, he sent an open letter, printed in the *Sheffield Independent*, announcing his intention to claim £500 against the Austrian Football Association. "I am quite broken down financially ... and I have a wife and three little children," he wrote. The way he handled the dispute at that time revealed him to be a man who did not let things drop if he felt slighted, bitterly persisting with the dispute for the best part of a year despite the fact that he did not have a snow ball's chance of getting money out of the Austrians. During that time, Hogan became aware of a fund that had been set up by the Football Association to help those footballers who had been caught up in the war. In a chapter entitled "The Ultimate Insult," Norman Fox writes that Hogan "was advised to go to the Football Association[8] ... to apply for help from a special fund that had been set up to give relief to professionals who had suffered financially during the war ..."[9] Fox states that Hogan wanted to get £200, which was basically an annual income for professional players. The "special fund" Fox was referring to was the Football National War Fund which was set up by the Football Association, under the guidance of Sir Frederick Wall, on 26 March 1918. Geoffrey Green, later, wrote: "The [objectives] of the fund were to aid Association football players and others who had rendered service to the game and their dependents, who were in need of assistance arising from the War and other causes."[10]

Those objectives would have been widely known to all in the football community. On 1 June 1918 the *Lancashire Evening News* stated that "[the fund was] established to assist those footballers who [had] been disabled in the war and, in the case of their death, their dependents."[11] This information would have come to Hogan's attention via friends who had played alongside him at Bolton when he returned to the UK. However, Jimmy Hogan either chose to keep himself ignorant as to the purpose of the fund or, possibly, thought it worth a gamble to convince the FA of an entitlement based on the spirit of the Fund rather than its actual wording before making the trip to London. In truth, as Hogan knew, he wasn't entitled to any money at all for he was neither physically nor mentally injured during the course of the war and it could never be said, at all, that he was financially disadvantaged by the war itself. After all, within the four years of the Great War, Hogan had led an existence of resplendent fortune. Up to the end of 1916, he was given food and free accommodation by the Blythes and had spent a good proportion of that time prancing about in borrowed tennis whites in a private garden in Vienna. For the rest of the war he was given cash and accommodation to coach footballers in Hungary and all the while this was taking place a lot of people in various places were doing their damnedest to blow each other to bits. Hogan did not see the irony of it when he wrote, later: "The time I spent in Hungary, was almost as happy as my stay in Austria. Budapest is a lovely city ... the most beautiful in Europe."[12]

The Austrians may have broken contract but that was a commercial agreement between their Football Association and himself. It would be a long stretch to say that the breach of that contract should have brought Hogan within the protections of the Football Association's War Fund which had been set up to compensate the families of footballers who gave up their lives for their country, or compensate footballers who were disfigured or maimed by the war. However, considering matters in the round I think the real story is that Hogan's application for funding was a front to seek audience with Sir Frederick Wall to help him get the compensation that he felt he was owed from the Austrians for breach of contract. The reason for this was because he felt that, as an English professional footballer, the Football Association had overall responsibility for his welfare and that included representing him in the resolution of disputes or, as he wrote in March 1919 "to see that justice is done to one who was a registered English professional."[13] Unfortunately, this has erroneously come to be interpreted as some type of dispute that Hogan had with the Football Association with the insinuation that Wall saw Hogan as a "traitor" to his country which is as far from the truth as could possibly be the case. Wall would hardly have viewed Hogan as conspiring with the enemy given the circumstances he had found himself in. The "traitor" remark also alludes to the well-padded story that Sir Frederick Wall, the FA Secretary, handed to Hogan some khaki socks as a substitute to any entitlement of funds, the implication being that Hogan's incarceration was a coward's way out of service. "Here," Wall is supposed to have said, "this is what we gave the troops on the front line." The fact remains however that, we don't know if there is any truth in the story about the socks and we don't even know if that conversation even took place.

# Jimmy Hogan

It is, however, at this point that there is a confusing aspect to the story. If Hogan had been declared a "traitor" then it would have made sense for him to have had nothing whatsoever to do with the FA from that moment forwards which was never the case. I say this for a number of reasons. Firstly, there was no fall-out between Hogan and Wall in relation to the alleged incident or, if there was, it did not endure. Hogan met Wall in later years in order to impress upon him the importance of developing a coaching programme for the country[14] and did this because, in truth, Hogan saw Wall, as historians should do, as a man who had an interest in developing a national coaching programme. In other words, Hogan saw Wall not as some high-minded old duffer who was out of touch but as a person who was intent on devising a strategic programme to develop football in England and on the Continent.

Secondly, there's little evidence to assume that Jimmy Hogan ever turned his back on the FA, least of all in order to help other countries defeat England. When the FA offered Hogan work, to lead the coaching schemes as instructor, he accepted the offer without hesitation. Finally, when Fulham summarily sacked Hogan in 1935, Hogan's first port of call was not to a local solicitor, it was to the Football Association to ask for their help to secure compensation for breach of contract. Yet another of those financial disputes, that seemed to signpost most of Hogan's professional career.

Thirdly, if we rely upon the contemporary evidence it is quite clear where Hogan's real antipathy lay at that time. In July 1921, whilst he was still employed by Walker's, Wiener AC, a leading club in Vienna, contacted Hogan and offered him a contract to coach their players. He refused.[15] That refusal was a case of Hogan having been once bitten. It was only in 1932 that he finally relented from his stance of refusing to work with the Austrians. Otherwise, as a direct result of what happened in 1914, Hogan was very cautious when it came to putting himself out for the Austrians, unless guarantees could be secured first which undermines the rather daft conception writers have about him and the *Wunderteam* because whereas many see Hogan as the great architect behind the *Wunderteam*, his engagement with the Austrian national association amounted to no more than six weeks in 1912, five weeks in 1914 and around a week in 1932. In truth, Hogan is but a footnote on their development.

This may have been the last we heard of Jimmy Hogan but for an advert that came to his attention in the spring of 1922[16] from Switzerland's Young Boys Club who were seeking a coach. Though the contract took him to little Switzerland, with its limited number of League teams, the job being offered was by no means a sinecure. Young Boys had finished a disappointing fourth in 1921-22, had last won the title in 1920 and were desperate to get back to winning ways and the management at Young Boys, intent on not letting the Zurich or Genevan clubs get ahead of them, set about strengthening their club. They offered Hogan enough money to persuade him to give up his store-man's income, bring his family over to Switzerland and sign up for a deal that would keep him in Berne until the Paris Olympic summer of 1924.

He arrived in May 1922 and was joined by Evelyn and the children three months later, after he assured himself as to the quality of the contract and was able to secure schooling for his children. The owners of Young Boys did a good job in pumping in enough cash to ward off repeat requests for his services from the Austrian teams[17] and also did a good job in saving Hogan from the realities faced by the game in Switzerland at that time because the game was in a sorry state there when he arrived. Writing later, David Jack said of a Bolton Wanderers tour,[18] "A thunderstorm nearly flooded the ground [in Bern] and dress-room accommodation for in those far-off days was poor in the extreme."[19]

There were also teething problems connected with player registration during those transitional years as Switzerland sought to assert itself on the football field. Up to then the Swiss had seen football as being an excuse only for "lung-busting." Players went in for kick and rush tactics as if their lives depended on it: "... of a system [there] was hardly any."[20] But very quickly, things were turned around and Switzerland, though the least well known of his stays in Europe, represented a huge turning point in Hogan's life. His reappearance in Central Europe was welcomed by the regional press agencies because, they felt, "he had endeared himself to the Viennese through his coaching ability, his 'gracious' nature and [had helped improve] Hungary's standing in football in the region.' "[21]

But Hogan was only one of many Brits operating in Switzerland at that time. George Handley, formerly of Bradford City, was coaching Brühl in St Gallen; Arthur Gaskell, of Bolton Wanderers, was working with Grasshoppers; William Townley was working at St Gallen and Sammy Lamb, formerly with Plymouth,[22] who had helped train the Spanish in preparation for the Antwerp Olympics was with Old Boys in Basle but the stand-out was Teddy Duckworth who found a place with Servette in Geneva. Duckworth, wounded at the Battle of the Somme, had been but a bit part player at Blackpool, but he brought with him such innovative training methods that soon the players were being enrolled in dance classes to develop their balance which encouraged fluidity over the previous, uptight military two-step.

Duckworth was to enjoy a spectacular run of success. In the 1922 Western Championship, Geneva went through the season undefeated and that summer beat the Blue Stars of Zurich and FC Luzern to win the national Championship. It was little wonder that the national Association

The Swiss Olympic team 1924

would hand him the reins to the national side in preparation of the 1924 Olympic Games.

The British were not the only foreign coaches there, since the Swiss had sent the call out for imports from all over to help them in something of an hour of need. Why the Swiss had started to import workers from around Europe was not hard to fathom. In June 1922 the Swiss national team had travelled all the way to Vienna just to receive a 7-1 spanking before travelling all the way back home again[23] so the Swiss did what the Swiss do, they imported migrant workers on temporary contracts to plug the skills gap. The Swiss clubs invited six Austrian internationals across the border to train them but the call went far and wide. Over in Basel, the small Second Division Nordstern club pulled off a remarkable scoop when they were able to entice Dori Kürschner from Frankfurt and from that moment on, under Kürschner's guiding hand, the club would rise like a bubble in a champagne flute only to go "pop" when he left. The Swiss decision to throw money at the game was helped substantially by the fact that their neutrality during the war had saved their economy from the battering that their neighbours had experienced and since they had money so people, like Hogan, came seeking work.

In light of the 7-1 defeat in Vienna, bringing over Austrian and mid-European coaches made perfect sense. Bringing over British coaches didn't since standards in the British game both professionally and in amateur terms were seen to be noticeably on the wane. At the Antwerp Olympics in 1920 the British team, the reigning Gold medallists, had arrived home before their postcards after a first round defeat. Later, in 1923, England came bottom of the Home International Championship without a win to their name. One could blame the war for robbing us of talent, or the creation of the Third Division, for diluting what talent was available to top clubs, but whatever the reason there were concerns about a serious erosion of skills within the British game. Previously, the sedate pace of the game had enabled some players to develop their skills but from the 1910s and into the early part of the new post-war decade, the game had quickened immeasurably. K. R. G. Hunt wrote, in 1923: "Players devote themselves far more to the destructive than to the constructive side of the game, which is fought out at such a pace that the clever, thoughtful player is given very little chance. One may say that generally the keener the desire to win, the poorer is the quality of the football served up. Brain is sacrificed to pace."[24]

Commentators, seeing the decline in playing standards exhibited by those teams on their continental tours, felt that coaching standards must surely reflect that of the playing ones. Hence why the Swiss decision to import so many British personnel caused bemusement. The *Bredashce Courant* in Holland reported: "While not every Englishman is a good footballer and not every good player a good coach, Switzerland seems to have become quite affected by [having English coaches]."[25]

However, notwithstanding the reservations the decision to invite the British would shortly come to represent an inspired decision on the part of the Swiss. For the band of British coaches working in Switzerland was representative of the earlier age and so in a very short period of time, science replaced speed and stamina replaced strength in the Swiss game. The Swiss still retained their love of kick and rush but after that heavy defeat to the Austrians positive strides would be made in the Swiss game both domestically and internationally, culminating with an Olympic silver medal in 1924 and those associated with that triumph, including Hogan, saw their own market value increase as a result. Hogan, particularly, was intent on holding firm to what he felt was his proper market rate and this would simply increase as a result of that triumph. Hogan took full advantage of that with the letter-head of his personal correspondence reading "Olympic coach."

The Young Boys club had developed a penchant for employing British coaches since the time they engaged William Reynolds as their trainer just before the Great War. Before Hogan they employed Bert Smith.

Once again Hogan's arrival was presaged with good fortune in that he

# Jimmy Hogan

inherited a team with a competitive spirit and one that contained three players, Hans Pulver, the goalkeeper, Paul Fässler, left half, and Rudolf Ramseyer, the left back, who were all good enough to win national and international honours within the space of a few years. Before the domestic 1922-23 season began Hogan accompanied the Young Boys side to Vienna where in a stirring battle they won 4-3 against Rapid in a match played with "hardly a foul."[26] Not one to miss an opportunity to promote the sport, and his part in it, Hogan penned a letter to the principal Viennese sporting newspaper after the game. In the letter he wrote:

> Excuse me, but maybe your readers would be interested to hear about the match between Rapid and the Young Boys that was played on Tuesday last week in Bern. As an old English player and coach I can assure you that this match was one of the best I have seen on the continent and people will talk about it for years. It was good exciting football from beginning to the end and even though Rapid lost 4-3 they played praiseworthy.
> 
> It's only fair to notice that my old friends from Vienna were ... tired after the long travel and the match versus Luzern, but we also need to admit that Young Boys deserved the win.
> 
> Rapid's excellent performance helped to evoke the best in our boys and [inspired] them to win. Rapid was 3:2 ahead just minutes before the end but thanks to an extraordinary effort, the home team scored twice and saved the match. There is only [one thing further] left to say that the match was played in true sporting spirit, there were hardly any fouls and Rapid proved themselves worthy of its reputation as a great team.
> 
> With my best wishes and regards to you and my old friends in Vienna, sincerely, yours Jimmy Hogan.[27]

Although, early results in the League were not startling, the official history of the club recorded the fact that "you soon saw ... that all assets are moving forward"[28] and his contribution was noted when, in the autumn of 1922, the Swiss national association asked Hogan to coach the national side for the international against Holland, the Swiss winning 5-0 at the Young Boys' Ground in Berne.[29] It went so well that he was retained for the match at Bologna against Italy.[30] Pulver, Fässler *and* Ramseyer played in both games for Switzerland but the match was less successful, for it was Ramseyer who saved Hogan's face in the second against Italy in Bologna with a late equaliser when the Swiss were facing a 2-1 defeat. Even so, those two matches altered the impression the continent had of Switzerland's footballing ability. Previously they had been there for a whipping, but those two matches drew praise from an Austrian reporter who remarked that the skill level of the Swiss was moving in "a noticeably ascending curve." And what did he put this down to? Foreign coaches working in Switzerland, "of whom Hogan had achieved great success in the country."[31] By way of confirmation, Fässler was the standout in a tie with Austria on 21 December 1922 when Switzerland won 2-0, a victory for which Hogan was again given credit.[32]

Hogan's first season with Young Boys, 1922-23, went remarkably well. There was the typical increase in the number of glory hunters was noted as the fortunes of the Young Boys club improved. In the February of 1923, *La Rhône* apologised for bringing a match report late to the "large audience ... anxiously following the adventures endured by the Championship contenders" for late publication of the news report of Young Boys' victory over Aarau. Throughout that season was able to bring in some young players including Bigler, of whom *Le Peuple* wrote that he was "a brilliant new recruit working to the methods of Hogan"[33] and the season even offered Hogan the opportunity of a winning swansong to his playing career when he played and scored a goal in the 5-1 defeat of Urania in the January of 1923.[34] The Young Boys' defence, with Ramseyer in the centre-half position, developed into a tight unit and it was only in March 1923 that the side fell to defeat against Basel by a solitary goal, a fixture in which Young Boys played "incoherently" according to a local report.[35] The following week, Hogan renewed his association with the Hungarians who had come to play an international in Lausanne. Stars from his present club, Ramseyer and Fässler were in the Swiss dressing room that day, but Hogan used the occasion to spend time in the away dressing room[36] where Kertész, Orth, Molnár and Plattko swore to give their all for their old boss and did so in a victory which saw Molnár and Orth share four goals. But for all that, the domestic season would end in controversy. Young Boys won the Central Division, dropping only six points in their fourteen games and looked set to play for the national finals[37] when it was announced that FC Biel had played unregistered players in their game against FC Bern.[38] This meant that there would need to be a play-off between Bern and Young Boys.

However, Young Boys refused to participate in that game and Bern became the focus of ire amongst the popular press.[39] "This is a bitch," wrote the correspondent for *Becsi Magyar Ujsag* (*Wiener Ungarische Zeitung*). "The conspiracy of FC Bern will not result in them winning the title, just because they got Biel out of the way."[40]

Hogan felt cheated by the way the season had panned out and for a while Hogan made it clear by his views, and actions that he wanted to leave Young Boys, reluctantly staying on only because he was indentured by the contract he had signed. During the close-season,[41] he returned to Budapest to open a football school with Willy Kertész, his old club captain at MTK.[42] There were grand plans at first, a grandstand for spectators, a fully appointed gym, washing machines and paid residences for the boys who would fund it all. Kertész was happy to forego his amateur status, foreseeing a time when he could be paid to coach.[43] In early July 1923, Hogan was interviewed by one of the correspondents working for the *Becsi Magyar Ujsag* (*Wiener Ungarische Zeitung*)[44] and made clear that his heart was not in his current post. He didn't feel great about being in Berne and would have preferred to have been in Vienna or Budapest "but my contract is until next May so can't move to another city until then."

The break in Budapest served to right his ill feeling. In the close season Hogan helped attract international clubs to Berne. Bolton had just won the FA Cup and their tour of Germany, Prague and Amsterdam enabled him to meet up with old friends. They stayed in the city for a week, playing Young Boys twice, winning the first, at a canter 2-0, converting a penalty and having Pym save a penalty from a Young Boys' striker and the second 2-1. In between times, MTK's old nemesis, Törekvés would also play a friendly and Hogan was able to enlist help from the Bolton lads with David Jack, Smith and Vizard helping for Young Boys in a 3-1 victory.[45] The signs were looking good for the coming 1923-24 season. Hamburg and Zurich Blue Stars were both defeated and before the break in the domestic season, Young Boys had been leading the Division in front of Kürschner's Nordstern. They toured Africa and Spain "where in addition to the football games all sorts of things happened" wrote the official club historian, "which we do not want to reveal here" and then when they got back beat FC Bern 2-1 - and kept top spot until the very last weekend when they met Basel. The small-sided League proved its worth ensuring that all were in contention until the end. And so it proved here. Young Boys could only draw 0-0 and were over-taken at the top by Kürschner's Nordstern who overcame Aarau to win the Division in the final game. As far as Hogan was concerned, that was that, leaving the club to join Lausanne-Sports in the April of 1924 as soon as his contract came to an end.[46]

At the turn of the year, the Swiss Olympic Association had asked Hogan to join a coaching team of four to help prepare Switzerland for the upcoming Amsterdam Olympic Games. The group of four would be "managed" by Teddy Duckworth and comprised coaches who represented regions within Switzerland and respectively these would lead coaching sessions staged in different parts of the country throughout that spring. The four coaches were Duckworth, Dori Kürschner, Hogan and William Townley. An initial squad drawn principally from their club sides had been whittled down from 36 in early spring 1924[47] to twenty "following classes held between 8 March and 3 May 1924"[48] that were led by Duckworth in

Geneva, by Hogan in Berne; by Kirschner in Basel and by William Townley in Zürich.[49] Duckworth was given responsibility of leading the squad in Paris. It was remarkably successful collaborative effort, orchestrated by Duckworth, who coordinated the work of the others, listened to proposals, agreed tactics and devised training and this led not only to a remarkable silver medal performance but also the development of a technically advanced defensive system that was to serve Switzerland for decades to come. As matters transpired the four contributed equally for when the squad was announced seven players came from "Duckworth's" Geneva "region"; six from "Kürschner's" Basel and a further seven from "Hogan's" Bern and Neuchâtel. Not to be outdone Townley, provided Max Abegglen, perhaps the most skilled player within the squad.

The defensive system was the "Riegel" WW formation. Some writers have attributed Kürschner with the development of this system but the truth is that no one really knows which of the coaches did what and what impact they had on the way the team played and performed. We don't even know for sure what the WW formation looked like. For instance, did the centre-half sit in front of behind the wing halves? Were the halves stationed out wide or close in to deal with the opposing inside forwards? Willy Meisl was particularly vague when describing it, later. Indeed the formation is shrouded in mystery. Kürschner, when he was later coach of Flamengo, in Brazil set his team to play in a WW formation, which required there to be a creative centre-half. The problem is, of course, that we do not know exactly if the WW formation that Kürschner experimented with was his idea alone or whether it arose out of his experiences in Switzerland when working alongside Duckworth.

We do not even know if the "Riegel", the defensive system that Willy Meisl vaguely attributes to Kürschner, and which was an early version of the Bolt system, was his idea either. What we do know however is that defence was not key in either system despite the fact that it was effective in stemming the amount of goals Switzerland had grown used to conceding because, at its heart, it was a system based on counter-attack, in other words how to best and most efficiently transfer the ball from a defensive situation to the attack. The clue is in the starting point of where the ball was when Switzerland first gained possession, for the Swiss, through clever use of their limited resources, were honest in their outlook. Facing historically stronger opponents than themselves they *had* to revert to stealth and strategy in order to unlock opponents; invite attacks into their lair and spring attacks from deep in the field. The transformation in the success of the Swiss in using the system was self-evident. In 1923 the national side did not win a single match of the six games they played and conceded nineteen

# Jimmy Hogan

goals.[50] In 1924, following the first of the training clinics, and up to the Olympic final, they played eight times, lost none and conceded only five goals (see table).[51]

| DATE | OPPONENT | SCORE |
| --- | --- | --- |
| 11 March 1923 | Hungary | 1-6 |
| 22 April | France | 2-2 |
| 3 June | Germany | 1-2 |
| 17 June | Denmark | 2-3 |
| 21 June | Norway | 2-2 |
| 25 November | Netherlands | 1-4 |
| 8 March 1923 | Training session 1 - Geneva | |
| 23 March 1924 | France - Geneva | 3-0 (a match played in driving rain) |
| 29 March | Training session 2 - Berne | |
| 12 April | Training session 3 - Basel | |
| 21 April | Denmark - Basel | 2-0 |
| 3 May | Training session 4 - Zurich | |
| 18 May | Hungary - Zurich | 4-2 |
| 25 May | Lithuania | 9-0 (Olympic 1) |
| 28 May | Czechoslovakia | 1-1 (Olympic 2) |
| 30 May | Czchoslovakia | 2-1 (Olympic 2) |
| 2 June | Italy | 2-1 (Olympic 3) |
| 5 June | Sweden | 2-1 (Olumpic 4) |
| 9 June | Uruguay | 0-3 (Olympic 5) |

When faced with European teams attacking the Swiss in the conventional British manner in the early 1920s, the defensive system worked well enough. Attacks in the 2-3-5 formation followed conventional patterns. Opposing halves would play the ball wide to the outside forward and inside forwards would run into the box in anticipation of the winger's cross from the corner flag.

Under the Riegel system, when the ball was played wide, the opposing wingers would be forced wide by the wing halves, impeded where necessary, so that the defence could organise itself. This had two outcomes. Firstly, if the defensive wing-halves won the ball on the wing the ball was then fed to the centre-half to start the counter-attack. Secondly, if the attacking winger managed to cross the ball, the inside forwards would be man-to-man marked in the penalty area.

Karl Rappan, later Switzerland's national coach, would overcome any confusion by ascribing the Swiss left-back to the attacking centre-forward so that the Swiss centre-half could be freed from defensive duties. Under Rappan's system, rather than allow the wing halves to be ascribed to the

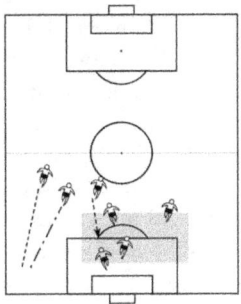

Fig. 6

mark or track the wingers, he brought them inside and much closer to the defensive unit. This was seen with the following diagram.

In this formation the halves are no longer in a position to mark the wingers. As a result, their role is to mark the inside forwards. Rappan kept his full backs inside rather than converting them to be wing-backs and attacks came through the centre. As a result, inside forward play would have been nullified by weight of numbers. The right half would have attacked the inside left 'A' and the left half would have tracked back to mark the inside right 'B'.

But say the wingers did not have such a say in the attack? Suppose, for instance, that instead of an attacking outside forward receiving a ball from an inside forward and haring off for the corner flag, the inside forward played a short diagonal pass to the inside left running into space *behind* the centre-half; what then? If the inside right could get behind the centre-half then Switzerland would find themselves exposed at the back and the inside right would have a clear run on goal (Fig. 7). Those are the questions that

# Jimmy Hogan

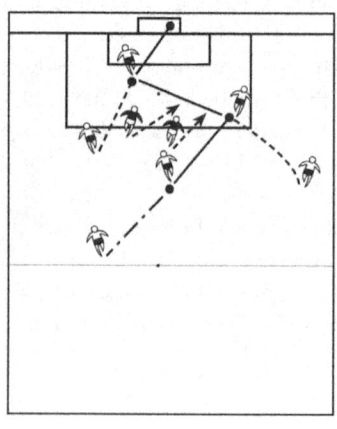

Fig. 7

faced Switzerland when they faced Uruguay in the 1924 Olympic Final, for the play of the South Americans was designed around a much tighter spearhead attack than the Europeans had become used to. For when Switzerland met Uruguay in the final it is noticeable, from examining film of the game, that two of Uruguay's goals[52] come from players running onto diagonal passes into the centre of the penalty area.[53] Uruguay had thus unlocked the Swiss latch.

Hogan's club players did play a key role for Switzerland on their way to reaching the Olympic Final, providing both the defensive backbone but also acting in a creative way too. "His" players included the 'keeper (Hans Pulver), the converted left back (Rudolf Ramseyer[54] and the left wing-half (Aron Pollitz). The role of these players of Hogan in this system was purely destructive. It was the centre-half, August Oberhauser, one of Kürschner's Nordstern players, who gave the side the creative force to attack; a deep-lying role ready to pick up the pass from the backs or the halves, a roving commission going forward.

The Swiss Olympic budget was finite. Townley, Kürschner and Hogan were not required to accompany the team to Paris and the latter two sat out the competition which should be looked at quite critically. In 1958, Dave Sexton, who played for West Ham and managed Manchester United in the late 1970s, grabbed a back-pack and some walking boots and paid his own way from London to travel around Sweden in order to see matches in the World Cup. He did this because he felt it was a sound decision to spend his own money to build his knowledge of the game. By comparison, Jimmy Hogan did lots of things connected to the game that provided him with his livelihood, but never did much for free. Ultimately, there were only two occasions when Hogan travelled to an international competition and that was in 1912 and 1936 for the Olympics for they were the only times when his passage and stay were covered. His attitude in these matters was pretty much straightforward. If no one else was going to pay, he certainly was not going to do it because investing his own money in building up his knowledge, seeing first-hand new innovations in the way the game could be played was not on his list of priorities.

In the spring of 1924, Lausanne Sports, arch rivals of Duckworth's Servette, offered Hogan a better deal than he was getting at Berne. He accepted terms whilst Evelyn set about finding suitable schools for Joe, Mary and Frank. There they would learn French to supplement the German language they had already acquired. The new contract would take Hogan up to the end of the 1924-25 season. The Lausanne club had already employed British when they engaged Hogan's old Bolton teammate Billy Hunter in 1922 and Hogan now arrived but the atmosphere at the club was poor. Just before Hogan's arrival there had been a huge turn around, famous old players left the club, amongst them Max Abegglen, and a few new ones arrived, including a young André Syrvet, who would go on to appear for the national XI in the 1930s. It was a reasonable season, made noteworthy in the summer before the season when Hogan turned out for what was a composite Swiss side to face the Egyptian national XI.[55] The Egyptians had just caused a massive shock in the 1924 Olympics eliminating Hungary quite easily, 3-0. The Hungarians could have few excuses since their team contained Orth, Gyula Mándi, Bela Guttman, Braun and Jeny. Having received invites from around Europe, the Egyptians stopped off to play the Swiss XI on their way to play to in Vienna. However, following the conclusion of the League championship, won by Servette, Hogan was being tempted back to Budapest.[56]

# Jimmy Hogan

## Notes

1 The greatest likelihood is that this would have been after July 1919.
2 Fox states that this work came about because Gordon Walker, the owner of the company, also found himself in Budapest during the War and "shared food parcels with Hogan."
3 The company was based at the Mersey Tobacco Factory, 217 Scotland Rd, Liverpool 5. The previous name of the company was Walkers Tobacco Market Limited and that company was wound up on 24 July 1919 and a new company took over the business and undertaking. That company was Walkers Tobacco Company Limited.
4 Otherwise Wilson calls him a "delivery foreman" Fox states that the family were living in the Knotty Ash area at this time. Why they decided to live in Liverpool at the time is not known.
5 The number of clubs increased to 66 from 44 at the end of the 1920-21 season. Charles Buchan wrote in *A Lifetime in Football* that it was : "... the biggest mistake in [the League's] history. ... [Because, notwithstanding] the ... war, there were not enough first-class players to go round. ... In my opinion, it was responsible for the deterioration in the standard of League play from which it has never fully recovered. In pre-war seasons ... scouts had only to go to the north east, the Birmingham area or any of the thickly populated districts to discover several players ... but in the next few years, these areas were practically drained of their promising material." (pp.64-65).
6 *Athletic News*, 2 December 1920. The letter was reprinted with Catton's remark on it in the *Derbyshire Courier*, 25 December 1920.
7 Matthew Taylor, Football's Engineers? British Football Coaches, Migration and Intercultural Transfer, c.1910–c.1950s, *Sport in History*, vol. 30, no. 1 (2010), 138-163.
8 We are not to know who advised Hogan to make the trip to London; one, evidently, that he could ill-afford to make for he stated that he had to borrow funds for the train fare to London.
9 Fox, 85.
10 Green, *The History of the Football Association* (Naldrett, 1953), p. 292.
11 https://playupliverpool.com/1918/06/01/the-football-war-fund/
12 Fox, 80, lifted from Hogan's life story in *Sport*.
13 *Sheffield Independent*, 12 March 1919.
14 They scheduled a meeting to see each other around 27 April 1934 at the Football Association to discuss the development of the coaching scheme (see *Burnley Express*, 21 April 1934).
15 *Wiener Sporttagblatt*, 16 July 1921. In March 1924 Wiener AC tried again to persuade Hogan to transfer allegiance to them. Again he refused (*Neues Wiener Journal*, 7 March 1924). This could have had something to do with the money that was being offered, but either way, Hogan did not take up their offer.
16 Young Boys provide that he was contracted to work at the club from 10 May 1922 having taken over from Bert Smith. News was first announced of Hogan working in Berne in the *Athletic News* on 8 May 1922. Confirmation was printed in *Tribune de Lausanne* on 14 May 1922 that it was a two year contract.
17 There were a number of bids for him to return to Vienna between 1922 and 1924.
18 He was referring to the May 1923 tour of Switzerland. Bolton beat Hogan's Young Boys 2-0 in their fixture on 21 May; and 2-1 in their fixture on 30 May that year.
19 *Soccer*, 305. On 12 February 1923 it was reported that of Young Boys' victory over Aarau that the players were sinking up to their ankles in the soft turf.
20 *Bredashce Courant*, 4 November 1922.
21 *Illustriertes (Österreichisches) Sportsblatt*, 3 June 1922.
22 Acknowledgement to Sandra Gill.
23 The international was played on 11 June 1922.

# 1919-1925

24 Hunt, *First Steps to Association Football* (Arthur Pearson, 1924), p. 12.
25 4 November 1922.
26 *(Wiener) Sporttagblatt*, 23 August 1922. The match was played on Tuesday 15 August 1922.
27 Translated by Claudia Schmidtt.
28 Charles Beuret, Archivist of Young Boys football club.
29 A game refereed by Hugo Meisl at Sportplatz Spitalacker.
30 *Illustriertes (Österreichisches) Sportblatt*, 20 January 1923.
31 *Ibid.*
32 *(Wiener) Sporttagblatt*, 26 January 1923.
33 1 September 1922.
34 *Tribune de Lausanne*, 1 January 1923.
35 Losing 1-0 on 22 March 1923.
36 Recounted in *Becsi Magyar Ujsag (Wiener Ungarische Zeitung)*, 6 July 1923.
37 The Swiss system was built on three divisions providing, three Champions for a League play off competition.
38 Bern won the Final Group and were declared Swiss National Champions. It was only in September 1923 (long after the Championship medals had been handed out from the previous season) that it was announced that in September 1922 - in the match between FC Bern and FC Basel (in the Central Championship) - Bern, themselves, had used an unregistered player. In essence, this meant that Bern would not have had enough points to qualify for the initial play off and Young Boys would have been in the national final group. Subsequently, the Swiss FA stripped Bern of their national title and the 1923 Championship was belatedly declared without an overall winner.
39 The arbitration committee met on 5 May 1923 to determine what to do regarding the no-show.
40 *Becsi Magyar Ujsag (Wiener Ungarische Zeitung)*, Saturday, 24 March 1923.
41 *Burnley Express*, 6 June 1923.
42 *Nieuwe Tilburgsche Courant*, 15 November 1922.
43 *(Wiener) Sporttagblatt*, 8 June 1923.
44 6 July 1923.
45 Charles Beuret, archivist for Young Boys.
46 *Tribune de Lausanne*, 19 April 1924.
47 Pulver, Ramseyer, Fehlmann, Haag, Reymond, Pülitz, Galler, Richard, Fässler, Oberhauser, Imhof, Schmidlin, Pichter, Mayer, Charpilloz, Ehrenbolger, Marienet, Pache, Matzinger, Perrenoud, Dasen, Sturzenegger, Lavallaz, Leiber, Dietrich, Abegglen, Schmid 1, Bouvier, Ruffle, Inaebnit, Schâr, Bühler, Maspoli, Dubouchet, Gottenkieny, Osterwalder.
48 *La Sentinelle*, 15 February 1924. The classes were held on 8 March, 29 March, 12 April and 3 May.
49 Townley, eventually, went on to coach the Dutch at the Olympics. For some reason, Townley's part in all of this has been airbrushed from history.
50 In sixteen matches dating back to 1921, Switzerland had won only two games.
51 *European International Football*, 201.
52 Cea's in the 65th minute and Romano's in the 82nd minute.
53 Indeed, Cea kicks his through Oberhauser's legs as the centre-half is tracking back trying to cover the ball for Pulver to gather.
54 Ramseyer had, the previous season, operated as an outside left.
55 *Le Droit du Peuple*, 18 June 1924.
56 Acknowledgement to Dr Gregory Quin, Université de Lausanne for assistance with this chapter.

# Jimmy Hogan

## NINE

## 1925-26
### 'The vast improvement reaped by Hogan has almost made him an idol.'

Hogan returned to Budapest in early May 1925[1] to take up a contract with MTK. Antal Frontz had just led the club to its tenth consecutive title. The club had not known anything but victory since before the Great War.

This season would feature a profound change to the Laws but how that alteration was reflected on the field of play depended on where you played your football. On 25 June 1925, at the International Board meeting in Paris, it was decided that the Scottish FA's proposal to limit the number of defenders to two needed to play an attacker offside was accepted. The alteration brought about a distinct change in the way teams organised themselves. Although administrators had removed the need for three defenders, clubs in Britain quickly decided to put one back there and so create the defensive third back role. It would take a while for a formation to reveal itself but at Chapman's Arsenal an inside forward, Alex James, whom Chapman would buy from Preston in 1929, would be sacrificed to provide the creative influence. Over on the continent, the approach adopted by the clubs Hogan worked for was to retain the creative centre-half. There was not the appetite to change the way the game had been played and in in Hungary and Austria, the alteration to a defensive centre-half was seen as anathema to how the game should be played. If the centre-half was nullified, came the thought, where would the creativity come from? As late as the 1954 World Cup, the centre-half still had a significant bearing on the game enough that Ocwirk would lead Austria to a third place finish.

Budapest was a much more conducive place for Hogan than Switzerland had been. He knew the players, the football "environment" and used it to his advantage. Press coverage in Switzerland by comparison had been sparse and although moving around the cantons had proved profitable while Evelyn raised their young family but it was not helping to keep his profile in the public eye. Within a couple of months of being in Hungary, Hogan had once more made attempts to promote himself and his work with the British media. He was now 42 years of age and had a keen eye on the future. For him, traipsing about in Europe brought in the money but he would need to settle and the best possible future was to secure a well-paid job in England. To that end, he went about creating a platform that would promote his work amongst readers and clubs in England.

He was happy to be back in Budapest, but 1925-26 proved to be a bad season, the auguries being poor from the off. Upon assuming the MTK coaching role, Hogan became embroiled in a public spat with David Jack following a feisty old game in which MTK drew with the touring Bolton side.[2] Braun was absent for the game and Orth had to forego his normal game, to play right-back because of an injury sustained by Mándi early in the first half.[3] What got Hogan's back up was a conversation he shared with David Jack after the game. Jack's insistence was that coaching was, basically, a con in that no matter how much was provided by a trainer you could not magically "produce" talented footballers; players, according to Jack, were born not made. What the argument really revealed was the British aversion to coaching. Jack distrusted coaching because professionals of his standard had been indoctrinated with the understanding that they were paid to play the game; it would undermine their status to be taught. The Continentals on the other hand saw coaching as an essential, enabling them to build on what they had, understanding that to succeed in football, one needed more than a background kicking a tanner ball as a youngster. Players playing for Continental teams would have been stunned if no formal training programme had been forthcoming and Hogan, being engaged in that cultural movement, was now fully sold on the benefits that such a programme could bring. The argument therefore marked a clear distinction between him and the prevailing British mood and attitude. He may have been British but he was anything but in his outlook on these matters and, at that time, was quite happy for Britain to go it alone and leave the Europeans to get on with developing their art and methods. Hogan and Jack's argument came to be played out in public, Hogan sharing his views in newsprint and Jack taking time to relate his experiences in his biography published in 1934. Neither came out looking clever in the final analysis. Hogan invalidated his own argument, when he later wrote:

> I only wish that [David Jack], who argued ... that swerving and feinting were natural gifts which could not be taught, had [had] the opportunity of playing against [Orth and Braun]. [He] would have very quickly changed [his view] on the matter ... after all is said and done, [their] body control was only learnt by simple exercises, such as dribbling the ball around sticks and controlling it first with the inside and afterwards with the outside of the foot, coupled with gymnastic exercises to make the body loose at the hips. [Can] you imagine asking a British player to do anything like [that]? Yet this is what Continental teams, who keep beating English League XIs, are doing to prepare their players for the battle of football supremacy.[4]

# 1925-26

His argument would have carried greater validity if the two players Hogan referred to had not been Orth and Braun, for everyone knew they were "born" footballers but Jack made an ass of himself too when referring to Bolton's defeat on that same European tour. For in one section of the book he clearly makes reference to the benefits that coaching can bring for certain players. A week after their draw with MTK, Bolton would lose 4-1 to Ferencváros[5] and of that match, Jack wrote in his book *Soccer*[6] that Ferencváros:

> 'were three goals up before we really knew where we were'. It was 'one of the finest games I have participated in ... on tour. I have endeavoured to find the name of the Hungarian centre-forward [Vilmos Kohut.] who was mainly responsible for our defeat that day – he led his line with fine judgment and was one of the very few Continental forwards I have seen or played against who shot at every reasonable opportunity. One of his goals, scored from well outside the penalty area, gave our custodian, Dick Pym, no earthly chance ... [7]

But there was another issue at play here. In the upper chambers of the Football Association and the Football League there were open discussions at the time as to whether all those Continental tours were worth it if "prestige" was being lost as a result of the number of losses sustained by British teams overseas. Bolton were a case in point. At the time they were enjoying a sustained high point in their life cycle, Cup winners in 1923, they would go on to lift the famous old pot in 1926 and 1929, but their form on tour was mediocre. Writing in the *Athletic News*, Ivan Sharpe, disagreed with the notion of a ban but an answer was not easy to conjure. The holiday mentality, the high bounce of the ball on a hard baked surface inducing a lackadaisical attitude in the players heading out on tour was hard to shake. After all, these were players who had endured a hard season and were out now to enjoy themselves, while still obliged to represent the clubs who were paying their wages: "Clubs should consider ... the prestige of the tutor in making their plans for the journey"[8] was all Sharpe could suggest. For his part Hogan did not see any self-imposed ban by British clubs as being productive for anyone. But against that felt that unless something changed the ill feeling between British and European teams would continue to fester. He agreed with Sharpe. The problem was one of attitude but until the implementation of a European-wide competition, the players' views on these matches would remain as they were. In September 1925, Hogan was interviewed by John Hodgson, in a curious article printed by

# Jimmy Hogan

the *Liverpool Echo*.[9] Hodgson, who was visiting Budapest, met a few of the British professionals working in the city and asked them their opinions about the state of the game but of those he only interviewed Hogan. The strapline for the article could have been "Foreign players and teams were a lot better than the British were giving them credit for." Hogan told Hodgson: "The reputation of English football suffers [when the teams come out on tours to the Continent]. The Continental treats all his sport seriously and if he imagines his opponent is holding him cheaply he resents the slight." He went on, "If English teams cannot come out to play the game seriously they should remain at home, because the continental wants to see the best and has no time for the tourist out for pleasure."[10] Hogan used the interview to explain how important he felt coaching really was. He explained that it was not just about getting players how to pass and trap the ball, it included tendering for the mental and physical well-being of the players: "So strong is the affection of the players for Hogan, that they will ask advice from him on mere domestic affairs and anything they can imagine that can affect their playing in the team is not undertaken until they've asked Jimmy's permission."[11]

Secondly, Hogan argued, coaching required innovative thought. If you want good players you need to train with the ball but you also needed to make them think, to engage them mentally in what activity they were undertaking. To this end, "Hodgson" described the training regime that Hogan had set out for his players which included the use of chairs placed strategically in the field and Hogan would get the players to dribble around the chairs with the ball using both feet: "Quickness in performing the task is an essential. Heading exercises are also part of the Hogan idea, all of which means better control of the ball in actual matches, and the vast improvement reaped by Hogan has almost made him an idol."[12] Perhaps it did, although now after fifteen years of coaching what strikes one is not the advent of some tactical masterplan but the use of stationary objects in a field for players to run past. It seems hardly innovative to our minds but anything that continued to move the responsibility of training from the mouth of the trainer to the minds of the footballers represented a step forward. Sessions were now becoming player-led rather than coach-driven. But the key message being conveyed by Hogan was that coaching was vital if the intention to create players who could think for themselves on field was to succeed. Continental players were becoming more skilled in the game compared to their British counterparts because of the way they were being coached. And Hogan was demonstrating his central role in this cultural movement for British readers as a result of the article.

Hogan had landed on his feet once again, MTK still had a roster of star players, but things were to come unstuck that season following the loss of György Orth. Orth was still the undisputed genius of the team, Hogan valued him to be worth as much as £6,000 on the open market,[13] but the flip side to that remarkable ball control as he rode effortlessly over the bumpy grounds of the club pitches was his sizeable ego, the type which commonly afflicts so many footballers and attracts those villains who seek to chop both player and ego down to size. "From a modest and nice boy," wrote the *Illustriertes (Österreichisches) Sportblatt*, "he became a moody and difficult to treat star, who was ready to forget everything at any moment, that his club had done for him."[14] Orth had already scored a hat-trick in the first game of the season before MTK played SV Amateure Wien in a "friendly."[15] Matches between the Austrians and Hungarians were never friendlies in truth and it proved so here for at the end of that game Johann Tandler, the Austrian international, deliberately stamped on Orth's outstretched leg following a tackle. The injury signalled something of an end for Orth who returned to competitive football after a long lay-off as a result of the injury but was never the same player as he had been prior to it. Hogan, famously, cried when he saw the extent of the injury but he may as well have been shedding tears for his own Hungarian career because he knew that without Orth the team could not hope to succeed. That Hogan openly cried at seeing the injury was not too surprising; he knew that his absence was one that MTK could not hope to fill. But further than that there was Hogan's close friendship with Orth even to the extent of teaching his son English. Orth, ironically, was soon to be followed by Braun, who again was lost that season through injury.

Orth's departure opened the door for a bank clerk to take over the outside forward role at MTK. Rudolf Jeny had no option but to work at the bank he was employed at in the city but outside work he came under the tutelage of Hogan. Jeny said of Hogan that he "was an excellent coach ... a master of technology, tactics and great human qualities. He [trained us to pass on the ground] and improved the ability to shoot. He practiced a lot of exercises - with MTK's running pace we were training high jumps and [doing] various body exercises. Of course, we [did] not train as much as they [do] nowadays. We had to work if we had the opportunity; at that time I was a bank employee, MTK helped me."[16]

But the setbacks in losing Braun and particularly Orth spelt the end of the great MTK era. The club ran out of luck in the League[17] and although they did manage to take the Hungarian Cup[18] in a game held over from the previous season it was not enough to stop the axe from falling, the inevitability of it causing Hogan to look to other jobs and contracts as the season ended. On 23 May 1926 the *Prágai Magyar Hirlap* reported that

# Jimmy Hogan

Jimmy Hogan, the English trainer of MTK, would break contract with Hungária to work with Sparta in Prague. Hungária allegedly wanted to get rid of Hogan's krn180m annual salary, the correspondent wrote. But they also realised another truth. That Hungaria were lining up the return of their former players Kálmán Konrád and Jeno Konrád who had both canceled their contracts with the Amateurs in Vienna, and neither were inclined to work alongside a British coach. The club however spent some time considering ways to reach an arrangement between all parties. In the end Hogan's departure would be engineered all wrong. On 5 June 1926, the *Illustrated Sports-paper* in Vienna reported that Hogan had been fired by MTK. The paper was critical of the decision. "... a scapegoat had to be found," they wrote, "and that was Jimmy."[19] The decision was certainly wrong, the editorial reported, because the main cause of the club's disappointing season was the injury to Orth and since the club had known Hogan for ten years it appeared strange that his inability to lead the team should only now be apparent. The job in Prague did not materialise. Instead Hogan was called to attend a football conference in Budapest. It was while he was there that he met Johannes "Hans" Hadicke of the Central German FA who enticed him to Dresden with a two year contract. The contract was signed in July 1926.[20]

# 1925-26

Notes

1 *La Sentinelle*, 8 May 1925: "Jimmy Hogan, the ... coach from Lausanne, left Switzerland for where he signed with M. T. K., the famous Magyar. Bon voyage and good luck." The contract was confirmed on 29 April 1925 by the *Prágai Magyar Hirlap* newspaper.

2 10 May 1925. Mándi was injured in a tackle with Vizard and was replaced by Orth who had to play at right back. Three of the Bolton players had to leave the field toward the end.

3 http://www.huszadikszazad.hu/1925-majus/sport/mtk-bolton-wanderers-11-10

4 *Daily Dispatch*, September 1925.

5 17 May 1925.

6 David Jack, *Soccer* (Putnam, 1934).

7 *Ibid*, 314.

8 25 September 1925.

9 *Liverpool Echo*, 12 September 1925.

10 *Ibid*.

11 *Liverpool Echo*, 12 September 1925.

12 *Ibid*.

13 As reported by "Hodgson".

14 1 July 1922.

15 Played in September 1925.

16 http://www.magyarfutball.hu/hu/szemelyek/adatlap/368/jeny_rudolf&prev=search

17 Losing to Ferencváros by two points.

18 28 March 1926, they beat Ujpest TC 4-0.

19 *Illustriertes Sportblatt*, No. 23.

20 *Burnley Express*, 2 March 1927.

Jimmy Hogan

## TEN

## 1926-1932
## 'We have nothing more to learn from the British trainer but this cannot be true.'

When Hogan first arrived in Germany in 1926, football was not the number one sport there.[1] When he left in 1932, it was becoming so or, as Kolb stated, it had "conquered a mass public."[2] How crucial Hogan was in helping that transition is difficult to gauge, but his influence should not be overlooked.

Football expanded exponentially in Germany in the mid-1920s due to a number of factors. Firstly, the war had exposed the game to more Germans than those select number of teachers who had previously imported the game after undertaking trips to England. Soldiers returning from the Great War had brought back footballs in their rucksacks, having seen the game played during moments when the fighting took a backseat on the front line. This led to a dramatic increase in the number who played the game and in the way the sport came to be viewed in Germany.

Secondly, in 1926 the prohibition against German participation on the international stage was relaxed, enabling Germany to participate at the Amsterdam Olympics in 1928. As a result, the DFB, the German FA, put in place a programme, led by Dr Otto Nerz, to search for and propose a coaching strategy that would be adopted throughout the country and so ensure that there was a coherent basis for the national selection of players to represent the country at the Olympics.[3] This idea however did not meet universal approval in Germany at first. Strong regional identities became a yoke under which German football endured for many decades which hindered success up to the 1960s on the basis that regional groups demanded that the national side be proportionately represented and that the game should remain devised on regional lines. This meant that certain regions played the game in a certain style and for some time the effect of this was that the national side was form of players impracticably suited. However, it says a great deal about his character that Nerz had the confidence to force through his proposals in the face of such entrenched opposition. As a Southerner, one would have expected Nerz to have been influenced by Bavaria's Nuremberg, the pre-eminent domestic German club of the time, but their dominance was coming to an end partly as a result of the fact that they were anchored to "a slow, considered [Scottish?] style of play centred on good technique and the stringing together of passes." [Tor! 43-44.] Nerz saw nothing particularly special about the Scottish style, feeling that it became a means to its own end with proponents more concerned with moving the ball about than actually scoring goals. [Der Kampf um den Ball, Prismen Verlag Berlin, 1933, 66.] In the North teams "stuck to [what they called] the [new] 'English' style, based on pace and directness. Fast, furious wingers dashed to the by-line and sent high crosses in ...". [Tor! 44.] But tactically speaking this was a mess for on the one hand you had the decisiveness of modern wing-play with its speed and haste and on the other rather than benefit from the dash of the outside forward cutting in toward the penalty area at the angle of the defensive third and having a shot on goal, the wingers instead were ceding what advantages they had in order to make off determinedly for the corners like some speeded up version of Billy Bassett. Considering matters in the round, Dr Nerz saw the whole thing for what it was: a mess. The South was playing a game made redundant by the offside law change while the North was furiously busting a gut. Something must be done!

Thirdly, around 1923-24 there was the great clash between the Deutsche Turnen movement and football. Turnen, a brand of group gymnastics, sometimes performed in large open spaces described by Meisl as being "fiercely nationalistic and regimented," [Association Football, vol. 4, 308.] had happily co-existed with football, with clubs having members who undertook either or both of the sports, despite the divergence of their under-pinning philosophies. Turnen was all about the group working cohesively, many following a single movement whereas football is about individuals separately operating within and for the team. However, that season saw the "reinliche Scheidung" in which the Deutsche Turnerschaft banned turners from being members of clubs that were members of the DFB, the German FA. This move was self-defeating to the turner movement, leading to the move of vast numbers of football players and turners away from gymnastic clubs to football clubs.

Fourthly, the change in the offside law in June 1925 brought about a hastier, less-punctuated version of football that appealed to a new modernity that the Germans had embraced since the War. This was a topic touched on by the German publisher, Samuel Fischer, who was concerned by the way the country had moved away from a traditionally, deliberate way of life, something Fischer argued could be seen in the waning interest for reading and a fall in the numbers of those who purchased books. Writing in 1926, Fischer wrote: "People go in for sport ... Our defeat in the war, and the wave of Americanism, have transformed our taste and our approach to life."[4] By 1930, the game of football in Germany was exhibiting all of that new "approach to life", demonstrating speed, intelligence and effectiveness which Hogan picked up on when, just prior to England's game with Germany in May 1930, he wrote: "The type of game we are playing in Germany is a productive one, with good hefty charging, and we have good scoring forwards. In general, the low combination game is in vogue, but we have players who are strong and clever enough to hold the ball either for an individual scoring effort or to providing openings."[5]

**Roving Commission And Lectures**

Hogan's contract[6] was with the regional football association, Verband Mitteldeutscher Ballspiel-Vereine (Central German Football Association – VMBV) as Vereinsfussballlehrer.[7] We are not to know as to whether the role that Hogan was offered was being offered to others in the other seven regional Associations at that time.[8] Fox informs us in his biography of Hogan that he was first informed of the vacant role within the VMBV, the Central German FA, by Hans Hädicke, the President of the Association, at a conference held in Budapest in 1926. At the time Hädicke was also Chairman of Hallescher FC Wacker 1900 and he had in mind a role for his new Vereinsfussballlehrer that would ultimately assist his club in achieving national status.

There were three chief responsibilities for the Vereinsfussballlehrer but it was a role that one person could hardly fulfill. The first responsibility was that it was a roving commission to promote football to the youth of that region covered by the Association.[9] The Association was a regional football association that included approximately the present day federal states of Saxony, Saxony-Anhalt and Thuringia, but also smaller areas in Bavaria, present-day Brandenburg and Lower Saxony and the former Sudetenland. It was during one of these jaunts that Hogan first visited the town of Meerane, near Zwickau where he was to first clap eyes on Richard Hofmann, the famous pre-war German goalscorer. Added to this, Hogan was responsible for helping to unify football coaching for the local football associations that had been set up in Leipzig, Dresden, Chemnitz and Plauen. Hogan soon realized just how well the role suited him, ensuring he held elevated status over a wide area of the country. In March 1927, he wrote "If one accepts a post as a private trainer ... they expect a championship the first year. But the work of an Association trainer is shown in improvements in different parts of the country."[10] In this way, it was a departure from that which Hogan was used to and it said much for his profound sense of self-worth that he felt himself suited to the higher level role than that of a club trainer because, although it brought in a sizeable salary, it offloaded from him the mundane responsibilities of club management.

To begin with, he was required to coach groups of student footballers connected with local football teams which would be staged at the Verbundhaus, the training centre for the Association located on Leipzig S3, Brandvorwerkstrasse 70. In addition, each fortnight he would be given a schedule of venues where he would give instructions to various numbers of students.

"The students," he later wrote, "[knew] when I [was] coming and [arranged] a week's holiday. I [stayed] in various towns ... Dresden, Leipzig, Halle, Magdeburg, Erfurt and Plauen" and gave lessons in football positional play and tactics from 9-12 every morning. He coached outdoors in the afternoons: "[to]show them how to trap the ball, how to swerve, how to dribble, and all the other little items which go to make up a footballer. Then we have a little side game, in which I referee, stopping the game when I see the students doing anything tactically wrong and explaining to them where their error lies."[11]

Finally on Friday afternoons there would be an exam. The Germans invested time and effort into their football and that particular appetite that the Germans brought to the endeavour would have recalled to Hogan that of the Austrians. It was a world away from the sunlit jollities of Dordrecht; this was no longer the game of fags and booze and a few keepy-uppies to the accompaniment of polite Dutch applause. His offer of fairly standard training fare, as outlined above, did not satisfy everyone. For the second time in his career, concerns were raised by players who criticised his methods.[12] In Austria, such criticism had been deflected due to the support he had got from Hugo Meisl, who had acted as his bridge to the players. Meisl contextualised whatever Hogan was doing for a circumspect audience. In Germany, however, Hogan was very much on his own; he had few allies. That was obvious enough when Otto Nerz and Carl Koppehel wrote their book on training and tactics, *Der Kampf um den Ball* in 1933, the year after Hogan's "triumphant" stay in Germany had come to an end. A comprehensive survey of football, Nerz discusses characters and tactics in the game but considered Jimmy Hogan so lacking in importance as to not mention him at all. As a result of the concerns regarding what he was teaching, Hogan was asked by someone connected with the VMBV to give a lecture and this led to him undertaking the second of his roles for the VMBV, that of football lecturer. Further to this he was given an ultimatum; provide a lecture demonstrating what you know or resign. Up to 1926 there had only been one recorded instance of him giving such a demonstration.

## 1926-1932

On 12 April 1925, Tufnell Park's touring side were beaten 8-0 by SK Vrsovice in Prague.

"The following night [Hogan] gave a demonstration [in Budapest, and was], howled down by the audience but undertook tricks until 'blood and perspiration' ran from him. That was his way of upholding British football prestige."[13]

The "lecture"[14] itself was "a fiasco"[15] starting with the words "Meine Sicht beschäftigt meine Damen und Herren," or "My very busy ladies and gentlemen" and, according to Hogan, it, and he, was only saved by one of his default demonstrations of technical skill[16] during which (at one point) he repeatedly kicked a ball at a wooden panel in the hall with such venom that he said he cut his foot. The audience which roared with laughter at his poor German, now sat spellbound in appreciation of his ability. Hogan put his refusal to retire from the lecture down to his hard-headed Irishness but do not get sucked in by that. He knew that failure at the event would have been curtains for the generous contract the Central Germans had provided him with. It was the best contract he had ever put his signature too and he was not going to let it go without a fight. What is curious about this is that during the lecture Hogan did not suddenly do anything new that he had not done before. The only difference between what he did that day and what he had done before was that the audience was larger and wearing evening suits. His coaching profile up to then had been built on him demonstrating repetitive exercises with the football to footballers. He had been practicing those skills for years so it was quite natural for him to show an audience what he could do with a ball. However, what he had never done, was go over these exercises to a massed audience and, as it transpired, Hogan took to the role of "stage performer" like a duck to water. Accordingly the lectures and the role he undertook for the Central German FA changed his outlook. Up to that point he had always had that level of confidence that marked him out. Happy for his face and name to appear in the newspapers. Happy to sign pictures of himself. Happy to present an image of himself as some kind of "idol."[17] But now, his ability and natural confidence in giving these demonstrations, instilled in him the belief that he could help shape a much wider movement.

Hogan was always interested in self-promotion and publicity; the lectures in Germany simply opened his eyes to where this confidence could lead him. It certainly bolstered his ego immensely. Now he was given an opportunity to put himself out amongst the people, to help drive a popular movement. The fact that there was a demand for these public demonstrations, in Germany, at the very time of the rise of the National Socialists, is an oddity that perhaps informs the narrative of some contemporaneous mania that afflicted the German people. They were hungry to be told and shown. The impact on Hogan's outlook, as a result, was self-evident. When he went back to England, he spent time agitating toward a "national" programme that he could be a crucial part of. That's why he went back and spoke to Sir Frederick Wall. That's why he worked with Stanley Rous in coaching at the Refresher Coaching Courses from the mid-1930s onwards. It was all part of a campaign to replicate what he had done in Germany, to revisit that sense of country-wide fame and influence that he had grown used to. It's irrelevant as to whether the national coaching schemes amounted to anything or why they ultimately failed in England. What is important is that Hogan saw his role, at that higher level, as being a calling for him; something that carried more purpose than a lowly club trainer. And certainly something that, in his mind, carried more purpose than being a Priest in a small diocese in a non-descript Lancastrian town.

All of a sudden, he could sell himself to large numbers of people and it did wonders for his ego to suddenly be so popular. After all, why otherwise would anyone keep tabs on the numbers of people who came to see them? From Hogan's life story, Fox remarks: "7,500 people saw [him] in central Saxony (in Dresden and in Chemnitz alone)." By the spring of 1927, the *Burnley Express* "reported'" that "… he has given lessons to no fewer than 13,500 players … sometimes he addresses no fewer than 200 or 300 [people]."[18] By May 1928, his demonstrations had been seen by 43,000 people.[19] That was an extraordinary number of people because after all, this was not a pop concert. It was a man on a stage kicking a football but it was proving popular possibly because it subverted the expectation one had as to how football could be taught, an expectation founded on the fact that it had been taught by strict Prussian schoolmasters barking out instructions to wide-eyed, petrified German schoolboys. This was noticed by Helmut Schön, whom Hogan was to teach in Dresden in the early 1930s. The youngsters in Schön's class were used to coaches with ramrod backs who assumed the attitude of military officers of old. But Hogan was different in style and form. He wore a *Rollkragenpullover*, a "roll-neck sweater," he allowed the lads a drink, he would even join them, the night before a big game to calm them.[20] Schön recalled, "One day Jimmy Hogan took me aside: 'You know you're going to be on the first team soon. That means you have to live a sporting life. A player should not smoke. But I don't mind you drinking a big glass of beer the night before the match. Then you sleep well and it doesn't harm you.' That's what I kept to. Some of my teammates [...] said they would have wished for such good advice once. I'm sure Jimmy had his reasons for being very reluctant to give such advice."[21] It is easy to undermine these side shows for being exhibitions of self-indulgence, with limited teaching value, but what they did do was to help increase the exposure of football to a wider audience.[22] Whereas football had been able to get a foothold in some of the famous German schools, purely because a teacher or a headmaster had undertaken some study or a visit to England, there were still difficulties establishing it within the school system. As an instance, the teaching of football was banned in Bavarian schools from 1912. Perhaps the reason for this was that it was seen as "undermining the main principle of education, discipline."[23] Hogan identified this himself: "The great drawback of German football was ... that it was not taught in ... schools. The teachers ... did not know football, and, for the sake of keeping their own jobs, tended to discourage its introduction."[24]

What Hogan did was popularise the game in the Eastern region with his travelling show of tricks and surprises and elevated it to a level of acceptance for a certain class of southern and eastern Germans. He "freed" the footballers in those towns and helped popularise the game, allowed it to breathe. Little wonder that Helmut Schön, born in Dresden freed from the drudgery of some militarised group exercise to comfortably earn a lifelong keep in football, was to sing Hogan's praises with such alacrity upon his death. Without that travelling show the rapid increase in the game's popularity, and the investment that went with it, would not have materialised as it did *throughout* the country. The game's popularity freed Schön, just as it "freed" Herberger, and it would also help propel a better Germany into the international consciousness following the horrors of Hitler's war. The battle that Hogan, inadvertently, helped to win was one that helped lead Germany toward a football-loving future and international acceptance. Yet, in truth, it was just entertainment that he was bringing to the crowds not some new form of "coaching." From that point on, Hogan would follow a set routine, like a stage magician constantly pulling the same bunny from the same top hat. The demonstrations did not necessarily promote the playing of the game, as a TV chef does not encourage people to cook at home, but it did promote to sport over gymnastics and, in this way, his stay in Germany is vital to our whole understanding of his impact on European football.

On 19 March 1927, Hogan began a strenuous six-week lecture programme with a demonstration to 2,500 people at the Exhibition Palace in Dresden.[25] This lecture was part of a bigger demonstration regarding over ten Olympic sports in preparation of the Olympics in 1928 and was the largest audience Hogan had ever spoken in front of. By the end of April he had given demonstrations to 5,000 players in Dresden, moved on to Bautzen where he gave a presentation to 450 students then went to the

# Jimmy Hogan

Police Club Sports ground at Chemnitz to show off to another audience. In fourteen days he had been seen by 2,050 "pupils." He then went to the towns of Naumburg, Zeitz and Weissenfels presenting to another 540 players.[26]

The way in which football was being structured in Germany at that time was giving Hogan cause to compare football there with that played and organised in England and his view in relation to England suffered as a result. After all, this is a country that would go from one that was considered a whipping boy on the European football field in 1924 to a semi-finalist at the World Cup in 1934. Hogan's job, the rarified, almost political atmosphere in which he worked, the acclaim and respect that it afforded him was something that he cherished and obviously worked hard to distance himself from anything that would jeopardise the contract. While on his lecture tour, in Chemnitz, he met an old playing partner of his, Norman Dickenson. Dickenson had played for Bolton in Holland in 1910. He used the meeting with Dickenson to send another letter back to the *Burnley Express* and warn his old team, Burnley, in regard to their "duty," a duty they had to uphold the British game but in reality he was referring to a duty they to help him and it would be wrong to mislead oneself as to his actual motives. He felt that these performances were undermining his prestige and as a result his market worth. In the Easter of 1927, Cambridge University had been on the receiving end of a 6-1 spanking from Hamburger SV.[27] Of that, Hogan reported, "the [Germans] were disgusted." He went on to write that whereas touring teams will be "well-treated and enthusiastically received in every town ... in return ... the German wants to see the real thing ... the game as it is played at home ..."[28]

The VMBV contract also required Hogan to make numerous visits to England to see how the game was developing there, as scouting trips. This was particularly important given the change in the offside law that had taken place in the June of 1925 and was obviously wholly welcomed by him. In February 1927, Hogan returned to Lancashire for a few weeks so that he might identify "new developments in the game" the understanding being that if there were any developments brought about by the 1925 Law change the British would be leading the way but it was a wasted journey. "I saw one match last week, but there was nothing new in it as far as I could see."[29] The game may have held nothing for his pay masters but Hogan was quick to let the English readers remember that their football was still number one in one regard at least. "Englishmen are still the best exponents of football," he wrote. "Germany [have] realised that [but]... other countries ... like Italy and Spain do not [and go to] Hungary [to get their coaches] ... which was a mistake."[30]

## 1926-1932

The only League game that he said truly impressed him around that time was the derby game that he attended in early March 1927 between Burnley and Rovers. "I felt quite down hearted after watching two previous games and imagined England football had gone down very much. This afternoon has revived me great deal. I am very surprised at the pace of the game compared with what I have seen today, Continental football is mere walking."[31]

He returned to the UK in the September of 1927 to report on the match between Manchester United and the reigning champions, Newcastle United, at Old Trafford. He wrote a letter to the *Burnley Express* to give his views on a game in which Newcastle won 7-1.[32] It would be one of the very few occasions in which he discussed the tactical side of the game which highlighted the influence of the recent change in the Law on thinking generally. In that letter, he set out his belief in wing-play; an antidote to what he felt was the mindlessness of players putting their foot through the ball and sending it in the direction of the opponent's centre-half. Possession was being given away through a lack of confidence on the ball. Players who did have confidence were able to find their colleague and in the case of Newcastle that meant a better-placed teammate out on the wing. Manchester United, meanwhile, were humping the ball forward. There was no cohesion and no sense of combination just a hefty hoof with the view that a forward may be able to gain possession close to the Newcastle goal. Manchester United had attacked for two-thirds of the first half, Hogan wrote, but Newcastle were always the better team, "because they played with more method."

"What I saw only convinced me more than the wing game, as played by Newcastle United, is much better than the haphazard 'get-it-if-you-can', down-the-middle game, as played by Manchester United and by many other teams in present-day English football. Newcastle's seven goals all came from well thought out wing-play, and not from the 'kick-and-rush' game down the middle. ... I am still a great believer ... of the wing game," he wrote "because it opens out the play and gives the forwards more opportunity for scoring goals but, of course, the 'push or low pass down the middle from time to time is also every effective. Take the Burnley team [of the 1920-21 season] ... would the effective play-to-the-wing game of that wonderful half-back line, Halley, Boyle and Watson still play in modern football? I say it would."

It was the first time Hogan had seen a stopper centre-half; he found it difficult to compute what he was seeing. "What interested me on Saturday was the game of Spencer [the Newcastle centre-half] who seldom crossed the half-way line and left his wing-halves to support the forwards, whilst he himself lay well back the whole game ... he is the first centre-half ... to adopt these tactics. I like a centre-half to support his own forwards and always keep within striking distance of the opposing centre-forward."[33] Hogan concluded his letter in the following way: "I think it is a great pity that our British football players don't have more ball training, or at least ball training of the right sort – simple trapping of the ball, trapping on the run, trapping on the turn, etc, heading, dribbling, and combination exercises. I am sure they would derive great benefit."

His returned to Germany and got arrested for his troubles. His visa allowed him entry until the September of 1928 but that was of no concern to an immigration official at Hamburg who marched him off to some hut at the harbour in order to frisk him to the tune of 7s 6d. But of greater interest to us was the fact that he was on his way to the VMBV offices at 9 Klostergasse, Leipzig in order to help write a book which would include different training exercises, positional play and tactics for boys, school teachers, trainers and selection committees.[34] He had already been responsible for overseeing the publication of activities and exercises that had been printed in the local press. As things transpired the booklet contained only information about training exercises. Hogan was never one to wax lyrically over tactics and positional play.

Hädicke was now to play a key role in engaging Hogan as coach for his club, Hallescher FC Wacker 1900, of whom he was the chairman. At the time the manager was Willy Kupfer and the club had never qualified for the national championships. Hogan worked with Kupfer to bring three of the youth team up to the first team. They were Reinhold Keidorf, Abi Heynmann and Erich Schlag, the outside left. Hogan introduced a training mantra "Think! Play flat! Combine! Operate the wings! No detours in front of goal! Quickly shoot in!" The 1927-28 season went well for the club although there were murmurings of discontent from those senior players at the club who were quite happy for it to remain a back-water club away from the glare of the national championship. These were the type "who trained in civilian clothes with hands in their pockets and with cigarettes in their mouths."[35] Hädicke was intent on driving the club forward and in the April of 1928, they won through to the regional Cup final where they would play against Dresdner SC, the dominant force in the region. At the time Dresdner were coached by Lorenz Polster who they had brought over from Hakoah in Vienna and the result seemed pretty much foregone given that the club regularly fielded German internationals at that time, three of whom, Berthold, Gedlich and Kohler, were in Dresdner's team in the 1928 Final.[36] However, Halle had carefully prepared for the game, engaging Dr Burgosch to take care of the health of the players and Hädicke ensured the team stayed at a hotel the night before the match. The result was a marvelous victory for Hogan; Halle winning 1-0 with a goal scored by Hansi Schleg and Hogan slipped quietly away before the celebrations, publically stating that he was taking a break but privately explaining to Hädicke that an offer had been made by Dresdner SC for him to join them for the coming season.[37]

As Hogan's contract wound down with the VMBV, he sent a letter to Ivan Sharpe's *Athletic News*.[38] A month before his letter was printed the Scots had arrived at a rain-soaked Wembley and had driven their English opponents into the turf with a display which was as classic as the Elgin Marbles. That was the day of the mighty Wembley Wizards, a class of Scottish footballer, now long gone, who were able to demonstrate that football could be an art comparable with any other cultural endeavour as players ghosted into position, playing one touch, mesmeric football, the like of which the English were not to see again until November 1953 and, after that, never again. A sport that could conjure such magic was hardly one in decline yet the Wizard's display was not on Hogan's mind at all. His concern was with his own prospects. It was a theme[39] that was a constant in his writings around this period in his life: "We need to maintain the prestige of British football," he wrote, "the successes of British teams on the continent are of vital importance to *us* ... Once upon a time it was a case of 'only British trainers required' but continuous unsatisfactory displays have completely altered matters, and competition is now very keen. At present ... the Britisher is easily outnumbered. A certain newspaper out here went so far as to write 'We have nothing more to learn from the British trainer' but this cannot be true, because our teams are still welcomed abroad."

Up to that point the VMBV was the best paid contract he had ever secured but Hogan had done his homework and built on his network finding himself chosen for the trainer's seat at Dresdner SC in 1928.[40] He made sure his family were well-catered for, Dresdner finding them a property on Blumenstrasse, a block or so from the Elbe. He would have happily stayed in Dresden for a number of years[41] finally leaving in July 1932 to take up a post in Paris only because of "the uncertain state of affairs in [Germany]."[42] In short, his contract was astounding 1500 RM per month representing a high mark in his career and served to raise his sense of self-worth no end.[43] Little wonder that he now saw himself as commanding a role above the type of work commonly expected of a "trainer" in England: "Here we have special men for attending to those matters," he wrote, haughtily. "The trainer's work here is to teach the game."[44]

Dresdner SC were a mammoth club when he went to work with them.

# Jimmy Hogan

They could easily compare in resources to MTK of their great period, and the success that Hogan enjoyed during his stay there has to be considered in light of the commercial strength the club enjoyed, even so his impact on their development must be acknowledged. When Hogan joined them they had 1,000 paying members, five grounds and fourteen different teams.[45] When he left, in July 1932, the club had 1,750 paying members, nine grounds, and 43 teams. They were an established commercial organisation run on a sound financial basis, having enough cash to pay Hogan's incredibly generous salary whilst at the same time funding the redevelopment of their main stand which had only just been destroyed by fire.[46] The club went on an amazing run under Hogan, for between 1927 and 1929, Dresdner SC won every game bar four. In terms of their organisational structure and budget, Hogan could not have landed more securely on his two feet. When Hogan arrived, the club had their own dedicated track and field coach, Woldemar Gerschler. In addition, they had their own masseur, Kurt "Lille" Kühn. Kühn is said to have been one of the best and psychologically most skilful masseurs in German top-football.[47] Dresdner SC became a hub for the city, their old stadium the Ostragehege, being a familiar backdrop in the movie *Das grosse Spiel* which featured René Deltgen. Money was also made available for a number of other endeavours. In his autobiography, Helmut Schön remembered Hogan engaging the world famous circus performer and juggler Enrico Rastelli to give a performance for all the players at Dresden. Hogan told them: "Observe exactly, what he is doing with the ball. Just like this you have to [be able to master] the ball." Schön recalled: "I still know exactly how Enrico was dressed when he gave his performance – the shirt striped black and white with white shorts, those were the colours of the famous Italian club Juventus Turin."[48]

The Germans had yet to embrace professionalism but that did not stop Dresdner's chairman, Arno Neumann, from introducing a new wage structure at his club which saw the players receive 7.50 RM per match and therefore keep within the limits set down by the DFB. Like MTK of old, they had the means to attract the best talent and it was hardly a shock when, following the 1928 Olympics, Hogan persuaded the striker, Richard Hofmann, to join Dresdner SC from SpVgg 07 Meerane, a small town club, located near Zwickau. Hofmann's "discovery", like Hogan's discovery of Orth and Braun before him, was peculiar because, like them, he was hardly an unknown when Hogan first saw him as part of his travels around Saxony when working for the VMBV. He would leave Meerane, having issued Hofmann with nothing more than a series of exercises designed to develop his technique rather than undertaking intensive tuition. This seemed a strange way to nurture a national treasure. George Raynor, later, would be up at the crack of dawn to coach Kurre Hamrin in Sweden; but here Hofmann was simply left a menu of offer by Hogan. Between 1925 and 1930, Meerane SV had, won the West Saxony Championship four times but Hofmann was quite happy to remain in the town, driving his cab for a living and terrorising defences at the weekend for fun. It was only when Hogan first caught sight of him striking a ball that he realised that he was destined for much bigger things in football, "when he shoots I don't want to be the goalkeeper," wrote Hogan. David Jack later wrote of him: "I have seen much cleverer Continental footballers ... but none who knew better how to round off excellent midfield play ..."[49]

Hogan had not taken up his post with Dresdner SC when he first saw Hofmann but he was impressed enough to send a reference to Nerz that Hofmann should be selected for the national side. However, in the early days, Hofmann was overawed by the responsibilities heaped upon him. He was sent off against Uruguay in the quarter-final loss in the Amsterdam Olympics, for which he served a year-long suspension from the national side. Perhaps his hot-headedness, his "parochial" nature warded off potential suitors because he caused a stir when he first played for Germany against Denmark[50] introducing himself to the Danish King with typical Saxony gusto, and received some castigation for doing so from the German delegation, shocked at what they saw as tactless informality. But Hofmann was unrepentantly a man of his state and his people, once advising young players, "they have to know who they are playing for, their community, their city, their country."[51] This attitude was fine as Hogan was concerned for it meant that other clubs were not inclined toward signing Hofmann and it was nothing Hogan could not handle, having become used to calming all those tempestuous egos at MTK. Hogan was also pleased to take the risk knowing that in light of the change in the offside law, Hofmann was a God-send since he could play both in a withdrawn role and also as a spearhead of the attack and was therefore the perfect player to play in the formation for which Nerz was trying to convert the country over to that "Chapman-style" of play, with its stopper centre-half. In June 1929, a reporter in Cologne wrote of Hofmann's performance against Sweden:[52] "It was his game, the game of the best footballer Germany ever had, a great technician, a tireless trawler, a gun, a gun."[53]

Between 1928 and June 1932, when his contract expired, the Dresden club won four East Saxony titles and three Mitteldeutsche Fussballmeisterschaften (Central German Championships). When the Central German title was won in 1929, Dresdner SC went through their regional championship without dropping a point. The confidence of the club was reflected that January when Frank, Hogan's son, wrote to *Athletic News* to report on the happenings in Eastern Germany.[54] His father had decided to referee an inter-club match but noticed that one of the linesmen was smoking quite intently just before the game was due to start and obviously Hogan wanted him to put the fag out.

" 'Zigarette! Zigarette!' called Jimmy Hogan. The linesman stopped smoking, stared at Hogan and started searching in his various pockets before calling out 'Sorry, aber das ist mein letzter' or 'Sorry, but this is my last one.' "

The club won through to the 1929 regional final against Chemnitzer FC,[55] which paired Hogan up against an old player of his from Budapest. He wrote: "My prestige as a British trainer was at stake, as our opponents had been prepared by a Hungarian, a pupil of mine in days gone by. Would Jack prove as good as his master?"[56] Hogan reported the event to the *Athletic News* as well on 20 May 1929, which states the attendance was 25,000. The master prevailed, but only after Dresdner SC came back from a two goal deficit and saw a Chemnitz penalty saved in the first half. In the second half, Dresdner SC attacked with such insistence that both Chemnitz inside forwards were withdrawn into their defence but it wasn't enough to stop Dresdner SC winning. Their players were chaired off by the supporters rushing the field and attended a reception when they returned to Dresden. Dresdner SC also won the Central German Cup final that same season against Wacker Leipzig. As regional champions, Dresdner SC would go on to represent in the national play-offs leading to a final which would declare the national champions. Local success, however, was not followed by national acclaim. In the June, Dresdner SC were defeated 3-0 by Bayern Munich which set the tone for the rest of Hogan's stay, taking the club to the national play-offs, only to be knocked out before the national Final.

Germany's technical development on the football field was based on the way they were thinking about the game and that was leading to rapid improvements. Hogan had experienced it at Hallescher when Hädicke booked the entire squad into the hotel before the Cup Final, at Dresden with the track coach and massages and it was a mentality that was distinguishing the Germans from their British counterparts. On 4 June 1929, the *Yorkshire Evening Post* informed its readers that the Hungarian press were circulating reports about the behaviour of the Huddersfield team during their infamous tour of central Europe that summer. English players on tour "travel about pompously, earn high rewards for their play and behave as if they were missionaries from the home of football culture who were condescending to honour inferior colonials with their visit." It was an attitude that was reflected by the British higher ups as well. In the

## 1926-1932

May of 1929, England had had their colours lowered for the first time by continental opposition following a terribly organised tour of Europe. As Raynor understood years later, Hogan appreciated in the late 1920s: a diminution of respect for British football might have been well and good if it led to an improvement in English football but of pressing, fundamental concern for Hogan was how this changing relationship would affect his future contracts. If British football was seen as poor so the attitude and respect for British coaches would similarly fall. This could have a big impact on Hogan which is why English performances were important to him not because he was some misty-eyed patriot, marching in his pyjamas to a wonky gramophone recording of *God Save the King* but because if English clubs continued to be shown up then when the next contract talks started it might be some Hungarian, or Czech or German, who potential employers would turn to. So his letters to the *Burnley Express* can interpreted in two ways. Firstly, to remind everyone back in Britain what a brilliant job he was doing. Secondly, to identify that standards were genuinely improving on the continent and that Britain must replicate those methods if they were not to be left behind. On 9 November 1929, the *Lancashire Evening Post* made comment on Hogan's article in the *Sporting Life*. In that article Hogan asked: "Why are we failing?" The answer was simple: because

> [British] training methods are all wrong ... The German player receives far more ball practice than his British cousin, and he does a hundred and one interesting exercises with the ball.
>
> I have always been a strong advocate of more ball practice for the British player. He gets far too little of it. As boys ... we learnt how to play ... by kicking the ball for hours ... and it seems strange to me that when we become ... league players ball work is dropped like hot bricks and we are trained for the game on the running tracks or the golf links. No wonder that many an English League player is unable to trap a ball properly!

And furthermore, Hogan wrote, before the German undertakes exercises there are theoretical discussions to ensure that the players understood the significance and relevance of any of the planned activities. Hogan felt throughout that you could never discuss the game enough, that there were always things to learn.

In early March 1930, he wrote another letter that was printed in the *Athletic News* which followed the same theme: "Foreign methods, ball training, simple gymnastic exercises and football instructions are proving themselves more successful than British condition training ideas," he wrote. It was not just the method of training, it was the type of player the training was producing that struck Hogan. Around this time he came across a young cohort of players which included Helmut Schön, later to become German national coach. Schön was a gangly, long-legged player which brought comparisons with the great Austrian player, Matthias Sindelar, and was struck by how Hogan's coaching methods improved his ability to shoot and demonstrated to him just how properly-taught technique could compensate for physical defaults. This was in addition to other elements that Hogan migrated into local thinking. '[He] taught us the rough but fair art of tackling, wrote Schön, 'Up to this time, the German players avoided tackling or they committed fouls. Hogan also taught us the football-philosophy when he told us 'run to the right, play the ball to the left', which is like answering the phone the wrong way up', the purpose of which, according to Schön was to enable players to gain control of the ball but keep the opposition guessing.

In the summer of 1931, Ivan Sharpe wrote that it was clear that the continentals were over-taking England and Scotland and he suggested that the only way to arrest the decline was for the FA to employ ex-players as regional coaches working with the clubs to a set programme so that the home nations would not fall behind further. It was a national programme and one that despite the FAs best endeavours took many years to bear fruit. Sharpe gave Hogan a soap-box to stand on: 'let us be honest about the matter' said Hogan, 'Get down to the facts. We are absolutely out of date as regards our training ideas, and the sooner we realise it the better. The foreigner, with far less talent, is being taught, and is a most willing pupil. There is only one remedy and it is this. The FA must employ coaches and send them through the length and breadth of the land giving [lectures] on football. Instructing the boys at school, the young men and first class players both theoretically and practically in the art of the game'.

Amidst all the debate and success that Hogan was driving and achieving there were clearly signs that matters in Germany in the early 1930s were taking a turn for the worse. Luxuries such as regular meat and foreign-born coaches could no longer be justified and Hogan started to notice that on the terraces fans who previously had lunch at restaurants every day had started bringing packed sandwiches, locals would come up to his door seeking food and attendances were starting to fall off, despite half-price entry being extended to the unemployed. On 23 May 1931, the *Lancashire Evening Post* reported that the old Newcastle United international Jimmy Lawrence had returned to the UK after 5 years in Germany. This may have been due to losing a contract to a cheaper contractor but, alternatively, it may have been another signpost toward the economic fall of the state as the clubs started to find that ends did not quite meet. By the summer of 1932, Hogan, that archetypal operator, was quietly seeking an out, laying the groundwork via his regular pipeline of letters to the newspapers back home. They were more than just postcards from a foreign clime, they had become a reminder that he was there and willing to do in England what he was doing in Germany:

"Why hasn't England a coach with each League club and others to help the boys? There's no coaching of youngsters on an organized scale; boys getting through is down to luck." Hogan said that at Dresden there were 40 teams – eighteen boys and juniors and 22 senior teams. "During ball training the training is done in groups of six ... trapping, shooting, heading, swerving and combination exercises are thoroughly practiced."

In late May 1932, the entire Hogan family made a big show of "welcoming" the visiting Everton team as they arrived at the train station. Hogan squirreled off to have a quiet word with Mr Will Cuff, the Chairman, as the players mingled around the newspaper stall and checked out the *fräuleins*. But if Hogan was seeking a job in England he was not going to get one with the Blues who had a full complement of internationals on their books during those halcyon days. Germany was going to the dogs and Hogan's final letter in those days leading to his departure from the Weimar struck a chilling tone, "[The Germans] are a great people," he wrote, "for walking about in uniform."

# Jimmy Hogan

## Notes

1 Acknowledgement to Markwart Herzog for help with this chapter. Hogan started his contract in July 1926.
2 Eberhard Kolb, *The Weimar Republic* (Routledge, 1990), p. 95.
3 Nerz became national coach on 1 July 1926.
4 *The Weimer Republic*, 95.
5 *Athletic News*, 5 May 1930.
6 *Burnley Express*, 2 March 1927. The contract began July 1926 but Hogan first started teaching on 15 August 1926. A month before Hogan began his new post, Camillo Ugi, formerly a German international, had his application for the post turned down on the basis that he could not show that he had practiced teaching football as a full-time occupation and so Hogan, despite a pitiful lack of spoken German, was successful and he secured a two year contract.
7 *Burnley Express*, 1 October 1927. He was given a visa by the authorities until 19 September 1928.
8 The others were the South German (from 1927 the South German Football and Athletics Association), South-East German, Baltic Lawn and Winter Sports Association (from 1927 the Baltic Sports Association), West German and North German (from 1927 the North German Sports Association) FAs. The Central German FA had 960 clubs and over 130,000 registered amateur players at the time.
9 On 16 August 1926 he was already providing one of his first lessons in Leipzig. http://www.leipzigerfussballverband.de/cms2/index.php?page=322&br=ro&
10 *Burnley Express*, 2 March 1927.
11 *Ibid.*
12 Fox relates that they stated that they had already been shown the training methods he was demonstrating by Otto Nerz. That raises the question as to whether the national programme Nerz was introducing required Nerz to tour the country or to send out directives to the local FAs.
13 *Gloucestershire Echo*, 17 February 1937.
14 One of the attendees was Otto Nerz whom Hogan presented himself to afterwards.
15 *Sport*, Vol. 16.
16 He also carried out a series of step-overs against a local player.
17 *Liverpool Echo*, September 1925.
18 *Burnley Express*, 2 March 1927.
19 *Athletic News*, 7 May 1928.
20 *Fussball*, 1978. Acknowledgement to Dr Andreas Hafer.
21 *Immer am Ball*, 1970, pp. 15-16. Acknowledgment to Markwart Herzog.
22 These demonstrations were to serve Hogan well for the next 30 years becoming a standard part of his nationwide tours throughout England.
23 Willy Meisl in *Association Football*, vol. 4, 308.
24 *Burnley Express*, 2 March 1927.
25 *Burnley Express*, 30 April 1927.
26 *Ibid.*
27 10 April 1927.
28 *Burnley Express*, 30 April 1927.
29 *Burnley Express*, 2 March 1927, 'How continental football is developing'.
30 He would also see the Burnley v Bolton match played on 9 March 1927 at Turf Moor. *Burnley Express*, 12 March 1927.
31 *Burnley Express*, 5 March 1927.
32 Match played on 10 September 1927, but reported by Hogan on 17 September 1927.
33 This is a curious statement within itself. Is one led to assume that Joe Spence, the

Manchester United centre-forward, played a withdrawn role and United were playing in a 2-4-4 formation? It would not be surprising if that was the case given the various modifications that had been taking place in the seasons following the alteration in the offside law.

34 *Burnley Express*, 1 October 1927. Jimmy Hogan, *Practical Football Teaching*, (Leipzig 1929). See Appendix.

35 Acknowledgement to Professor Jurgen Hermann, *Mythos Hallscher FC Wacker 1900* (Arete Verlag, 2019).

36 Rudolf Berthold, Richard Gedlich, Martin Haftmann, Georg Kohler, Willie Kress, Rudolf Leip and Hugo Martel were all full internationals.

37 Played on 22 April 1928 at Dresden-Reick in front of 25,000.

38 7 May 1928.

39 "When our teams are beaten [on the continent] it means the dismissal of more English trainers." *Leeds Mercury*, 7 July 1936.

40 *Burnley Express*, 23 June 1928. The same day, it was reported that Nelson, his first club, was in dire straits owing £19.

41 His Dresdner contract would have seen him through to August 1933.

42 16 July 1932.

43 That calculated out at approx. £75 per month; £900 p.a., compared to a professional footballer in Britain at that time would earn approx. £208 p.a.

44 *Sport*, vol. 16.

45 *Ibid*.

46 Peter Salzmann, *Fussballheimet Dresden* (1995).

47 Acknowledgement to Dr Andreas Hafer.

48 *Fussball*, (1978). Acknowledgement to Dr Andreas Hafer.

49 *Soccer*, 315.

50 2 October 1927. Germany lost 3-1.

51 http://dresdner-sc.de/content/conpresso/inside/detail.php?nr=12529

52 23 June 1929, Germany won 3-0, thanks to a Hofmann hat-trick.

53 http://dresdner-sc.de/content/conpresso/inside/detail.php?nr=12529

54 28 January 1929.

55 12 May 1929.

56 *Burnley Express*, 22 May 1929. The match was played on 12 May in front of 30,000.

Jimmy Hogan

## ELEVEN

## 1932-1933
'Experience as a player, coach and as a manager has shown me his ideas were right.'

In May 1931, England were defeated by the improbable score of 5-2 by the French in Paris. It was remarkable victory that did much to inspire some French businessmen to form a professional league in France the following year. In Paris, the owner of Racing Club de Paris was Jean-Bernard Lévy. Although the club was otherwise amateur, Lévy had foreseen the potential in having a professional League in France for a few years. In 1930 he met Herbert Chapman and agreed a plan to bring about a friendly, rather romantic, competition between the two premier clubs of London and Paris from that autumn,[1] ostensibly to raise funds for those disabled by the Great War ("au profit des invalides de guerre"), but both he and Chapman saw football's future in international terms and realised that the game could not hope to survive indefinitely if its financial footing was reliant solely on pitch side adverts, programmes partly paid for by sponsors and terraced regulars. Around 1931, Chapman wrote:

> I understand that a scheme for a West Europe Cup competition on the knock-out principle is to be formulated. The idea is that the competition should comprise the champion teams of six countries ... The proposal has much to recommend it. I predict that it will be launched within the next year or two, and it will be a big advance on the holiday tours which England and Scotland have undertaken in the past. The enthusiasm for the game on the continent is amazing, and we cannot afford to treat their enterprise with indifference or even lukewarmness for the result of such an attitude would only be that we should be left behind in the development of the game.[2]

When the French League was being formed, the general view of the owners was that they must invite foreign players over to play for the clubs. This made commercial sense because when it came to the French spectators, France was simply not good enough for them. David Jack later reported that when Arsenal played in Paris they "have been cheered to the echo by an admiring crowd, but the cheers have quickly turned to jeers, derisive laughter, and whistling when the French players have made mistakes."[3] In the case of Hogan, his arrival was hastened by the fact that he needed to get out of Germany for the sake of his family because neither of his sons nor daughter could find work there: "All foreigners [were] barred [from working] on account of the great unemployment in the country," he wrote.[4] The family had squirreled away his earnings and his daughter, Mary, had sewn a small fortune into the lining of his plus-fours in order to hoodwink the German authorities. Hogan had considered going to Vienna after leaving Dresden but finally decided to take the family to Paris, no doubt as a result of the better financial guarantees that Lévy had provided.[5] His family was provided with a nice house on a terraced street in Colombes[6] and he appeared in press photographs looking resplendent in the best suit he owned. In that press photograph, he could be seen standing in his backyard poised as if to kick the ball but there was no way he was going to spoil the sheen on his newly polished brogues for the purpose of the picture was to announce to all and sundry just how well he had it compared to those back home. It suited him to be so seen as being materially comfortable but at heart he saw himself in constrained states as he had at Berne because the Racing job was another in a line of club positions that never quite suited Hogan. There was too much interference from the owner which served only to undermine the authority Hogan was trying to instil. Fox proposed that Hogan once wrote "[Lévy] would spoil the players with money and gifts so that discipline became impossible."[7] That may have been the case but the role of the coach is to overcome such obstacles and make do with available resources, something Hogan was not able to do.

How much Lévy put into the club is not known but his generosity was, through English eyes, staggering in some regards and mean in others. He invested in air travel to transport his stars over to England throughout the season for a series of friendlies[8] but that investment must be offset against the type of players he brought over from England to satisfy Hogan's requirement that the team needed some backbone.[9] Perhaps they did but none of the players, including Hogan's own son Joseph who played for the club, could be termed "top drawer." Nîmes, by comparison, had signed Alex Cheyne and Andy Wilson, two full Scottish internationals from Chelsea, while Hogan had to make do with Fred Kennedy and Arthur Phoenix who were both on their uppers. When Racing came calling, Phoenix was struggling like mad to get out of the reserves at Mansfield Town and Kennedy was kicking footballs for Northwich Victoria in the Cheshire County League. As Hogan, later, wrote: "Kennedy was out of work at the time, not even a third division team would give him a job and he had a free transfer. [But] although he was as fat as a pig when he came to us I quickly recognised his abilities."[10]

Under Hogan's tutelage, Phoenix developed into a sound right-back and Kennedy, like Hogan before him, became a competent inside-right. Otherwise, Hogan possibly had a hand in the purchase of the centre-half Elemér Berkessy,[11] a former Ferencváros player, but that is only on the understanding that Hogan still had ties over in Hungary. Formerly an international, by 1932 he had lost form and then his place in the Hungarian international side despite still only being 27 but he was a splendid runner when in possession of the ball, happy to burst forward as well as spray passes from his deep-lying position. The club goalkeeper during the 1932-3 season was André Tassin, one of those prewar continental goalkeepers who would throw himself through the air with gymnastic gusto even when the ball was blasted yards over the bar. Tassin's occasional replacement between the sticks was the great French-Guyanan migrant, Raoul Diagne, a French international defender who was the best player at the club.

**The 1932-33 season**

What we know of that season and of how Hogan marshalled his team can be ascertained from contemporary match reports. The French Championship was divided into two groups of ten teams. Racing's splendid home form was mirrored perfectly by their rubbish away record and finished third, seven points adrift of the Division winners' Lille. But it was how they played against the English sides, in friendly matches, during the course of that season that offers a good insight into some of the tactical concerns that resonated throughout Hogan's teams. They played twice against Arsenal. On 31 October 1932, at the new Parc de Princes Stadium, Arsenal easily beat them 5-2,[12] thanks to Bastin's four goals and a virtuoso performance from Alex James who moved about the field while Racing's half-backs respectfully ceded ground to the gentrified applause of the crowd. The return match between Racing and Arsenal at Highbury was scheduled for 30 November. Prior to the first game,[13] Hugo Meisl had sought agreement from Lévy to release Hogan so that Hogan could stay on in London to coach the Austrian side which was due to meet England at Stamford Bridge that December.[14] Chapman's friendship with Meisl and his appreciation as to the potential significance of the friendly international was such that he set out a series of proposals to Hogan including offering the training area behind the North Bank to enable the Austrians to train.[15] On 11 November, Meisl wrote to Chapman and thanked him for linking Hogan with Tom Whittaker, Arsenal's trainer. The two trainers would work together, agreeing terms as to how and where the Austrians could train and what apparatus they could use at Highbury.

Against Arsenal at Highbury, Racing were again found to be lacking.

Basically, within the month between the two games against Arsenal, Hogan had instituted nothing new to counter the threat of the Arsenal team. The London press noted that the team Hogan picked was remarkable for the fact that "most of [the players were] lithe and light, built as it were for speed, [but] could make little headway on the wet and heavy ground, and were quickly caught up once they got away."[16] They had only two shots in the first half and what was noticeable was the failure of the forwards to turn quickly on the ball, steady themselves and shoot.[17] Remember, by this stage, Jimmy Hogan this great wizard of technique, had been intensively coaching the side for the best part of five months and yet still the forwards had trouble when exhibiting the most fundamental of skills. The one stand-out was the performance in goal of Diagne, Tassin's replacement, in goal.[18] With almost miraculous timing, the goalkeeper would pluck the ball from a crowd of players as the ball pinged about the goal area. Arsenal finally won by three goals to none, two of them coming from Reg Stockhill, formerly the great *wunderkind*,[19] the second of which saw him run straight down the middle of the field, after Berkessy had been dispossessed, and shoot past Diagne. Stockhill was a good young player but by no stretch of the imagination would any historian say that he was an integral cog in the Arsenal machine of the early 1930s, yet here he was against Hogan's Parisien all-stars running around pleasantly, knocking in a couple of goals; granted freedom of the Highbury pitch for the afternoon.

**The weakness of Racing Club**

So from those two matches you can see that, under Hogan, Paris had a half-back line without a defensive bone in their body; inside forwards who couldn't shoot for toffee and had the sort of Gallic insouciance which, once the ball was lost, ceded reliance to the saving grace of a three-man defence. But wasn't that was the essential problem with the attacking centre-half game? As an attacking option it was creative, engaging and effective; as a defensive formation against the WM-tactic, or those sides with a more physically, destructive bent, it was a disaster waiting to happen. It says a great deal about Hogan's lack of tactical "inventiveness" that when he came to work in England with Fulham in 1934 that he had not considered any real alteration to the defensive frailties inherent within that system, feeling only that five across the front attack was required. It was laudable to think you could score more than your opponents but was completely out of kilter with the attitude in Britain which had seen the introduction of a method of playing that valued victory over defensive recklessness. It was also out of step with the tactical progression of the game which demanded that the chief responsibility should rest not with the centre-half but the inside forwards.

That's where an essential comparison between Hogan and Raynor, for instance, would show Hogan to be tactically naïve. Raynor, by comparison, would have tried to work out defensive options aimed at extracting as much advantage from the opposition. Raynor's take on it, taking a leaf from his mentor, Norman Bullock, was to have a roving forward connecting with the half-backs and the forwards, his G-man theory. He saw no purpose in having a creative centre-half because there's no point scoring goals if you've got a defence that leaks like a sieve. Raynor's theory served a variety of functions but two stood out. Firstly, it's much less disastrous should a centre-forward lose possession when trying to be a smart arse than it is for a centre-half to do so in the opponent's half of the field of play. Secondly, that there's far less fetching and carrying required if the roving commission is undertaken by one of the inside forwards. The ball can be quickly transferred, first from the half-back line and then swung out to the wings or passed inside, but, importantly, the attacking side's defence maintains shape regardless. This is not the case if the formation is 2-3-5 and the centre-half is give licence to move forward when the mood takes him and leave a vacant lot behind him. The only people who made much of an attempt to counter-act against the inherent problem within the attacking centre-half system were Kürschner, when, arguably, introducing "the Riegel," and Rappan, when developing the "Verrou" system, as a later version of "the Riegel." In both cases the essential element was to withdraw the centre-half, box up the opponent's target man with man to man marking and springboard a fast counter-attack from a deep-lying position. The inside forwards would track back and the whole system would operate almost like the vent of a concertina, withdrawn halves supporting the centre-half and short passes to forwards in close proximity. But this was missing in Hogan's teams where, as an instance, Berkessy would be off with the daisies once he had lost possession, Hogan's inside forwards would allow the opposing halves to go past them like the wind and opponents would arrow their passes at a centre-forward who might be marked by no one at all. In 1931 Chapman wrote: "It used to be thought that the centre-half was the key man of a team. To-day, I think, there are four key men – the two wing-halves and the two inside-forwards. The centre-half may *still* play an important part in a constructive sense, but under the altered conditions (brought about by the change in the offside law) the wing men have more scope as schemers ... "[20]

Hogan never really got his head around this concept; hence the problems he encountered at first askance with Jimmy Allen when Hogan took over the coaching duties at Villa in 1936.

Hogan, Chapman and Sir Frederick Wall were all there to greet the Austrians off the train when they arrived at Victoria from Dover. Charlie Buchan made his way over to Hogan to ask him his opinion as to what the outcome of the international would be. "Will it be another Spanish Armada, Jimmy?"[21] referring to Spain's 7-1 defeat in December 1931. Hogan said he didn't think so,[22] but the simple fact was that Hogan would not have known what to expect of the Austrians because he had not seen the *Wunderteam* in action in all the time he was working in Germany and Paris and though they had beaten the Swiss, 3-1 in their most recent international, which Hugo Meisl had admitted was a "rather poor game,"[23] it was an open secret that the *Wunderteam* had passed their peak. Meisl admitted such in a letter to Chapman: "Unfortunately, is our team at present far from the last year's form."[24] True, they had won the 1931-32 International Cup but whatever traction they had built up on their unbeaten run would now be put to the ultimate test against the most physically domineering of all the sides they had so far faced. They arrived in England fearful of a sizeable defeat conscious as to what had happened to the Spanish at Highbury the year before.

The touring party stayed at Oddenino's Hotel in Piccadilly, where the chef had prepared a Viennese-style menu especially for them. On the 3 December, thanks to Chapman's intervention, the players and Hogan gathered at Highbury for a practice session, and on the morning of Saturday, 5 December they went to Stamford Bridge for another training session, led by Hogan. Later that afternoon, the Austrians and Hogan took their seats at Stamford Bridge to see the fixture between Chelsea and Everton. Chelsea just edged the game 1-0, but Fox, in his biography of Hogan, described the game as being played out by two teams intent on kicking the ball long to the two strikers: Hughie Gallacher, the Chelsea forward, or Dixie Dean, the Everton striker. The Austrians apparently turned to Hogan in askance as to what they had just seen and he was not in a position to answer their queries. It makes good copy to think that English football was played by idiots but it would defy the convention of the WM attacking formation, which would never have countenanced a straight kick from defence directly toward the centre-forwards, and in any event, Dean's strength, as every schoolboy knows, lay in his ability to head the ball away from goal to an onrushing inside forward from a cross.[25]

The city of Vienna, seemingly, had become obsessed by the game. The *Burnley News* reported that "the economic depression is gladly forgotten for the time being and the chance of a victory for Austria are being considered from every point of view ... Every word that has been written in England relative to the forthcoming match has been eagerly read in Vienna."[26] The day before the match, Hogan held court in the ballroom of the hotel in Piccadilly, placing a shirt over a chair and asking questions of the players as to what to do if England attacked down the wings. The *Daily Herald* reporter listened as Hogan went through different scenarios: "What pass would the inside forward make if he went here?" Hogan told the reporter, "Win or lose, we will play football which the English spectators will appreciate, he said, "because it is highly constructive, fast playing and fast thinking."[27]

Of the England v Austria game enough has been written elsewhere for me not to write yet another match report. The enduring significance of the game, however, is that it represented one of the very few occasions when a British football audience were obliged to consider the performance rather than the result. Though England won, it represented victory by score-line alone because the Austrians brought to English eyes a beguiling and bemusing way of playing once they had overcome the shock of falling behind. Football for the English was a means by which a ball should be kicked into a goal and to achieve that aim the understanding was that the quickest method of achieving victory was the best. In football, as in trench warfare, the British had operated in straight lines. Austrians, and later Hungarians, did not see themselves bound by such rules. In essence, the Austrians wanted to play their own way because to play football in the national shirt of Austria, to them, meant nothing if the only differentiator from the opponent was the colour of the shirt. Running in diagonal lines, withdrawing themselves far back down the field, one touch passes to play the ball into space where a player had magically appeared, seemed a more effective and certainly more entertaining way to play than the way the English had shown them.

What the Stamford Bridge crowd saw that day was a way of playing that was distinctly Austrian. It was the Scottish style, to a degree, but Meisl's decision to mix up the dynamic long and short passing game with that

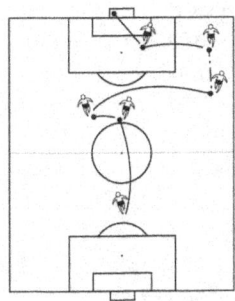

Fig. 8

## Jimmy Hogan

lightness of touch that Hogan had first noticed when he had visited Vienna way back in 1912 gave the performance a veneer of otherness that wowed the paying audience. What Austria brought to Stamford Bridge that day:

> was the '*Wiener Schule*' of football. Vienna, as opposed to Austria, being the operative term 'since all players within the Austrian national team played in Viennese football clubs and the Austrian national football league consisted exclusively of Viennese clubs. It was a means of playing football, specific to the Austrian mentality, a kind of game, which is based on beauty, on a wonderful aesthetic, in the public discourse, often compared favourably with the *Wiener Walzer*, the Viennese waltz.' In expectation of the game, the Viennese newspapers drew comparison between the so called *Zweckfussball*, football orientated only to the aim of winning a game, the type played by England and Germany and the Viennese aesthetic. That is football which was directed to beauty not necessarily to the goal of winning a game but to the beauty inherent within it. The game at Stamford Bridge was seen as the fight between these two styles of football. The Vienna School also carried an inherent value. Players who were school in Vienna were not as brutish as their British counterparts. So artistic performance could "compensate for the physical deficits the Austrian players had, compared with that of their English opponents.[28]

This sums up the reason as why the Austrians, though defeated, felt emboldened to promote themselves by reason of their difference. On 25 January 1933, for example, the SC Wacker Wien director wrote to Herbert Chapman requesting a friendly: "Our team plays the well-known Viennese School, the typical ideas paired with flat combination," but there was a problem amongst all the art-work and David Jack referred to it in his book *Soccer*: "[The Austrians] are, without a doubt, the most natural footballers on the Continent, their ball control, individualism, positioning, body-work, and combination being reminiscent of the true Scottish footballer ... but they have one outstanding weakness: they lack thrust near goal and are inclined to attempt to walk the ball into the net."[29]

When Hogan returned to Racing, technical faults also remained with his own team. One of them being their complete lack of fight, a factor Hogan which felt was based on the over-indulgences of Lévy. In mid-February Racing[30] played Portsmouth[31] and the *Times* reported that they were fortunate to take the lead when the referee ruled that a Pompey defender had deliberately handled a cross but once Portsmouth had got on level-terms, Racing's resolve simply dissolved. Pompey won 7-1 drawing the French defence late in the game with impunity. The lack of tactical sophistication was enough to raise the eye-brows of a reporter who, like all the British of the early 1930s, now expected more from Johnny foreign footballers when he noted that "the wing half backs did not drop back as the Austrians [of December 1932] did. Nor did the players retreat before the man with the ball like Spain in 1931'. Racing lacked dash; the close passing of forwards was easily broken up by Pompey half-back line; their shooting was bad and erratic. At the end, it is true, that Berkessy dribbled the ball "with the action of a high-stepping dancer, and achieved partial success because half the Portsmouth side stopped in admiration to watch the performance" but "otherwise it was ordinary football."[32] That represented a damning indictment of the coaching methodology of Jimmy Hogan. If the coach is unable to surmount what are common-place problems, i.e. due to the owner's undue interference and players lacking motivation, then there is limited validity in arguing about what a great coach he is or was. Fox argues that Hogan had influence over the players being brought to the club yet Fox then concedes that Lévy ran the club his way and Hogan had to put up and shut up. So which is it to be? Racing's last match[33] against English opposition that season saw them get on the receiving end of yet another walloping.[34] They went to Sunderland, where Raich Carter would perform with such high virtuosity at inside forward that the Rokerites won 5-2 and, partly as a result, Racing's[35] performance was notable on for some comedic play at the end of the game when Galley took a pass from "Momo" Delfour and shot past Thorpe after palming off in pure Rugby style as Murray as he came across to tackle him. There were crudities within the French game and weaknesses, but none of them appeared to be resolved by the time Hogan departed at the end of that season.

## Jimmy Murphy

That May, whilst undertaking a morning coaching session for Racing[36] in preparation of the game against Wislaw Krakow,[37] Hogan met Jimmy Murphy, the future coach of the Busby Babes under Matt Busby. Murphy, the young West Brom and Welsh international left back, visited the Colombes stadium the day before Wales played France[38] and for the first time in his life saw a football coaching session. "I was a fully-fledged professional player and international," he wrote, "yet this was the first time I ever saw a coach at work. What interested me more was all the teaching was based on use of the ball, an object we never saw from one Saturday to the next." Hogan and Murphy, the Englishman and Welshman but both Irishmen, fell into conversation and quickly developed a friendship that would endure down the years. At first Murphy was not convinced by Hogan's views, that the Europeans would overtake the British, but became mesmerised when attending one of Hogan's innumerable technical sessions.

# Jimmy Hogan

"I saw him," wrote Murphy, "white haired and fitter than most men half his age, performing miracles of ball control, he once drove a ball through wood panelling with his bare foot. He could hit a mark at 30 yards, ten times out of ten. Whatever basic skill he was teaching he could perform it to perfection."[39] This led to a definite form of rebellion in Murphy: "After our first meeting I *always* tried to break away from British custom and sneak out with a ball. Experience as a player, coach and as a manager has shown me his ideas were right, mastery of the ball and of the simple way of doing things were the basics of football, I used a lot of Hogan's ideas when I joined Matt Busby at United, he was a very influential coach."

Hogan left Paris to return to Lausanne in the autumn of 1933 but his sudden departure to claim a better paying contract showed him to be duplicitous when he needed to be. Just before he did so he was asked by Lévy to assist in the transfer negotiations which would see Hiden and Jordan come to France. During those negotiations with WAC Austria Hogan gave Hiden and August Jordan[40] his word that he would be coaching at Racing that season. Hogan returned to Paris and both players followed him on the understanding that they would work under him that season. However, within days of their arrival they were informed by management at Paris that Hogan had left the club. Lausanne had made Hogan an offer and he had accepted a new contract in Switzerland following weeks of private negotiations. *De Dordrechtsche Courant* commented, "If Hiden and Jordan had foreseen this, they would certainly have remained in Vienna, they supposed that because of Hogan they [would] have [received] good support. Indeed, with Hogan they could [be understood] in their own language, while he could also act as an interpreter [for them] in Paris. Now Hogan has left, the two Austrians feel like a cat in a strange warehouse. One who dwells in a foreign language and neither speak, nor can understand, is always gripped by a vague feeling, [that] impact[s] on [their] whole personality."[41] The chicanery of Hogan would go some way to breaking the trust that had existed between him and the two players and their early season performances for Racing showed uncertainty and a lack of thrust, factors that must have had something to do with Hogan's departure.

"A Swiss magazine has made the remark that Hogan will offer a contract to Hiden and Jordan (on behalf of a Swiss club), but it's not very likely that the players involved are willing to [accept], considering the attitude of Hogan. Anyway, from above, it is clear that even professional footballers, even when they have a job, face with all sorts of difficulties."[42]

# 1932-1933

## Notes

1  The first Racing v Arsenal match was played on 11 November 1930.
2  *Herbert Chapman on Football*, 170.
3  *Soccer*, 312.
4  *Burnley Express*, 30 July 1932.
5  His started date with Racing was on 16 July 1932.
6  9 Villa Marie, Rue Des Cerisiers.
7  Fox, 105.
8  Rounding off their spring tour with a short flight to Paris on 30 April 1933 in time for an afternoon kick off against Club Francais. (*Lancashire Evening Post*, 29 April 1933.) Interesting that at this stage Hogan was already announced as the Austrian coach for the Scotland international in Glasgow in November.
9  5 November 1932 in a letter to the *Burnley Express*.
10  *Burnley Express*, 29 November 1933.
11  Fox calls him Emilio Berkessy.
12  Tassin – Durbec, Capele – Gauteroux, Berkessy, Emil Scharwarth – Diagne, Kennedy, Veinante, Delfour, Galey.
13  This is also the date on which the Austrian XI was announced to the British press. Hiden (WAC), K Rainer (First Vienna), Sezsta (WAC); Mock, J Smistik(Rapid SC), W Nausch (FussballKlub), K Zischek (Sport Klub Wacker) F Gschweidl (First Vienna), A Schall (WSC Admira) M Sindelar (FC Austria), A Vogl (WAC Admira). Note that Hiden was still at WAC during this season – undermining the view that Hogan took him to Paris when Arsenal could not get clearance for him.
14  Hugo Meisl letter to Herbert Chapman, 26 October 1932.
15  Letter from Chapman to Meisl, 2 November 1932. Acknowledgement Andreas Hafer.
16  Diagne – Phoenix (Durbec), Capelle – Gauteroux, Berkessy, Scharwath – Defeue, Kennedy, Bamburger, Delfour, Galey. NB: Phoenix broke his leg early on in a challenge with Bastin and Durbec (operating as the linesman for Racing) came on to replace him.
17  *Times*, 1 December 1932.
18  Diagne would become the first non-European to appear for the French national XI.
19  He made his Football League debut at fifteen years of age; when he played against Paris, Stockhill had just turned nineteen. Perhaps Chapman foresaw another young star in the making (as he had with Bastin) but Stockhill's career at Highbury wouldn't last ten first team appearances.
20  *Herbert Chapman on Football*, 33.
21  This was reference to the game played the previous season when England beat Spain 7-1 at Highbury. The Spaniards had come to London on the back of their famous 4-3 victory in Madrid. Expectations were high that England were in for a tussle but the Spanish froze on the day and England ran riot in the Highbury mud.
22  *Aberdeen Evening Express*, 31 August 1956.
23  Letter to Herbert Chapman, 26 October 1932.
24  26 October 1932 letter.
25  See Nick Walsh, *Dixie Dean: the story of a goalscoring legend* (Macmillan, 1978).
26  3 December 1932.
27  *Daily Herald*, 6 December 1932.
28  Email from Andreas Hafer.
29  *Soccer*, 317.
30  Tassin – Diagne, Scharwarth – Gauteroux, Berkessey, Delfour – Borsenberger, Kennedy, Delesse, Viennante, Galley.
31  Letter printed in *Portsmouth Evening News*, 24 February 1933.
32  *Times*, 20 February 1933.

## Jimmy Hogan

33 Played on 26 April 1933 at Roker Park. Hogan went to Burnley after the game to visit his mother.

34 It shouldn't be assumed that their problems were exclusively foreign in origin. They went out in the French Cup to Montpellier before the quarters.

35 Tassin – Jean Gauteroux, Diagne - Scharwarth, Berkessy, Edmond 'Momo' Delfour - Ozenne, Kennedy, Delese, Viennaute, Galey.

36 Cabanis – Gauteroux, Calmels – Dagne, Berkesey, Delfour – Opala, Kennedy (44'), Delesee, Veinaute, Galley.

37 Racing won 1-0.

38 Wales played France in Paris on 25 May 1933. A Tommy Griffiths' goal earned Wales a 1-1 draw.

39 Jimmy Murphy, *United, Matt and Me* (Souvenir Press, 1968).

40 A team-mate of Peter Platzer, the famous goalkeeper.

41 5 September 1933.

42 *De Dordrechtsche Courant*, 5 September 1933.

## TWELVE

## 1933-1934
'To carry their finesse to excessive lengths.'

But Switzerland like Paris before it, in the end, presented more problems than it solved for Hogan. He had gone there on the back of the understanding that another new professional league would offer him a relatively easy pay day; that he would have time to build on the success of his earlier time in Switzerland; that it best suited his family to be back in Lausanne than to stay in Paris. "I have left Racing on the best of terms, but Switzerland, the climate and things in general, are more beneficial than France to my wife and children."[1]

At the start it seemed perfect. The correspondent for the *Gazette de Lausanne* noting that Hogan's ability to identify several good young players when coaching sessions for the 1924 Olympics boded well at a club where Faugel and Syrvet were coming to the fore. "We haven't just employed a coach," the reporter announced, "but a pedagogue."[2] The affability of Hogan married to the pay structure, M. Manuel[3] paying the players 100Fr. each per week, and a new professional approach, in which the players were gainfully employed[4] compared with the "doubtful strolls" of their predecessors would surely guarantee success. But it was not to be. The previous coach, Robert Pache, had guided the club to a third place finish[5] and, for a number of reasons, that benchmark proved impossible for Hogan to exceed for a few reasons.

Firstly, because of the money available in the Swiss League, a better class of coach was being attracted to the League. For instance, Duckworth's old club, Servette, were now led by Karl Rappan, who instituted his bolt defensive system. Secondly, there was the wrong mix of players in the Lausanne team at the time. There were too many Indians and not enough Chiefs. In early October, the *Gazette De Lausanne* correspondent wrote that "Jordan [though not Auguste] was a great player but lazy and Joseph Hogan was excellent on the wing [but only] when he wasn't being shoved by his opponent."[6] Thirdly, the professional game no longer permitted the charmingly generous attitude once displayed by the press. In 1923, victories were acclaimed with shocked surprise but now the press were now demanding of instant success. A 2-2 draw with Berne ensured a perfectly equitable record for Hogan's Lausanne, one win, one draw and one defeat but, given the expense in securing him and the investment pumped into the club, the local newspaper felt duty bound to ask why the club was going backwards.[7] "It's been two months since Hogan took over so we asked him how it was going," the reporter wrote. "It will take time, we are devising a new way of playing," Hogan replied with his hands held up and palms showing. The writer left and finished the piece with an unconvincing statement that the local populace had "confidence in Hogan"[8] but time was not going to be granted to Hogan. The owner of the club, a grocer, was not one to sit idly by. Hogan later wrote, bitterly: "[The President] should have stuck to his trade. He thought he knew everything about football but what he really knew you could write on the back of a half-penny stamp."[9] The reason for the bitterness was that the President interfered at training sessions and had caused real ructions when openly suggesting the poorly performing players should be fined which hardly made for happy campers.

In the November, Hugo Meisl asked whether Hogan would like join the Austrian *Wunderteam* touring party that was to play Scotland, Arsenal[10] and the Netherlands.[11] The tour was not as successful as Meisl or Hogan would have hoped. Scotland were able to snatch a 2-2 draw with the Scots the better team on a soft Hampden pitch[12] and Austria lost against Arsenal despite playing well at Highbury where their stand-out player was Seszta, their left back, scorer of an unfortunate own goal in Glasgow but the best man on the field in London. "It did not matter at what height, pace or angle the ball came to him – he was consistently sure in his kicking" and "in the place which would cause the Arsenal forward line the maximum of inconvenience."[13] That same year, David Jack wrote of Seszta's performance: "[it] was the best defensive exhibition given by a Continental footballer [in England]. I do not think Seszta made a single mistake; he tackled keenly, strongly, and quickly; he kicked cleanly and accurately; and despite his comparatively small stature, he was very successful in the air ... [he] was a great little player that day."[14]

In addition, one of the first moves of the Austrian forward line: "brought that gasp of appreciation ... which is the equivalent ... of the cricket spectator who sees a batsman, with a late-cut, beat both first-slip and deep third-man. The move was carried out along the ground with the ball moving methodically from man to man ... "[15]

But the quality of the Austrians could only take them so far. Arsenal two up at the break were the more clinical; and clinical won out with the correspondent noting that the Austrian "heading was not so accurate either in length or direction as that of Arsenal." Added to this was an issue that David Jack noticed. Jack wrote, "I think it would improve the Austrian game considerably if [Hugo Meisl] could persuade his inside forwards to adopt more responsibility as regards defence. The five-in-a-line attack should not be rigidly adhered to, even if the centre half-back has a roving commission! The inside-forward should never allow the opposing wing half-backs to come through with the ball unchallenged!"

The Austrians had been preparing to head back via Amsterdam but, just like 1932, requests and invitations came in, this time rather than stare the gift horse in the mouth they took up the offer with games against Liverpool and Manchester City and lost both of them. At Anfield[16] they bemused the *Times* reporter. "... on several occasions the Liverpool goal appeared to be at [the Austrians'] mercy, but the Austrian forwards approached with short passes and tried to walk the ball through the goal instead of attempting a direct shot."[17] The Austrians play "was not so effective, for the Austrian forwards began to carry their finesse to excessive lengths and to spend valuable time in merely tricking an opponent without obtaining any solid advantage." At Maine Road,[18] they took ages to thaw out as the bitter wind whipped across the ground: "The Austrians showed more cohesion in the later stages of the game"[19] but by that stage City were already two-up.

The tour had given Hogan a splendid opportunity to take a well-aimed shot at the President of the Lausanne-Sport Club on the public stage. While he was in England on his way to Scotland Hogan wrote a letter to the *Burnley Express*: "A good trainer-coach is more important than a President or a Manager. [The trainer] should be the chief man in the club."[20] But the letter went further than just slighting the people who were paying him to coach their team. He also used the article to set down his thoughts on how ludicrous it was that British football clubs, in 1933, were intent on signing ready-made foreign imports, from South Africa and Canada, to play the game young, local English lads could easily do if they were given the right training and opportunity. Hogan was incredulous when informed that Burnley had signed, "a player from the West Indies."[21] "Is this a sign of weakness in British football or are we getting too lazy to develop our own talent,'" wrote Hogan.[22] Hogan reiterated his firm belief that British players were the best natural footballers in the world, the only reason young, local, enthusiastic lads were getting squeezed out was because the clubs employed no formal structure to coach them. Instead the clubs were happy to persist with an "agency" rather than an "academy" model, whereby agents were bigging-up some "star" player on behalf of a club before an overpriced transfer was enacted. It had always been so and Hogan explained that when Burnley replaced Tommy Boyle, their title winning centre-half, they did so by spending £6k on Jack Hill rather than investing in a young lad to emerge through the ranks as a deputy for Boyle. That was a business model unsustainable over the long-term so Hogan offered a simple remedy:

take 100 lads from the Burnley School League and coach them but "for heaven's sake don't send them on the running track or give them a pair of skipping ropes and after three months at night school tell them to go their way." Instead, find a good coach to train them in the cardinal skills and "train their minds too" because cognitive engagement was a fundamental step in the process for within discussion and theoretical debate lay the tools which gave purpose to all that running about. Otherwise, "a couple of power lamps on the practice ground for these lads and an intelligent coach is a better outlay than giving thousands of pounds for so-called stars."[23] That Saturday, the sports' editor of the *Burnley Express* was unequivocal in his support of Hogan's position: "There is considerable truth in what he says," the editor wrote. "... football training [of juniors], mentally as well as physically... is not carried out as systematically as it ought to be. There is a haphazard atmosphere about the business that results in the whole affair becoming a sort of lucky bag in which clubs dip, deeply or otherwise, according to financial circumstances, and in most cases hope for the best."[24]

Just why there was a call for a systematic national programme at the time was not surprising. The idea had gained traction in some quarters possibly because of the strides that one could see Germany making, economically and in the sporting field at that time, now that Hitler had taken control of that country. Many people at that time felt that the National Socialists with their national programmes in Germany were on the right track, tapping into an ethos that was popularly acclaimed throughout the Western world. As A. N. Wilson wrote "[the] zest for the modern, [the] belief that humanity would become more reasonable when it had cast off the shackles of the past and embraced science and modern roads, was a belief shared with almost all forward-thinking people at the time ..."[25] And this was true of sport and football, just as it was true of the building of the Autobahns. Football in Britain, wrote the correspondent of the *Liverpool Echo*, could benefit by placing "a dictator" in charge of the way coaching was organised here, beneath whom someone like Nerz could be "responsible for all football coaching throughout the whole of the country."[26] The editor of the *Burnley Express* had also alluded to the point in his article: "The Football Association ... should be prepared to sponsor a system of preparing junior footballers along the right lines." But this was also not just an issue pursued by blow-hards in the press rooms. Sir Frederick Wall was calling a meeting of the FA's General Purposes Committee to look into the feasibility of developing some type of national coaching programme. Could it work in Britain? Sir Frederick Wall entered into discussion with a number of people, not least of whom was Jimmy Hogan, presenting himself to the FA's offices during April 1934.[27] The two men discussed the scheme but nothing came of their meeting immediately. One of the reasons being that Hogan simply priced himself too high for the FA to give him the responsibility to manage the programme.[28]

Jimmy Hogan's work in Germany had convinced him of how scandalous the situation was in English football where so much waste and lost opportunity could be avoided by introducing a national coaching scheme. After all, from Hogan's point of view the current transfer system created a status quo that did not benefit the long-term health of the game and retarded any serious stride toward a comprehensive improvement in the standard of football played in Britain. All that appeared to happen in Hogan's view was that clubs with more resources purchased skilled players from smaller clubs and completely abnegated their responsibility to institute a coaching programme themselves to bring through their own youth contingent. He exemplified that point when referring to how Burnley had replaced Tommy Boyle, their title winning captain from 1920 with Jack Hill, a £6,000 purchase from Sunderland. Why, Hogan asked, had Burnley not trained a youngster from their own ranks to take the role of Boyle? In Holland, Switzerland, Hungary and Austria, with their limited resources and a public interested in games other than football, clubs had no option but to intensely train, coach and inveigle whomever they could find and treat each youngster interested in football as a precious resource. The benefits of taking a root and branch approach to such things was there to see within a few years because in 1937 little Switzerland would beat mighty England in Zürich: an almighty shock result but one that just went to prove that if sewn correctly and assiduously a threadbare lawn can produce a decent turf of grass. The question, and one Hogan was never able to answer, was what form should the strategic change take? In the early 1930s, he was inclined to feel that the change should be enacted on a local basis, that clubs should implement local programmes. It was only with the intervention of Sir Frederick Wall and Stanley Rous that Hogan saw and finally participated in a programme with a wider vision.

Hogan's visit to see Sir Frederick in London that April had come soon after his dismissal from Lausanne. In April 1934, the *Gazette de Lausanne* reporter was diplomatic when saying that there had been a difference of opinion between the club President and Hogan over "technical issues." Issues which no doubt could be seen in the team finishing sixth and losing every other week. Hogan was out the door followed by a number of the club's players[29] but trouble had been brewing for months beforehand.

Early that spring, Meisl had asked Hogan if he wished to join the Austrians for the Italian World Cup that summer but Hogan's heart and mind was not in it. The Austrian national association could not guarantee funds to pay for his passage and stay in Italy and the side had been denuded of some serious talent when some of their key players had signed contracts with the French professional clubs rendering them beyond the scope of selection.[30] To add to their problems, Nausch was injured in the qualifier against Bulgaria[31] and had not the time to recover his lost place in the side. But the key reason Hogan backed out was that his Joe, 22, and Frank, 19, were finding it difficult to secure work in Switzerland. "It was impossible," he said "to find a position in civil life overseas."[32] He went onto say that if he couldn't find work in the UK he would be forced to continue to work in Switzerland but arrangements would have to be made for his family and none were forthcoming while other offers were just not agreeable. In the second week of April he received notification from Dordrecht, the club where he first got his start as a coach. They needed his help but Hogan was rudely dismissive of them[33] explaining that there was no way he would be returning given the money they were offering so the family returned to the UK in April 1934.

On 19 April, while "visiting relatives" in Burnley he gave an interview to the *Lancashire Evening Post* and used that opportunity to announce that "he [had] entered into negotiations with a view to obtaining an appointment as manager and coach with an English club"[34] but he would not say which. Was this the moment when he was in discussion at Highbury? The club were still reeling from the loss of their leader Herbert Chapman, who had died in January, and were led not by any manager but by the trainer at that time. Hogan explained that he was still in negotiations with the Austrians but you could sense that it was but a secondary option for him. He wanted to stay in England but he did use the column to set out his demands for his new employers. "I think ... [in the] not far distant [future] first class teams in England will employ a manager-coach," he said. In the end that first class team would be Fulham. "There is considerable scope for improvement in developing of young talent in this country. Continental football is forging ahead because the players were taking it seriously and following intensive training from an early age. The services of coaches were in great demand abroad and a thorough system was followed. As a result, the mechanical side of football such as trapping, heading and passing, came as second nature to the experienced players, and he was able to concentrate fully upon constructive play. Particular attention is paid to schools boys and every facility is offered to stimulate interest and enthusiasm while at the same time intensive training is proceeding."[35]

# 1933-1934

## Notes

1 *Burnley Express*, 16 August 1933.
2 *Gazette de Lausanne*, 7 September 1933.
3 The President of the club. The financial manager was Gueleve Mayer.
4 Joe Hogan was found a job in a confectionary shop.
5 *Gazette de Lausanne*, 12 February 1934.
6 2 October 1933.
7 *Gazette de Lausanne*, 12 October 1933.
8 *Ibid*.
9 *Sport*, vol. 16.
10 The Football League forbade clubs from playing national teams and so the Austrians were retitled as a Vienna XI for the match.
11 *Gazette de Lausanne*, 17 November 1933, which stated that Hogan would leave on 24 November and return on 12 December 1933.
12 Hogan – when asked – had wanted a frosted surface to help the Austrians whip the ball about to pitch but the weather played up and the surface was muddy when the players emerged from the tunnel.
13 *Times*, 4 December 1933.
14 *Soccer*, 321.
15 *Times*, 4 December 1933.
16 Wednesday 13 December 1933 – Liverpool won 3-0.
17 *Times*, 14 December 1933.
18 Monday 18 December 1933 – City won 3-0.
19 *Times*, 19 December 1933.
20 *Burnley Express*, 29 November 1933.
21 He was referring to Alf Charles, one time manservant of Learie Constantine. Burnley signed him in November 1933, consigned him to a stint in the reserves and sold him on. He made one League appearance for Southampton. Acknowledgement to Ray Simpson for this information.
22 *Burnley Express*, 29 November 1933.
23 *Ibid*.
24 *Burnley Express*, 2 December 1933.
25 A. N. Wilson, *Hitler: A Short Biography* (Harper, 2012), p. 187.
26 *Liverpool Echo*, 3 March 1934.
27 *Burnley Express*, 21 April 1934.
28 *Burnley Express*, 29 November 1933.
29 *Gazette de Lausanne*, 9 April 1934.
30 https://de.wikipedia.org/wiki/Matthias_Sindelar&prev=search
31 Played on 25 April 1934, Austria won 6-1 in their only qualifying game.
32 *Burnley Express*, 21 April 1934.
33 14 April 1934.
34 19 April 1934.
35 *Burnley Express*, 21 April 1934.

Jimmy Hogan

## THIRTEEN

## 1934-1935
### 'By leap and bounds.'

The story of Jimmy Hogan's stay at Fulham can be condensed into the story of one man, one transaction and an injury that cost the Cottagers their dreams of First Division football for two decades. The man was Frank "Bonzo" Newton who went to Fulham from Stockport County and by the end of the 1932-33 season had scored 154 goals in just 177 League games. That rate of goal-scoring was almost without parallel in League history but Newton was to be underdone by two managers at the Cottage: James McIntyre and Jimmy Hogan.

Hogan's predecessor at Fulham was McIntyre who benefited from the changes that had come into English football following the rise of Herbert Chapman at Huddersfield and Arsenal. Chapman had helped alter the mind-set of Chairmen and the Directors who ran football clubs in first class football in Britain. Prior to Chapman's ascendancy, the directors, generally, had negotiated transfers and kept a firm grip on the money but during Chapman's time the status quo was transformed as clubs, enviously eyeing the commercial and tactical success of Arsenal, gave their manager's licence to assume more administrative responsibilities, just as Chapman had, and this ushered in a new era. But Chapman was a character who always seemed to be linked to shady dealings. He has been treated with blind reverence by football historians but you do sometimes wonder if they're talking about the same man who got up to all manner of scrapes during his career. After all, he received a lifetime ban from the Football League when he was found to have committed fraud at Leeds City by burning the financial records of the club. That led directly to the disqualification of club from the League. He had not been back in football for many months after somehow getting that ban overturned when he craftily conspired to get Ambrose Langley the sack at Huddersfield. He then worked with that crook Sir Henry Norris at Arsenal where he quite openly engaged in the sort of commercial shenanigans that would make your eyes water. Ensuring deals by intoxicating the directors of other clubs was just one trade secret he openly rejoiced in. Heaven knows what else he was getting up to. Away from Arsenal, Bury's directors, for instance, gave team manager, Norman Bullock, power over coaching, selection and scouting around 1935 and

# Jimmy Hogan

under him Bury came within a hair's breadth of recovering their place in the First Division. Therefore, even in the right hands, success was not a guarantee; in others it was a move replete with danger for giving the club's cash and control of assets to the manager meant that the directors were beholden to whether the manager knew what he was doing or was doing things in the greater interests of the club. Unfortunately, for Fulham, James McIntyre fell into this latter category.

On 19 September 1933, much to the shock of Fulham's supporters, McIntyre offloaded Frank Newton to Reading. For some unknown reason, McIntyre got it into his head that what Fulham needed was not Frank Newton, standing on the precipice of legendary status, but Arsenal's Jack Lambert, who was over the hill, and, in some eyes, had never really surmounted the summit in the first place. One would have hoped that McIntyre would have cashed in on the considerable investment that Newton represented, after all players averaging nearly a goal a game don't grow on trees, but when the dust settled, the £600 McIntyre got Reading to pay for Newton suddenly made Fulham everyone's favourite Musical Hall joke. To put this into some sort of perspective one would have to go back to the early 1920s to discover that Bob Kelly had cost Sunderland ten times that amount to move him from Burnley. Just what inspired McIntyre to make his ill-judged foray into the transfer market is still a matter of conjecture but the fall-out was all too clear when, at the end of the 1933-34 season, McIntyre was dismissed primarily on the basis of that transfer. As a result, Fulham's irate directors spent a considerable part of their summer break charming and cajoling Reading's upper brass in order to bring Newton back to Craven Cottage.

It was during that same close season that Fulham's chairman, John Dean, made his interest in Jimmy Hogan known. At the time Hogan and Austria were in final training for the upcoming World Cup to be held in Italy but Hogan's interest was easily swayed now that a chance to coach in England was being offered. The irony of this appointment could not be gainsaid. For years he had lathered on that poor English club performances on the continent represented a threat to him finding further work in Europe. However, now, when it came to working in England his reference was the performance of the Austrian national side over here at Stamford Bridge in December 1932. On 12 May 1934, the *Burnley Express* reported that Hogan would be taking up a position with Fulham,[1] the appointment finally confirmed on 2 June, the day prior to the World Cup semi-final between Italy and Austria, when the *Sheffield Independent* reported that he would be appointed as manager-coach and that his duties would begin "immediately." On 30 July he met with the players at Craven Cottage and set out his

## 1934-1935

vision for the coming season alongside John Dean over a few cups of tea. A London *Evening News* article[2] set the scene and reported Hogan saying "I don't want you to have the impression that I have come over from the continent with lots of new-fangled ideas." He went on, "It's natural to work with your hands. If a footballer is to kick a ball with the same dexterity as he can handle it, he must have plenty of practice." He concluded: "I want constructive football, with every pass and move made towards one definite objective, reaching the opponent's goal by the shortest possible route. I will have no aimless kicking."[3] To assist Hogan, Dean had offered him Joe Edelston as a trainer. Edelston, the old right half for the club from the 1920s, had stepped into the manager's seat when McIntyre was sacked and would now form a coaching partnership with Hogan, who would take him with him to the Coaching Refresher Courses that were to be held in Chelsea and Leeds starting the following summer.

What game would Hogan be returning to after all his years spent traipsing about on his Grand Tour? Well, by some accounts, it was a sport with its face set firmly to a bright future. Chapman's passing in early January of that year, led some to view that future with optimism since it meant that Chapman and the pervasive negativity surrounding the WM would now hopefully be consigned to history. On 24 September 1934, the *Sunderland Daily Echo and Shipping Gazette* reported that a record of number of clubs had posted profits, that women were becoming interested in football in far greater numbers than in previous years and, with the passing of Chapman's vast shadow, football's future seemed "brighter" because without Chapman's overbearing dominance, there would be less defensive football and more inclination toward attack. Was this the moment when football could regain the art that it had lost since the change in the offside law in 1925? "The W-formation was falling into disfavour," the *Gazette* reported, reviewing the mood of local supporters "and there is a strong feeling that all five forwards should be forwards." The argument seemed to be that by increasing the manpower up front, with five or even six men forward, with the centre-half moving up, more goals would result.

In 1937, F. N. S. Creek, set out a logical response to that in his book *Association Football*. Creek argued that since there was only one ball, one passer of that ball and one recipient, having all five forwards streaming forward in each attack would result in inside forwards soon getting tired and disinclined to keep running. What was required to transition the game away from Chapman's tactical plan was to introduce more inventiveness as to how to unhinge defences, not to simply throw more strikers forward. The Austrians had demonstrated this beautifully at Stamford Bridge: a double centre-forward game, with one centre in a withdrawn role and

# Jimmy Hogan

blind side movement by the outside forwards: it was well-thought out stuff but simple: "Run to the left, pass to the right." Surely Hogan would challenge the hegemony crippling English football with Austrian thought and application that would bamboozle the opposition and race Fulham to the top of the Second Division without much ado? And yet when it came to setting out his great tactical primer, Hogan announced that Fulham would "spurn all ideas of third-backs, W-formations and the rest and play with five forwards in a row. '[Fulham]', wrote the correspondent, 'will also concentrate on ball control, and it will be most interesting to see how successful this type of football is in the Second Division, where certain teams rely on pace and a power kick ahead."[4] In the *Bystander* "Mark Over" was excited by the change:

> Hogan ... has decided to scrap the very fashionable 'third back' game. Indeed, Fulham are to revert to the old time plan of playing an attacking centre-half. This idea should please the fellow who pays the money that keeps football on the go. Too often have we seen matches which have become nothing more than wars of attrition, with each side hoping against hope to get a snap goal and then sit on the lead by dogged defence. Now, that isn't the idea of the game to my mind; what I, and I daresay you, have been wanting to see is the spectacle of five forwards up in a line, with the centre-half helping to initiate attacks. Blood-stirring football that: a sight better than some of the soulless sort of stuff we've seen of late years. And here is Fulham bringing back some of the old glory of the game. Will it pay them to throw everything into attack? A difficult question, and one that can only be answered by Fulham's playing record in the campaign now on us.[5]

However, all this pre-season optimism soon hit the skids once the season started and Hogan's reversion to the pre-1925 style suddenly had the press questioning the wisdom of it all. On 1 September they had beaten Plymouth, drawn with Brentford but were said to be "likely to lose to Norwich."[6] Even when they performed well the press were quick to point out failings in the opposition as was the case against Blackpool at Craven Cottage on 22 September. The *Lancashire Evening Post*'s "Hermes" reported of the match: "the Fulham forwards played to a plan conceived by [Hogan] ... expounded to the team in the form of a lecture the previous day ... from the start the home forwards tried the 'direct to goal' method and played it with success. They cut out the frills, lambasted the ball from wing to wing and were fast enough to keep in touch with it. Result – a harassed and badly-positioned opposing defence with gaps in it yards wide."

But you're only as good as the team you're put up against and of Blackpool, the *Post* reported: "[they] never seemed to get the proper run of the ball," passes were "too often misplaced and useless." The forwards were "incompetent." By the end of September, Fulham had won just three times and the club sat anonymously in tenth spot but Hogan was apparently unperturbed by the travails besetting the club. Others would have thrown themselves tooth and nail into correcting the problems. He, on the other hand, chose, at that point, to lead two lives: building his public profile at the very time when he should have been strengthening his position with the players. At that time it was very much unknown for managers to offer anything other than a nod and a wink to reporters when discovered scouting on a match day at a rival ground. In Germany, his profile had been raised continent wide by his lectures; *over there* his public demonstrations had complemented the contract he was on but in England the two roles were in conflict with one another. In late September, he gave a lecture at Southborough's Royal Victoria Hall, just north of Tunbridge Wells.[7] He showed real guts when telling the assembled audience and reporters that British footballers were, essentially, "thick." That was a bloody brave call to make when your team was tenth in the Second Division. "The system today is wrong. There is far too much aimless passing. You say 'get rid of it' but where is a player going to get rid of it if the others are marked?"

"There are two types of attack," he said, "wing play and down the middle ... at Fulham we play with five forwards up if we are attacking and five forwards back if our opponents are attacking ... Teams [in Britain otherwise] try to overcome the third back with three forwards against two backs, the centre-half and the goalkeeper [but] if you have five forwards against these four you are bound to draw the centre-half out of position." Hogan announced his separation from the herd: "I'm a great supporter of the wing game – there is plenty of room there." By playing the ball wide teams could maintain their shape; swing the ball from inside forward to opposite wing and by alternating the direction of the attack lure the centre-half away from his lair. "I still like the old triangular game if played quickly. The cross pass from say the right half to the inside left is one of the best moves in football." But, said Hogan, "forwards have got to work. If they want to play good football they must remember the first rule – if you run to the right, pass to the left."

It is hard to say whether the decision to give lectures was taken for financial or egotistical reasons. Perhaps we would be on firm ground if we said it was a combination of both. It could easily be argued that public lectures would offer him maximum publicity more in keeping with the view he had of himself as the great coach; the internationalist who stood apart from the insular English around him. Lectures were a great vehicle to broadcast insights and experiences as well as the outlandish views he had on training and coaching; contemporary British values no longer

# Jimmy Hogan

being applicable but, of course, there was the flipside to all of this: his day job. The work that fed the kids and paid the rent saw him as just another club manager struggling to make headway against the likes of Norwich and Brentford. It is true, some were convinced he was on the right path. The *Sheffield Independent* of 29 September reported that they would not be "surprised if, before the season is over, other clubs were watching Fulham closely with a view to imitating their style of play ... Fulham were coming to the front by leaps and bounds." On 3 November, the same newspaper said that Hogan "was good enough to become the Herbert Chapman of present-day football" but Sheffield is a long way from the banks of the Thames and power lay not with the press but by the players and owners of Fulham. Simply put, all was not sweetness and light at dear old Craven Cottage. There was an increasing disconnect between the image he was portraying of himself and the mood at the club. He was advocating one thing to the press, and the players at the club were holding on to the view that they did not necessarily give a stuff for his great ideas. Fulham players simply did not see themselves as being the guinea pigs to Hogan's great experiment and he revealed as much when, in late October, he spoke to the Fulham Rotary Club[8] and gave away clues to the problems he was facing in trying to change the prevailing mentality amongst club professionals in superfast time. "The game is going down," he said, "players train like they did in Victorian times. On the track and on the golf course. [We have] first class footballers who can't control a ball ... I think it is ridiculous." The problem was that notwithstanding all the pre-season promise and the alterations in style, Fulham were not making the type of in-roads into the leading pack that the directors were seeking. The team's performance was comparable with McIntyre's side up to the turn of December of the previous season; but Hogan's influence had not brought about the dramatic improvement that his persona appeared to guarantee. If Fulham were leading the march, and making a mockery of players "who couldn't control a football," such sentiments would have been fine but since Fulham were playing a type of game that was easily overcome in 1930s England, and had a manager who was slagging off professionals his side was facing, the same sentiments only caused Fulham's opponents to up their game. Playing an attacking centre-half was sound in theory if you played against opponents playing the same way. But having a centre-half go walk about when the opponent just wanted to kick the ball up to a big brutish centre-forward standing on his own in the penalty area was like leaving the silverware on the welcome mat for the burglars.

Hogan continued to gratify the press; the provincials lapping up his offerings. Other managers of the day put up and shut up; Hogan, by comparison, couldn't stop himself telling all and sundry what he felt about things. On 10 November he gave a speech in London. "He actually said he was 'disgusted' with Second Division football," the *Sheffield Independent* reported. It was a laudable sentiment and he was probably being sincere but it all meant nothing in the tough commercial world of Second Division League football; opponents were not going to play some arty-farty version of football just in order to appeal to the *aficionados* that might turn up to pay their farthing. Fulham were still motoring along in second gear while the Division's front runners asserted themselves. On 24 November Fulham went to Turf Moor to play Burnley, it should have been an emotional return for Jimmy Hogan but the match was played in a torrential downpour. The *Burnley Express*, ever so graciously, gave their prodigal son some sound, Northern advice, "Fulham should not try to do too much with the ball on a heavy ground such as Turf Moor'." They know their football up north. Fulham lost. On 28 November, Hogan in resolute mood wrote to the *Burnley Express*. "I should like to congratulate my old club on the splendid display of constructive football which they gave against 'my new love' Fulham. We were fairly and squarely beaten [Burnley won 4-0.] ... We at Fulham are not discouraged in the least. *We still think we shall 'get there' one day by trying to play the game as it should be played*, but, strange to say, we are rather a poor side away from home at present." Unfortunately, no record was kept as to what John Dean felt when he read that he was not "discouraged in the least" by a 4-0 thumping in the bloody rain after travelling all day to watch a football match.

The following Monday, Fulham played host to FK Austria, featuring the famous Sindelar. For the first half-hour Fulham gave a good account of themselves. It seemed the perfect panacea for all, taking thoughts away from the present travails in the League. The *Times* reported that Fulham showed "more purpose and with equal science, began to fight back" after going behind. Gibbons, the Fulham centre-half:

> took advantage of Sindelar's wandering licence, and attacked from a high position on the field ... the Austrian's played, for the most part, a close-passing game, kept the ball on the ground as much as possible and show an instinctive knowledge of each other's whereabouts. Sindelar, the centre-forward, *contrary to the modern tradition in this country*, played well back, [but] the fault of the forward line, which showed admirable ball-control, was that not enough of its members were up in the goal-mouth when the Fulham defence was harassed.[9]

However bad news was close at hand. Frank Newton who had been playing his way back into the first team after his return from Reading was seriously injured just before half-time. In those days footballers were not precious snowflakes but there was an immediate awareness here that Newton's injury was serious. He was Fulham's ticket out of the Second Division particularly so given their stuttering attack [In nine first team games that season (out of eighteen matches) Fulham had scored just one goal or nothing.] but the early diagnosis was dreadful and as things transpired it would be the last time he played in a competitive match. In light of that, Hogan did himself no favours in travelling north with the Austrians in order to report on their 3-0 victory over Sheffield United and, true to form, gave yet another speech that evening. "The game proved one thing ... that the Austrians can play the ball on the ground and take up position far better than the average First Division side in this country."

But after this a further set back bad news was to follow. Hogan informed the club that he would need to be operated on for appendicitis. The operation would take place on 28 December[10] and he would be out of action for the foreseeable. The club were without a manager or a coach but that did not bother the players one sausage. These were seasoned, pre-war professionals not the modern day type who look to the bench for askance whenever an opponent starts posing a few questions and Hogan's absence led to a curious case of revival at the Cottage. They reverted to the W-formation that they were familiar with and dispensed with the theorem. The team freed from his tactical restraints and reverting to default – lost once between 19 January and 30 March, including a thumping 7-0 victory over Notts. County. This obviously set John Dean and his directors a bit of quandary. If Hogan was absent and his ideas not being employed then what was the point of paying him? On 15 March, Dean announced that Hogan had ceased to be their manager and that the running of the team would revert to a three-man team of directors and coaching would be led by Edelston. Hogan was given the news while still recuperating and in those far-off days of hiring and firing the club felt it right that he should not receive compensation. He immediately resolved to take the matter up with Stanley Rous, the newly appointed Secretary of the Football Association's, who represented Hogan in securing severance against Fulham and from that initial conversation, Rous brought Hogan in to the inaugural FA coaching programme that was run that summer in Chelsea.

It may well be said from this distance that more time should have been afforded Hogan at Fulham but this is from the stand-point of observers whose money is not intimately tied up in the business of running a professional football club. Indeed one could argue that the directors, in putting pressure on Hogan and bowing to "player power," had a point. After all, Austria had come to England and, under the supposed "guidance"

## 1934-1935

of Hogan, had given the old country the sternest of tests. So now that the directors of Fulham had that same Hogan within their pay they should have expected, with some confidence, that Second Division make weights would be easily routed for did not Hogan know the closed secret of football: brilliant, sterling play, mesmerised opponents and a run of success at the highest level within the game? Yet to where had he led the club?

Fulham would have deflated egos far less resilient that Hogan's but he was irrepressible. As it was Hogan hardly broke stride. In April, the *Portsmouth Evening News* was reporting that he was in negotiation to go "to another London club." It might have been Arsenal or it might have been fake news provided by Hogan to keep him in the public consciousness. In June the *Burnley Express* was reporting that he was involved in filming some training sessions.[11] During the filming of this Hogan was approached by a local schoolmaster who recommended fifteen-year-old Reg Lewis as being ideal for the film. He was, remarkably so, for Hogan felt that Lewis had greater potential still. So he recommended Lewis to George Allison, manager of Arsenal who drafted Lewis into the fabric of that great London club. That particular story would reach an awkward conclusion some years later.[12]

# Jimmy Hogan

## Notes

1 The club found him a nice family home to move into at 14a Oxford Road, Wandsworth with Evelyn and George, Joseph and Mary. Acknowledgement to Shirley Ashton, Lancashire Libraries. The house is a gentle stroll across Putney Bridge and along the Fulham embankment to the ground.
2 Later reported to the *Burnley Express* on 4 August 1934 by H. J. Palmer.
3 *Burnley Express*, 4 August 1934.
4 *Times*, 28 August 1934.
5 *The Bystander*, 28 August 1934.
6 *Times*, 1 September 1934. Fulham drew 0-0.
7 26 September 1934.
8 *Sheffield Independent*, 31 October 1934.
9 *Times*, 31 November 1934.
10 At Putney Hospital. (*Leeds Mercury*, 23 January 1935).
11 *Burnley Express*, 1 June 1935.
12 *De Sumatra Post*, 9 February 1939.

## FOURTEEN

## 1935-1936
### 'A kind of travelling circus.'

It was one of the great football ironies that the country that did so much to export coaches and introduce the culture of coaching overseas should be so poor at implementing a programme in their own country. But that the case with Britain until the 1930s. The reason why the development of a national football coaching programme came to prominence in the 1930s was because the visit of the Austrians in 1932 had highlighted the benefit of a systematic coaching programme of what came to be called "scientific football," otherwise the coaching of the fundamental skills every footballer needs to succeed.

The person responsible for starting the ball rolling in regards to the first national coaching programme in Britain was Sir Frederick Wall, who formed the General Purposes Committee (GPC) at the Football Association in January 1934 to inaugurate "Instructional Classes for Boys in Association Football." Although the visit of the Austrians was fundamental to this it should be noted that the real motivation behind the development of these classes went much further back in time, to 1907. It was in that year that the great divide took place between the professional game in the north and the amateur game in the south. The Middlesex, London and Surrey FAs were charged with registering professional clubs into their Associations and because of the predominance of privately educated officials and private schools within their associations, all of whom saw professionalism as a threat to the amateur traditions, they unilaterally withdrew from the Football Association. This led to the development of the Amateur Football Association in the same year and an exponential increase in the number of private schools that exclusively played Rugby Union. To counter this, Wall felt that the GPC should undertake a review of what facilities and resources were available and seek input from headmasters as to how football could be best promoted within the education system. Football had, by default, became the national sport because it was commonly played in the public school system but it was only with the introduction of the GPC that there had ever been a review as to how football was actually taught in schools. In addition to the review, the FA proposed that ex-professional players on central FA contracts should be sent out to the schools to coach football and that led to another of a number of problems that the review had identified. The first issue involved who would administrate the coaching programme:

"At the outset two methods of ... coaching ... were considered – either full-time, centrally controlled experts who would travel round the country giving first-class tuition, a kind of travelling circus: or a series of decentralised schemes making full use of part-time coaches. The latter was decided on ..."[1]

The FA had to decentralise the scheme because they could not afford the manpower required to contact each school in turn throughout the country and position one of their players within each school. Far too much paperwork would have been required and the negotiations would have swamped the FA, which at that time did not have the type of payroll it can afford nowadays. There was also the cultural distaste that the British had for centralising such schemes generally, in Germany it could be achieved but it was too much for Britain at that time. The idea was therefore to hand over the responsibility to each County FA (CFA) and this required the FA to provide the CFAs with guidelines and then have them enact the programme in their region. One of the first schemes was held by the Kent FA who utilised the services of Len Graham, previously with Millwall, who in the spring of 1935 started working with Dover County School.[2] Such a scheme relied on the goodwill, commitment and complete assistance of the CFAs and, finally, local schools.

That was not naturally forthcoming since both the CFAs and schools had their own agendas that they were intent on delivering and those did not automatically align with the FA. For their part the schools were not necessarily in favour because they had enough to do when teaching their pupils without promoting emphasis on football at the expense of other curriculum activities. Secondly, the scheme relied on the County FAs to commit to persuading local schools as to the benefit of the programme and place footballers in those schools. And since the County FAs were short of funding and resources themselves it was not something they were wont to do. But a bigger problem still involved the use of the ex-professionals. What Wall did not seem to grasp was that whereas the likes of Graham had presumably been coached, there were no assurances as to what level or how this coaching had been discharged. In other words, in the absence of any standardised course there were no guidelines as to how coaches should go about teaching footballers. In essence, although those players knew their trade, what those players took to be acceptable coaching practice was determined very much on what they themselves had learnt at their clubs and in the main there was no coaching of "scientific football" that was going on at that time. All in all, the idea of sending these men out to teach

# 1935-1936

others was ill-conceived.

Sir Frederick was replaced as Secretary of the Football Association by Stanley Rous in the summer of 1934. Rous had been made the Games Master since 1921 at Watford Grammar School so had knowledge of the difficulties faced in implementing such a scheme. "As a schoolmaster I had seen how little was done to encourage youth or to provide any training and coaching facilities."[3] Rous introduced the County Youth Championship and also what became the FA Youth Cup. "The next and most important step was to develop training courses for coaches and referees. As far as coaches were concerned this was a new idea for any sport."[4] So following his introduction, Rous proposed what came to be the Coaching Refresher Courses which were designed to coach the coaches. In preparation for this first course, which was a three day course held at the Duke of York's Headquarters in Chelsea in the June of 1935.[5] Rous assembled a team of "experts." These were Tom Whittaker, Arthur Grimsdell, Norman Creek, the Rev. K. R. G. Hunt and Jimmy Hogan, who was then out of work. Creek was still a player with the Corinthians and the Reverend Hunt, also an amateur, had been a member of Wolves' Cup winning side of 1908.[6] They would be giving lessons to a number of ex-players or those who were coming to the end of their playing career.

The first course was not the success. Rous had rightly expected Whittaker, Grimsdell and, particularly Hogan, to be proficient in providing clear instructions and delivering effective lessons. The expectation had been heightened in the case of Hogan because he had, by that stage, been "coaching" continuously for over twelve years. However, upon viewing Hogan's "lesson" Rous described the group's reaction to the exercise: "What alarmed us was how ill organised Hogan was when it came to taking the practical periods ..."[7] Hogan "took the class to the furthest pitch, wasting five minutes walking there." Secondly, "[Hogan] had forgotten to arrange for the balls to be [at the pitch designated for training]." Thirdly, "he talked and demonstrated for so long that there was no time for practice." If Hogan was purposefully wasting time in order to foreshorten his lesson, to limit what information he was prepared to divulge, that would have been understandable, but it was the outcome of the conversation Rous had with Hogan following the lesson that the Emperor's wardrobe was laid bare. Rous explained: "*In discussion with Hogan on coaching matters* I came to realise that his great reputation abroad was in part fortuitous [my italics]. Because he could not speak the Austrian players' language he had to content himself with endless demonstrations of his own high skills. ... Hogan himself was content with the demonstrations ... [but] the players ... soon became disillusioned and bored ... It was then that Hugo Meisl ...

would take over and compel the players to go on practising the skill until they were as proficient as Hogan. ... it was clear that Hogan, on his own, lacked many of the organisational skills a coach requires."[8]

That is an astonishing admission and raises the understanding that following his stint in Vienna, Hogan would have travelled onto each successive contract and explained that the process he followed was 'x' and the clubs, knowing no better, had simply followed suit and nobody had challenged him or interrogated his methods until Rous finally did. Remember Schön's analysis of Hogan was of some benign Svengali and the appetite of the Continentals for training, added to the view that the English quintessentially knew *their* football, limited the opportunities for those who opposed or sought to challenge Hogan's methods. Another interesting aspect of that is that what passed as being practicable in Vienna did not necessarily equate to being suitable in Lausanne or Fulham. The watch, learn and practice method suited the Southern Germans who were socialised in order to view "the main principle of education" as being "discipline."[9] They therefore followed, studied and learnt by inculcation. But that culture did not simply translate to other countries and cultures.

Despite all that, Rous persisted with the courses and also with Hogan who came to refer to himself as the FA's chief instructor and would serve on the annual courses all the way up to 1939. That's possibly the case, but he was assisted in the following summer's course by representatives from Carnegie Physical Training College, in Leeds, where the course was held[10] and a number of professional and amateur players.[11] For the second course "the emphasis was on the *proper organisation* of coaching and the pooling of ideas and methods"[12] so that players could understand how to deliver effective coaching to pupils and students. This was an outcome directly related to the failings that Rous had identified at the first course. Therefore it can be said that Hogan's part in the development of the national coaching programme was definite, it was just not in the way he would like it to have been recorded.

Rous would gather the thoughts and teaching of the group on the second course in order to produce the *Football Association Coaching Manual*,[13] that went on to be translated into German and French. It is a thorough examination of all the things that young footballers need and, barring the odd reference to enjoying the pleasures of cigarettes, I would contend that it is still as valid now as it was when it was written. I would even wager that if a young player today was to follow the Manual religiously they would no doubt end up to be a perfectly skilled footballer. Stanley Rous wrote the Preface to the *Manual*: "It cannot be denied that the coaching given in other countries by past British players has borne fruit; present players, who

[have] received instruction as youngsters give ample proof of the value of scientific coaching."

The expert personnel on the course were each made contributions to the *Manual*. Dr Ronald Cove-Smith, an ex-England Rugby player, provided information regarding health, hygiene and injuries, Ernest Major and Stanley Wilson provided instruction regarding activities that went to exercise technical skills[14] and Hogan provided the text and exercises regarding kicking competently with both feet, ball control, tackling and heading, the four fundamental skills every single footballer must master if they are to be considered to be "good." I won't use this platform to enquire as to how many professionals are able to kick equally well with both feet but it does lay bare the understanding that those who cannot be classed as being competent in their primary function.[15] A number of Hogan's exercises are reprinted in diagrammatic form in the *Manual*, dealing with accurate shooting practice and also that famous chair slalom activity that he first trialled in 1925 in Budapest.[16] Sticks spiked into the ground now replaced the chairs but the exercise was archetypally Hogan: short constant control, use of both sides of each feet to manipulate the ball at speed around a short circuit as part of a group exercise.

If dispute did eventuate in the composition of the *Manual* then it did so between Creek and Rous about the extent of information that should be provide regarding the tactics within the game. Rous informed him that there was space only to discuss the third back game and the attacking centre-half game within the *Manual*. As a direct result of this, Creek was to write *Association Football* in 1937 which set out "the most complete modern analysis of the game"[17] and in that book he discussed a number of tactical methods that were being tried and applied in the UK in the mid-1930s. Creek's view was that WM and the third back could only be effective if you had the players to be able to execute those tactics. Even at the highest levels, clubs were struggling to replicate what Arsenal were demonstrating which would have been devastating for those less skilled sides in the lower echelons. Creek wrote "it is doubtful if one in a hundred had the necessary talent to carry out the essential features of [their] plan."[18] So therefore rather than just teach those two methods, which would have been impracticable to lower skilled sides, Creek used his book to suggest that there must be a wider analysis of tactics and that teams should find one that suits the resources at their disposal. All readers are absolutely encouraged to go study copies of Creek's book which is lays bare the fallacy that British sides in the 1930s only played WM and nothing else.

Added to this were two further books that were produced by the Football Association. These were *Association Football: an Instructional Book of the FA* and *Recreative Physical Exercises and Activities for Association Footballers and Other Games*. The first included diagrams and pictures of proper technique or exercises designed to assist in developing a high standard of technical skill and in these we see further examples of Hogan's technical exercises. In the end, despite the laudable aims of the Football Association the coaching course moved away from its primary objectives of putting skilled footballers into the education system to improve technical ability of young players of school age. Instead it became lost in a series of lectures provided by Walter Winterbottom to club coaches who would turn up pick up the hand outs, sit as passengers and offer nothing in return.

# 1935-1936

## Notes

1 Geoffrey Green, *The History of the Football Association* (Naldrett, 1953).
2 15 March 1935.
3 Stanley Rous, *Football Worlds* (Faber & Faber, 1978), p. 57.
4 *Ibid.*, 57-58.
5 Between 15 and 18 July 1935. Reported in *Leeds Mercury*, 21 June 1935.
6 He was the author of *First Steps in Association Football*, published 1924.
7 *Football Worlds*, 58.
8 *Ibid.*, 59.
9 Meisl in *Association Football*, vi, 308.
10 Held between 6 and 10 July 1936.
11 Creek and Norman Christie of Blackburn Rovers were there to help with the instructions.
12 *Football Worlds*, 59.
13 *The Football Association Coaching Manual*, (Evans Brothers, 1936.)
14 *Leeds Mercury*, 7 July 1936.
15 Puskás was a single right-footed player, Cruyff was two-footed. Who was the better player?
16 *Liverpool Echo*, 12 September 1925.
17 F. N. S. Creek, *Association Football*, Editor's Note, (Dent 1937), reprinted 1947.
18 *Association Football*, 49.

Jimmy Hogan

# FIFTEEN

## 1936-1939
### 'A man who could teach the players how to play football.'

Jimmy Hogan at Aston Villa
(Photo courtesy of Aston Villa FC)

Jimmy Allen was one of the great British footballers now, alas, lost to history. A centre-half of immeasurable talent, he was the subject in 1934 of a huge transfer which came about because of his performances for Portsmouth in their Cup run of the same year. That he was a talisman for the famous south coast club is unquestionable. At Wembley, before departing with an injury, he single-handedly kept Manchester City at bay, held Portsmouth's half-back line steady and was chief orchestrator in what should have been a famous 1-0 victory for Pompey. But in his absence Portsmouth fell apart and two late Fred Tilson goals sent the Cup back to Manchester City for the first time in 30 years.

As a result of this, Aston Villa made Portsmouth a headline-grabbing offer of £10,775 for Allen's services in the summer of 1934. Unfortunately, the price tag became an unremitting burden to Allen and gave the Villa Park crowd a convenient excuse to send a barrage of abuse Allen's way if matters did not go to their liking. Behind closed doors, the ire was not directed at Allen but at the person who had brought him to Villa Park, the manager Jimmy McMullen.[1] McMullen, like Jimmy McIntyre at Fulham, was another who was hamstrung by the changing times and became associated both with Allen's transfer and the failure of that transfer to deliver any immediate benefit. As Peter Morris wrote, "[McMullen's] first job was to assist in the signing of Jimmy Allen,"[2] and when it came to Jimmy Allen, things would never right themselves while McMullen was still in the dug-out. Even as late as the 1935-36 season, when Allen had had the requisite time to bed himself in, it was noticeable that he "could not" in the words of Morris "settle down."³ That failing had a knock on effect throughout the team. In late October 1935, Villa shipped eleven goals against West Brom and Leeds in two successive matches, results for which McMullen paid with his job and the running of the team was transferred to the Directors.⁴ Villa had won only three games since the start of the season and the signs were that the team was in trouble. They had never dropped down to the Second Division and there were fears, even at that early stage in the season that their splendid record might fall. There then began a spending spree the likes of which had never been seen in English League football history as the directors set about trying to save their club. Between 6 November and 9 January, seven players arrived at Villa Park to the tune of £35,500. This was a rash move but the players coming in were star performers; seven were internationals. The high quality of the players that Villa purchased that autumn guaranteed a high return at the turnstiles as the curious and expectant were drawn to Villa Park. Peter Morris wrote of one of the recruits, George Cummings, an £8k buy from Partick, that he was the "cleverest full-back I have seen, Cummings was an artist at bottling up wingers, a wonderful kicker of a ball at any height or angle and the cagiest tactician of his day."⁵ The quality of the new staff could not be faulted but the speed by which they were expected to combine and produce a winning formula was unrealistic. The defence, marshalled by Allen, was in disarray. In December Arsenal went to Villa Park and Ted Drake, the Gunner's centre forward, scored seven goals and hit the bar with his only other shot in a 7-1 battering. The Villa faithful was obviously wound up to the nth degree by all of this. Before their eyes their club, the grand old yacht of the Victorian age, was being buffeted in the wake left by a sleek, powerful, modern speedboat in its red and white livery. Yet, despite the fact that, in the middle of the Villa Park pitch was £49,000 pounds of the finest British talent, the enduring image that season was the unedifying sight of seeing goalkeepers Harry Morton and Fred Biddlestone presenting their arses to the sky 56 times as they picked the ball out of the Villa net.⁶ Villa simply couldn't find their form, and the waves pulled them under for the first time since the club was launched into the welcoming estuary that was the Football League in 1888.⁷

At the time this was all going on Jimmy Hogan was in Europe and was not a feature of Villa's future plans at all. Hogan had gone back to Vienna in late 1935, summoned by Meisl to coach the Austrian senior and Olympic teams but he had no firm plans beyond the summer of 1936, apart from hankering for a return to the UK. In the January, Hogan was in Madrid to see Austria's famous victory over Spain when they took the Spaniard's home record but his primary function during this period was to cast his eye over and prepare the national amateur squad for the Berlin Olympics which were to be held in the August of 1936. The national side was populated by the Viennese but it was his role leading and coaching the amateurs which required him to start touring the country, assessing and constructing a team almost from scratch. Admittedly, three key players were from Salzburg, two of whom were brothers, one being the goalkeeper and team captain, Eduard Kainberger. But both the towns of Leoben and Kapfenburg were represented by two players each and from the far western border hamlet of Lustenau came Ernst Kunz, the left-back. As a result, Austria's Olympic side was represented by amateurs playing for genuinely second and third string clubs. In that regard they would go to Berlin and scrupulously uphold the Olympic ideals which is more than could be said for some of their opponents they met there in Berlin.

In early May, Hogan had also helped in the preparations of the Austria v England tie which Austria won 2-1. Hogan then made two visits to England in short order, the first enforced on him, the second scheduled. In mid-May 1936 he paid a short visit to 43 Todmorden Road, in Burnley to visit his dying mother before returning to Vienna the same week.[8] He had been released from his contract on compassionate reasons but that did not stop him from visiting the *Burnley Express* offices in order to fire off a quick broadside at Fulham's directors and remind the readers of the local lad made good. "He's known throughout central Europe as Jeemy Hogan," the correspondent wrote,"the way the crowds go crazy over him is a thing that Fulham would marvel at. When Herr Hogan goes to a town the entire populace turns out to meet him."[9] Then in early July, he returned for the 1936 Refresher Course in Leeds.[10] England had just returned from their Continental tour with their tails planted firmly between their legs having lost both their games in Vienna and Brussels but a more worrying sign was that they had now gone four matches without a win, their longest ever. Surprisingly, the clamour for change was not as deafening as one might expect, despite that Hogan's name was mentioned in the same breath as the Führer as part of one man's confused campaign to put England back on the right track. Even though Hogan was in town for the FA's course a correspondent of *The Green 'Un* wrote: "The Germans [are] showing us what can happen when one man takes control of a nation's main roads. Nerz is doing the same [with their] football. We are going to [need] Jimmy Hogan to start a summer course."[11]

In the same month that the refresher course was being held, the Independent Aston Villa Shareholders' Association were holding their general meeting in a rancorous atmosphere. They had two principle aims and reached consensus fairly quickly. The two aims were for the appointment of a manager, in whom the qualities of tact and initiative – as well as football judgement – should be outstanding and who should be given a generous measure of control; and complete overhaul of training and scouting systems and change of policy which will result in building the team from the bottom up, instead of from the top down.[12] The shareholders had little faith in the current board and so elected Fred Rinder back onto the Board to deliver the aims on their behalf. At the time, Rinder was vice-president of both the Football League and the Football Association and in this second role he would be travelling with the Great Britain team for the Olympic Games, where he would meet Jimmy Hogan.

Meanwhile, in Vienna, the squad Hogan had been training for the Olympics were found to be in a terrible mental state prior to the Games. Self-analysis had served only to convince themselves that they had no chance. When he was interviewed, Hogan explained that the Austrians were "the biggest outsiders in the whole competition, because our players are provincial boys. Six of them are unemployed, and the rest have very poor jobs in Austria.[13] The low status of the players possibly explains their rather shaky performances which seemed to follow a pattern: Austria would take an early lead, would then tire and allow their opponents to come back into games that should have been won and dusted, informing an impression that they were tactically naïve and lacked stamina. One thing the squad did have in abundance, though, was a fondness for Hogan, a fact which was borne out when, following their semi-final victory against a good Polish side, the Austrian players swarmed as one to the bench to proclaim their great father-figure. It was obvious by that gesture alone that they were as surprised as any to have reached the Gold-medal match.

The turning point came in their second round match against Peru; a game that was to cause rancour and produce one of the biggest Olympic controversies of all time. Austria had taken a two-goal lead into the interval but then indulgently allowed Peru to come back into the game in the final quarter of an hour. The game remained tied with five minutes left of extra time when Peru scored twice and it was the second of these goals, scored with just a single minute left on the clock, putting the Peruvians 4-2 up, that was to cause all the trouble. After Villanueva's goal, some spectators entered the field and one of these spectators, reportedly, kicked an Austrian player, although we are never to know which one and never to know who the spectators were.[14] With seconds to go, the referee decided to abandon the game. Hogan said the next day: "It was an insult to world football. I had hoped to relinquish my association with football abroad without any incident of this kind ... I shall not be sorry now when I return to England .. Five of my players were badly injured by Peruvian spectators who invaded the ground."[15] The following day a Jury of Appeal sat and decided that the game should be replayed which was extremely harsh on Peru. The fact that Peru were two goals up with less than a minute remaining led most to assume that Austria would not have had time to recover the game in any event. Even so, the Jury concluded that the invasion onto the field "caused a decrease of the fighting energy of the [Austrian] team, and ... such an incident cannot be reconciled with the spirit of the good sportsmanship ..."[16] Accordingly, the Jury of Appeal informed all parties that a re-arranged match should take place behind closed doors on the 10 August. Then, when Peru failed to show up on that date, the Jury extended the invitation to the 11 August. Once again the Peruvian delegation failed to appear and it was subsequently made known to the IOC that the entire Peruvian Olympic Squad had formally withdrawn from the Games. Faced with that withdrawal, the Jury of Appeal had no alternative but to progress Austria through by means of a walkover.[17] In Lima there came to be dark mutterings about a stitch up, that Austria's reprieve and progress seemed more than coincidental following the surprise elimination of the German side the day before but there has never been any conclusive evidence provided to support such an opinion. Hogan did some smart tinkering for the semi-final, bringing in Kainberger and the teenager Mandl and he would be doubly vindicated when both rewarded him with goals, Mandl's coming with two minutes to go as Austria made the final. They were to lose that game, 2-1 to Pozzo's Italy, but once again Hogan had been cute when changing the team and selecting Stienmetz, a player who went onto score the equaliser with ten minutes to go.

At an early point in the Games, Rinder pulled up a chair with Hogan in the Athlete's Village and set about convincing him to sign with Villa. The objectives of Rinder's shareholders appeared to be met in the person sitting before him. That was to be made clear by the performance of the Austrians under Hogan in Berlin because there Hogan demonstrated tactical awareness in altering his line ups and had a persona that engendered such affection amongst the players playing under him that they overcame their lack of initial confidence and won through to the final. As Rinder would have noted, if Hogan could get a bunch of amateurs to the Olympic final then he surely had the capabilities to drive £49,000 worth of talent to the First Division. Hogan did not take much convincing.[18] Repeated goes on the European merry-go ride had confirmed to him that the bolts were coming loose, particularly in light of the fact that in Germany and Switzerland chauvinism was forestalling working opportunities for his family. Rinder was interviewed by the press and later said: "I have known [Jimmy] ever since he played for Bolton ... and I know from actual observation what he has done for Continental football since the War. I have been over to the Continent many times and .... I came to the conclusion this was the very man to engage in the circumstances."[19]

To begin with however, the two men seemed at odds. When interviewed, following notice that Hogan had been appointed manager, Rinder said "[Jimmy] has very distinct plans for Villa's future and will certainly introduce new ideas ..."[20] but Hogan dispelled talk of some tactical revolution: "I have no new ideas on training to introduce to Villa. My ideas are those of common sense and I didn't learn them on the Continent," he said.[21]

A few days before on the 10 August 1936, the *Evening Despatch* made the announcement public "Jimmy Hogan appointed manager," the very day that it was announced that Britain's latest Olympic football journey had come a cropper to continental opposition. "He is an expert tactician," commented the correspondent, "and it is largely through his skilful coaching that the standard of Continental football has made such rapid improvement in the post-war years." Almost immediately after the Olympic final, Hogan would make his way over to Birmingham before the round of press interviews began in earnest.

Hogan's lifestyle on the Continent had clearly imbued him with a set of cultures that marked him distinct from his fellow managers. There was none of the typical British restraint of the day. He was open and happy to discuss with the press and news outlets. He said:

> The first thing that struck me when I arrived at Villa Park was – despite our relegation last season – that the average attendance for our games was 40,000 [note the pronouns]. Such loyalty – under adverse circumstances – simply staggered me ... I know the class and style of football you require and to which you were always accustomed. Let me say right now you are going to get [promotion] so long as I hold the position of manager. I am a teacher and lover of constructive football with every pass, every kick, every movement, an object.

The Birmingham *Evening Despatch* likewise started puffing up the dreams of the Villa fans with a glowing piece about the new manager. One did not need to search too far to find out the source of their copy. Hogan, they wrote, could have joined half-a-dozen prominent clubs, including Arsenal and Burnley. The newspaper also said that "thanks to Hogan - *more than anyone else* - association football ... [in Europe] has reached its present high level." Hogan, they wrote, had - in total - coached 50 teams prior to coming to the Villa. The *Despatch* went on went on to embellish Hogan's playing career: "He was one of the finest forwards of his day" ... "He nearly played for Ireland," the paper wrote, "but just as he expected to be called up by that country, they decided not to pursue that route on some technicality." It is almost as if Hogan himself was his own press office for this information could only have come from one person.[22] Following this, on 20 August 1936, the *Evening Despatch* printed a very candid interview between Raymond H. Hill and Hogan. Hogan gave an assurance that he could give the Birmingham public the football they longed to see but he also had this to say: "It is my opinion that the whole secret of football is this need for a complete suppleness of the hips. Once that is secured, a man can swerve, head, tackle, fall, with the utmost comfort. You ask me what is wrong with English football? That is what is wrong. English players are generally too stiff."

Hogan went on "In six weeks I'll have these players accustomed to my style – and you will see the difference." And with that Hogan proceeded to run around Villa Park nodding "invisible footballs." It was all very strange but curiously compelling.[23] Villa started the League season well and one suddenly saw the benefit of the great relationship Hogan shared with the press coming to the fore. In September, the *Sheffield Independent*'s correspondent wrote in glowing terms about him and his impact at Villa:

> It was obvious that all that was required at Villa Park was for someone to bring the best out of the players and it was obvious that Jimmy Hogan was the man for this job, in spite of some of those derisive references to 'Hoganisms' that have been heard already. There is no getting away from the fact that far too much rot has been written and spoken about tactics of late years. A little less tactics and more straightforward football would have done the game a world of good. But Hogan has never suggested himself to me as a mere talker. He has always left the impression that he is a sound judge of the game and this is why I maintain he will get the best out of the Villa.[24]

Nevertheless there were problems in the offing and they involved Jimmy Allen. There was clearly a disconnect between Hogan's insistence on using the centre-half in an attacking role and Allen's preference for staying put. The *Sunderland Daily Echo* went so far as stating that Allen's departure up-field was the cause of at least one loss that season.[25] The issue seemed to be one that at first look seemed irresolvable with Hogan persevering despite the reticence of the player and his team-mates to revert to a style of play that – in England, and certainly in the Second Division – was by and large redundant. "Hogan," they wrote, "won't have a stopper centre-half." By

# Jimmy Hogan

late January the situation had hardly improved. "When Doncaster Rovers - undisputed wooden-spoonists of the second-rate class - can visit Aston Villa and hold them to a draw there can only be one conclusion, which is anything but flattering to the Villa." By springtime the team had steadied themselves and looked odds on to scale the heady heights once again back to the First Division.[26] Then the roof fell in. In Villa's last six matches they didn't pick up a single point, finished ninth and a season which began with great promise ended in bewilderment. The fans may have felt bemused at the lack of bite at the end of the season but Hogan's relationship with Rinder saw to it that he should be retained. At Fulham he was not given his fair dues but at Villa, saddled still with the debts emanating from the madness when buying the magnificent seven, the decision was taken to stick rather than bust.

For the 1937-38 season, Hogan suddenly saw the light and finally relented in relation to the attacking centre-half game. From here on in it would be done away with. This change drove Villa onto promotion and led to the development of a confidence within their play that Hogan was to refer back to for years to come. Jimmy Allen had weathered the abuse and come out of the dark tunnel of the 1936-37 season, in which he had only appeared sporadically, to become the main stay in the centre of the field. At the end of that season Johnston wrote: "Allen, now finding his form at Aston, was *the* pivot of the middle line, and he was well supported on the flanks by Massie and Iverson."[27] Hogan had reached agreement with the players that all should play to their particular strengths. In Allen's case since he was one of the country's top stopper centre-halves he would remain so and Bob Iverson and Alex Massie would now come to the fore as "attacking" wing-halves,[28] confident that in Allen they now had a stay at home centre-half to protect the back line should the attacks break down. Given Allen's assured presence, confidence soon spread to the other players. At full-back "Callaghan and ... Cummings were such a formidable pair that they frequently indulged in such 'risky' pastimes as heading back to Biddlestone from the edge of the penalty box and inter-passing with one another to play themselves out of danger."[29]

But there was a further tactical plan that was unveiled that season. Frank Shell, signed from Dagenham's Ford Sports in May 1937, had been on the fringes of the first team since the start of the season and suddenly became a regular feature of the first team when he struck three times against Stockport in a 7-1 win.[30] On that performance alone Shell had to be retained given that Villa had not been able to tie down a regular starter in the forward role and as the season wore on so Hogan's side triphead a scheme whereby Shell and his inside forward partner, Frank Broome, would switch positions during their games. This would see Shell apparently drift aimlessly and take the centre-half with him whilst Broome, from inside right, would move quietly into the centre-forward position vacated and smash home the chance presented. The interesting aspect of this was the use of Frank Broome who was the archetypal "Hogan" player, "too light and too frail to occupy the major place throughout the afternoon" but then again, given the wiles of the constant switching between the front two men, he didn't need to be in the "major place."[31] What Broome lacked in bulk he made up for in thought and as the perfect fall-guy he would wander here and there taking his marker with him as he went, releasing Shell in turn. In physique Broome represented an alternative to the big, burly strikers of the day but that and the fact that he was playing Second Division football all season did not stop the International Selection Committee from taking him with them on England's foreign tour in the summer of 1938. That fact alone gives the lie to the notion that the Selection Committee were reticent to gamble on any of the "new" stuff being produced by the clubs.[32] On 1 March 1938, the *Sheffield Independent*'s correspondent wrote: "the public are just beginning to awaken to Jimmy Hogan's scheme of things in having Shell at centre for the bulk of the time and then swinging Broome into the centre so that he can bring his speed to bear. Villa realise that defences ... have a one-track mind outlook ... and it is this sudden switch over ... with something completely new that does the damage." One might say that this tactic had its foundation in the play of Sindelar and Gschweidel when playing up front for the *Wunderteam*.[33] At one time Sindelar would take "the lead" at another his team-mate and such circuitous confusion would baffle those sophisticated continental defenders no end. Given his proximity to the Austrians, it would be a fair argument to say that Hogan was responsible for the tactic but the introduction of any new tactical idea requires insight and understanding by the players to make it work and so the success of the scheme says a great deal about the personnel at Villa Park in those days.

Broome was not the only frail player Hogan nurtured. Like Raynor after him, he had time for players who did not necessarily "look the part." A case in point was Jackie Martin. A part time footballer and school teacher, he could hardly withstand the heavy physical work required of being a half-back when he arrived, but within a couple of seasons he was considered of a standard worthy of international recognition. To bring about this transformation Hogan "turned to a gym teacher in Birmingham, called Platenauer" and asked him to build up Martin. "The effect has been amazing and the player, who not long ago was rated by many as too weak and useless ... [has been] outstanding."[34] Elsewhere the likes of Martin and

# Jimmy Hogan

Broome would have been discarded; too much hard work, time and money required, others would have argued, but Hogan's stay overseas had opened his eyes to the idea that precious resources in whatever size and shape should be cherished and nurtured. In Europe, the clubs had to utilise the few players that came their way. In Britain, where everyone wanted to be a locomotive train driver or a footballer, the clubs were less efficient with the resources that came their way. There were loads of players; but it took courage to spot and nurture the type of talent that Martin and Broome represented.[35]

It has been fashionable for some time now to just accept the hackneyed belief that English football was peopled by idiots who played one way only, that the only inventiveness within the game at that time and into the 1950s was exclusively foreign in origin but this premise is wrong. It didn't take a great deal of time for people in England to realise that WM required certain types of players for it to work and various clubs – for whom it couldn't work – sought to counter it. The delay in the introduction of different ideas in the English game was as a result of a lot of factors, one of which was that given that since some managers only saw Arsenal play twice a season it took them some time to work out what was actually going on. Others, meanwhile, came to their own conclusions as to how to counter the third back. Norman Bullock at Bury trialled playing a "false 9" in Ernie Matthews, giving him a roving commission and playing four up front. At Kenilworth Road, "Bunny" Bell had formed one part of a dual spearhead during the previous (record-breaking) season.[36] Such ideas as these became commonplace once managers and players realised that Arsenal's tactics were especial to them alone. At Villa, the two centre-forward game was perfectly effective, as shown when Broome and Shell worked to dramatic effect in the January fixture against Sheffield Wednesday, a game which was heading for stalemate. As "thousands were on their way out of Villa Park believing the result was a 3-3 draw ... the Broome-Shell switch worked once again for Broome to snatch the winning goal."[37] But this wasn't the only new idea that Hogan introduced at the club that year. On 27 August 1937 the Hartlepool *Northern Daily Mail* reported that Hogan "was organising a series of debates to stretch the minds of the younger, single players." By March these debates had become a feature of first team club life. The players were now used to "weekly tactical talks"[38] led by Jimmy Allen, the now popular captain of the side, and Hogan himself reaped the rewards. The improvement in fitness was evidenced in that reserves were hardly called upon to play in the first team and promotion was assured from a relatively early stage in the New Year. Villa, wrote Johnston, "had a sound, reliable team, which always gave an impression of mastery over their rivals."[39]

## 1938 tour of Germany

That close season Villa travelled to Germany for what turned out to be a controversial three-match tour. The team played in the same Olimpiastadion where England had routed the Germans 6-3 the day before in a controversial match. Frank Broome, later said of the decision to ask the players to give the Nazi salute: "The dressing room erupted. All the England players were ... totally opposed to [it]."[40] The following day Villa met a combined German XI, however this time it was not a representation from the British Ambassador or the Secretary of the Football Association but Jimmy Hogan himself who – Broome recalls – said "They'll expect you to perform the Nazi salute."[41] Hogan's point was probably based on showing due deference to your hosts, rather than aligning yourself with their politics. Player power, however, dictated that there would be no such thing. Those two resolute Scots, Massie and Cummings, refusing to bow to the pressure the team were under. Even after the match Hogan said that "he would have asked them to go back and give the salute."[42] On the field, Villa gave a demonstration that brought rave reviews from the German News Agency which stated that Villa "played marvellously [and] gave a demonstration ... which was many-sided and elegant."[43] Another German newspaper reported: "The utilisation of advantageous situations with lightning speed ... aroused our enthusiasm time and again."[44] But it was a performance not without some evident bite from Massie, who injured Schmaus in a tackle forcing the German to be removed from the field. In Dusseldorf three days later, against a combined German XI,[45] and in Stuttgart on the 22 May, against a Greater Germany XI,[46] Villa actually did consent to give the salute. The reason being that as Houghton later recalled "... we had a meeting and said that, for peace and quietness we'd give the Nazi salute ..."[47]

That summer in June, at the Annual General Meeting of the club, Rinder gave a self-promotional speech about the decision to bring Hogan to the club. Rinder spoke glowingly about the purpose behind retaining Hogan. "It was not so much a manager we wanted," Rinder said, "in my judgment the directors ought to manage the club and if they are not capable of doing so they ought not to be there. What we wanted is what we got – a man who could teach the players how to play football. It had become the system to get a young player and put him in the first team; if he had the 'guts' he made good; but if not there was nobody to help him. That was what the game was suffering from."[48]

But, peculiarly, under Hogan, Villa had become characterised not by some conveyor belt from the youth team but of a side built around those key imports that had been brought to the clubs in the previous few seasons. For the 1938-39 season, Allen was *still* the centre-half; Iverson and Massie *still* the wing halves; Callaghan and Cummings *still* the reliable backs producing that calm, measured approach while the penalty box was a mass of bodies and flying boots. Yes, it could be said, that Hogan had done away with the lack of security that McMullen had brought to the club by reducing the numbers of players being tried in the first team, but it was a team that harked back to 1935. Would it be good enough for the First Division?

In the first few months of that campaign, the answer to that question was no. By the third week in October (their eleventh match) they had won four times and lost three times and when they welcomed Leicester City to Villa Park, the pressure was starting to affect even the normally reserved Hogan. In the days following the game, he was summoned to appear before the Football League disciplinary committee to answer charges regarding his conduct during that game, which Leicester won 2-1.[49] Hogan had taken it upon himself to enter the referee's room after the match to "[express his] opinion,"[50] infuriated that a Villa player had had his name taken for returning onto the field without a signal from the referee. Hogan's dispute proved that the old proverb will always be true; weak teams always rely on indulgent referees. The FA charged Hogan £5 for the offence which he accepted with good grace but Hogan's ire revealed concerns about the actual quality of the team in the best company. The season was punctuated here and there by minimal success but the crowd was none too convinced that a corner had been turned.[51] There were even doubts whispered as to whether Hogan's coaching methods were ultimately up to much, a *Daily Herald* correspondent taking considerable time before announcing that "the coaching wizardry of Hogan was tried with the seniors, it didn't work ..."[52]

It didn't work in the Cup either, when Villa went out to Ipswich after a replay. The Villans were saved from a home tie defeat[53] when one of their scurrilous players chucked mud at the ball just as Ipswich's Fletcher ran up to the take a penalty. He missed but Hogan was all angelic innocence when declaring "I never saw anything ... I have asked our players about it and they say they observed nothing at all."[54] It was not the best of times at Villa Park, Frank O'Donnell, the England international, had been bitten on the leg by a stray dog whilst playing golf with Starling and Houghton.[55] Worst of all, for Hogan particularly, was the loss of Fred Rinder, who died on Christmas Day 1938. He had been ill for some time previously and

## 1936-1939

his ill-health was mirrored by a particularly bad run of form the previous October when during a run of six games without victory, Villa scored just twice. If Fred Normansell did actually say "I've no time for all these theories about football. Get the ball in the bloody net, that's what I want," (there's no evidence that this comment was ever made) then this is when he would have said it, as the Chairman started to assert himself at the club in anticipation that Rinder's final days were upon us.

But the bad news affecting the club did not stop Hogan leaping onto the nearest soapbox whenever he was within sight of one. "English players[56] play with speed," he said. "Continentals play with their heads."[57] Hogan would have done well to have heeded his own lessons for Continental coaches also 'play' with their heads when spotting decent young talent. Hogan had first recommended Reg Lewis to Arsenal in the February of 1938 during the making of one of those FA coaching films and here he was – the same Reg Lewis – scoring a brace of goals at Highbury ... against Hogan's Aston Villa.[58] What could Hogan do but smile, hold his hands up to the heavens and congratulate George Allison, his opposite number?[59] So there were some pleasant moments but they were few and far between. Against Brentford in the League their performance earned rave reviews: "Hogan's men produced the rarest football of all. Classic, cultured ... every talent, every elementary principle of the game was exploited. Ball along the ground ... subtle positioning ... uncanny-control. In short, science all the way. That was one good reason why the Brentford defence looked even worse than it is ..."[60] but the long and short of it was that there was trouble at t' mill. The rumour of Starling's transfer request rumbled on and suddenly there were question marks about the future of both him and Hogan at the club. Perhaps it was the intention of the Shareholders to place pressure on the Board now that the summit of the First Division had been regained? Perhaps it was more to do with the loss of Hogan's one true ally in the Boardroom, Fred Rinder. Were the Board seeking another manager to lead them onwards? The press remained curious.[61] On 21 February 1939, the *Western Mail* printed the story that the Villa board were denying that Hogan's contract would not be renewed; if there were grounds for discontent with Hogan's methods then the news was kept quiet but for two long months the negotiations carried on until the directors finally presented Hogan with a two-year contract deal on 25 April 1939.[62] It represented a marked relief to Hogan and would give him the springboard to help challenge for title in 1940 and 1941. The outcome of the contract talks were doubly propitious, book-ending a month in which his daughter had married[63] and celebrated news of the contract with another summer at chief instructor for the Football Association at their July course.[64] He was now 67 years old but still in fine fettle. Prior to the course, he told the press that there were thirteen ways to trap a ball and went about expertly demonstrating each and every one of them to the cohort looking on:

> With the sole; With the inside of the foot With the outside of the foot; Trapping and passing at the same time; With the shin; With the inside of the foot on the turn; With the outside of the leg; With the thigh; With the stomach; With the chest; With the head; Taking pass from behind with the right foot kicking forward; and, Pulled down from the volley.

It seemed a splendid way to spend the summer playing nothing but football outside in the peaceful July sunshine but there were growing concerns about the international situation in Europe. In early August, hope for peace was winning out, youngsters had convened at Villa's training ground in preparation for the 1939-40 season but Hogan's mind was elsewhere.[65] His son, Jimmy jnr., was recovering from an injury in Southern France[66] and back in Birmingham he had concerns regarding the Villa centre-forward, Albert Kerr, who was suffering from some form of malady which would result in him collapsing after every game.[67] The matter had still not been resolved when news came that following Hitler's decision to invade Poland that a state of war existed between this country and Germany. Once again the future was thrown into doubt by conflict. In the spring of 1939, Hogan's next two years had been assured and a pathway set out for him. Now in October he would be joining the likes of George Jobey, Scott Duncan and Jack English, all coaches of repute, as one of the great unwashed.[68]

# 1936-1939

## Notes

1 Previously captain of the Wembley Wizards.
2 Peter Morris, *Aston Villa* (Naldrett Press, 1961), p. 150.
3 *Ibid.*, 152.
4 McMullen was sacked on 28 October 1935.
5 *Ibid.*, 154.
6 They would concede 110 goals in total that season.
7 It is ironic that that same season Frank Barson was leading the Villa juniors to three junior titles.
8 Margaret Hogan would die on 23 May 1936, and her place within the community was such that the mass requiem held on 27 May was reported in the *Burnley Express* which carried her obituary. Hogan was represented by a "beautiful floral wreath." *Burnley Express*, 30 May 1936.
9 13 May 1936.
10 *Leeds Mercury*, 7 July 1936.
11 18 July 1936.
12 *Evening Despatch*, 2-4 July 1936.
13 *Evening Despatch*, 15 August 1936.
14 The Olympic report refers to one Austrian being kicked, regardless of what Hogan reported.
15 *Sheffield Telegraph*, 11 August 1936; interviewed by Capel-Kirby.
16 *Official Report of 1936 Olympic Games*, 1048.
17 8.8 – 2-4 v Peru 2-0 h/t; 2-2 f/t. There are two versions of events firstly in last fifteen minutes spectators ran on pitch attacked Austrian players and scored "in the chaos." Secondly, spectators ran onto the field in the 119th minute, one minute before the end after Villaneuva's second (Peru's fourth goal). Werginz 22' Steinmetz 36' [Alcalde 75' and Villanueva 81'] E.Kainberger(cap) - Kargl, Kunz - Krenn, Wallmuller, Hofmeister - Werginz, Laudon, Steinmetz, Kitzmuller, Fuchsberger.
18 The terms of his contract were revealed by the *Nottingham Evening Post* on 21 August 1936. They stated that Hogan had signed a seven-year deal worth £1,500 p.a.
19 *Evening Despatch*, 14 August 1936.
20 *Ibid.*
21 *Evening Despatch*, 15 August 1936.
22 Throughout the season Hogan helped the press with a smattering of views and news – commenting on introducing new footballs every fifteen minutes to reduce the risk of head injuries (November 1936) and giving a speech regarding the way the game was heading and showing off his physical fitness (February 1937).
23 *Evening Despatch*, 20 August 1936.
24 9 September 1936.
25 14 October 1936.
26 From Austria – at this time – came the news that Hugo Meisl had died on 17 February 1937.
27 W. M. Johnston, *The Football League: the Competitions of Season 1937-38* (Association of Football Statisticians, 1984), p. 85.
28 Morris, 176.
29 *Ibid.*, 175.
30 The match was played on 11 December 1937.
31 *Utrechtsvolksblad: sociaal-democratischdagblad*, 29 September 1938.
32 The FA – under Stanley Rous – were happy to bring Hogan into their developmental programmes at various opportunities at the time. In February 1938 he was asked to assist in the preparation of a coaching film. It was on that occasion that he first saw young Reg Lewis,

who Hogan recommended heartily to George Allison at Arsenal and then, later, regretted his stupidity in handing a young starlet over to a major rival.

33 This was the tactical idea that Meisl had discussed with the Viennese journalists at the Ring cafe in Vienna.

34 *Utrechtsvolksblad*, 29 September 1938.

35 On 12 February 1939, the *People*'s correspondent wrote that after Hogan had dropped Martin back to the reserves and used his physical culture instructor to get him back into shape that the "Result now is that Martin is a stone heavier and has an increased chest expansion of five inches. And what a ball player! Here's one who will play for England or I'm a blue blooded Rumanian." Meanwhile Brentford spent £18,000 on purchasing Cheetham, Boulter and Gorman in order to save themselves from the drop.

36 All these alternative ideas – bar that outlined by Bullock - were set out by Norman Creek in *Association Football*, printed in the Autumn of 1937. For more information about Bury in the 1930s see George Raynor, *The Greatest Coach England Never Had* (History Press, 2014).

37 Morris, 175.

38 *Gloucestershire Echo*, 25 March 1938.

39 Johnston, 84.

40 Rogan Taylor & Andrew Ward, *Kicking and Screaming: an oral history of football in England* (Robson Books, 1998).

41 German Select XI: Raftl – Streitle, Schmaus – Wagner, Mock, Skoumal – Hahnemann, Stroh, Binder ('43), Jerusalem, Neumar. Ten of them were Austrians; second goalscorer not recorded. Villa: Biddlestone - Callaghan, Cummings – Massie, Allen, Iverson – Broome ('6, '30), Haycock, Shell ('67), Starling and Houghton.

42 *Sunderland Daily Echo*, 18 May 1938.

43 http://www.birminghammail.co.uk/sport/football/football-news/great-games-german-select-x1-181054

44 *Ibid*.

45 Villa lost 2-1.

46 Villa: Carey - Callaghan, Cummings – Massie, Allen, Iverson – Kerr, Haycock, Shell, Starling and Houghton. Won 2-1.

47 Taylor & Ward.

48 Acknowledgement to John Lerwill.

49 Fox mistakenly reports this as taking place in October 1937.

50 Fox, 149.

51 The average attendance being 6,000 down on the previous season.

52 *Daily Herald*, 23 December 1953.

53 7 January 1939, 1-1.

54 *Coventry Evening Telegraph*, 9 January 1939.

55 *Northern Daily Mail*, 13 December 1938.

56 It depended on who was English. Fred Haycock was wanted by the Irish FA to play for Ireland. Hogan sent them the depressing news. Haycock was English. *Evening Despatch*, 27 February 1939.

57 Speech at Stourbridge, *Birmingham Mail*, 31 January 1939.

58 4 February 1939.

59 Perhaps that would explain why in late February the *Mirror* revealed that Hogan was wearing a charm from his wife to keep a 'flu bug away from the Villa players. He didn't want bad news affecting the club and denied that Ronnie Starling had put in a transfer request.

60 *People*, 12 February 1939.

61 In the *Daily Mirror*, 4 Feb 1939, Hogan was quoted as saying "I am living the greatest years of my life, Villa management and players alike have always treated me like true sportsmen."

62 *Daily Mirror*, 26 April 1939.

63 10 April 1939 at St Augustine's Church, a ceremony in which Jimmy Murphy also attended. *Birmingham Daily Gazette*.

## 1936-1939

64 11 July 1939. Portsmouth's captain Jimmy Guthrie (who had led Pompey to their FA Cup success that season) would be seriously injured during the course. The injury hastened the end of his playing career.
65 *Daily Herald*, 9 August 1939.
66 *Birmingham Daily Gazette*, 19 August 1939.
67 *Daily Mirror*, 24 August 1939.
68 *Sheffield Evening Telegraph*, 3 October 1939.

Jimmy Hogan

## SIXTEEN

## 1939-1945
'The proof of the pudding being in the eating of it.'

The war and Villa's decision to suspend his contract forced Jimmy Hogan to return to Europe when he otherwise had no intention of doing so. Hogan, like a lot of people within the football business, was left kicking his heels for a while because, given the uncertainty of the times, Football League clubs could not issue direct contracts. Villa's ground was closed by order of the Home Office and so Hogan took his leave of Birmingham and moved south finally ending up at 39 Pendine Avenue in Worthing on the Sussex coast. Worthing, like Brighton in thos days, attracted those retirees seeking the quiet life. If that was Hogan's intention then he could not have made a worse decision. In lieu of a possible invasion and the understanding that the first battle ground would be fought across the skies over the Channel and along the coast, one would have thought there were safer places to lick ones wounds, but that's where Hogan lived out the winter of 1939. Even then his recalcitrant nature saw to it that before the excitement of wandering down to the Brighton Road to see the waves started to ebb he would be off seeking more work. And so in the early part of 1940 he contacted Stanley Rous to see whether there was a role he could undertake as a physical training instructor. Rous, however, referred him to the Entertainments' National Service Association (ENSA) who had made a special request to the Football Association.[1]

The purposes of the ENSA are self-explanatory and are more commonly associated with costume shows and plays put on to entertain troops overseas. In the early part of the 1940, the ENSA were notified that a very strong French Air Force team wished to play a match against the RAF. The French had already staged a match against the far stronger British Army team, which was of international standard. Therefore the ENSA contacted the FA to see if a coach could be sent "somewhere in France" to assist in organising a coaching programme so that a competitive RAF XI could be gathered, trained and give the French a good game. Hogan was flown out to France in March 1940,[2] provisionally to oversee a series of trials which would lead to a fixture between possibles and probables on 24 March but he was also charged with organising and presenting a series of lectures to members of the British Expeditionary Force (BEF).[3] As matters

## Jimmy Hogan

transpired, the French fixture that should have been held on 31 March in Paris never actually took place. It was rescheduled for the 21 June 1940 but by that stage the Germans were already goose-stepping along the Champs Elysée. What the postponement did bring about was an extended eleven-week stay within France for Jimmy Hogan which comprised lectures and demonstrations amongst the billeted staff.

In the April, while lecturing some of the troops who were on stand-by, the siren called out and when the troops returned Hogan said he hoped they had seen to their duties. "Aye," said one Lancastrian, "mind tha' [allow] time for interooption, Mister Hoogan."[4] In those eleven weeks, Hogan worked out that he lectured to over 4,500 troops, during one of which one wag made a fair point after Hogan informed the gathering that they must keep the ball on the carpet: "but what happens if you come to a ground and they haven't got any carpet?"[5] But jokes aside, things were becoming hairy. Over the border the Germans were massing for attack and in May, the Low Lands fell in spectacularly quick fashion. Within days they had invaded France, and Hogan and all the British troops now found themselves in occupied land. He had already had a narrow escape when a lecture he was giving to 250 men was halted while the area was dive-bombed and machine-gunned by a passing squadron. He displayed that war-weary resilience when another set of fliers tried to intimidate a match he was refereeing in front of small contingent of service personnel for the match passed off without "interooption." But now with the Germans getting close enough that his hotel had been decimated it was decided that he be shuffled in amongst those troops to be evacuated back to Blighty. Initially he stayed in London picking up some paid work there but then moved back down to Worthing, fearful of the London Blitz that was gathering pace. It was not the most astute moves one could make because Worthing was directly under the flight path of the German bombers heading to London from the airfields in France and became a dumping ground for any of their left-over bombs so in October 1940 he and Evelyn returned to Burnley to stay with his sister, Kathleen.[6]

He stayed in Burnley for Christmas and in January, at St Mary's Assembly room, Yorkshire Street, Burnley, entertained some members of his late mother's congregation, when giving another of his lectures entitled "Fifty years of football at home and abroad."[7] It did not pass his notice that the male contingent in the town had been sent overseas to fight the good fight. "He introduced quite a great deal of humour," wrote the *Express'* correspondent "to entertain the many women-folk." He followed this with many interesting demonstrations, thanks to assistance from a number of St Mary's schoolboys with whom he had carried out detailed rehearsals.

One of those who had been posted overseas was his son, Joseph, who had been sent to the Middle-East and led men in battle after achieving the rank of Sergeant. In August 1942, Hogan was informed by the War Office that Joseph had been taken prisoner by the Germans and was being held in Italy where he would serve out his sentence for the duration of the conflict.[8] Hogan did his bit to maintain morale but one could not help thinking that he seemed to be frustrated by the lassitude caused by the war. The lectures revealed a mind still busily fretting over a way to win football matches, as if he was at a post-match news conference; that the war was simply a distraction. "With the destructive centre half-back game today it was very difficult to get through down the middle but if the winger could draw the backs to the [side] line[,] gaps would be created in the defence." He went on to explain why he was so successful at Villa. I know "the wing game rather than down the middle was the better policy in attack."[9] Typically he ended the lectures with one of his demonstrations, introducing the segment with a told-you-so anecdote. "When [I returned from working on the continent and] showed how the ball could be killed with every part of the body [I] was laughed at, but [in the end] everyone ... followed suit, the proof of the pudding being in the eating of it." He would re-join the ENSA lecture circuit around Britain in the April of 1944, producing gasps of astonishment from gathered audiences that someone at the age of 61 could be so physical strong, so enthusiastic in his outlook.[10] One soldier wrote to the *Liverpool Echo* from "a destination unknown": "For two hours he kept us enthralled. You ought to see him skip with a rope and his amazing agility and command of the ball. The thing that he emphasised throughout was 'constructive and intelligent football' as opposed to big kicking. He showed every possible kick with either foot and twelve different ways of trapping the ball while his heading was amazing."[11]

In the late autumn of 1945, Hogan came back into the wider public consciousness as a result of the arrival of the Soviet's Dynamo Moscow team. On the eve of the tour Hogan was asked to write a comment piece in the *Daily Dispatch* but he revealed a bitterness for British football when he did so. "We ... have thrown our constructive and intelligent football aside," wrote Hogan. "Gone are the days when the ball went from man to man ... we taught the world how to do these things and then flung them away as if they were scrap."[12] The Soviets would create huge interest during their matches, displaying an attitude that seemed at odds with how football should be played. They presented bouquets to their opponents on the field at Chelsea, while wearing white trim on their shorts. Their training session at Craven Cottage the day before the game and had been so lackadaisical that one reporter claimed "you can almost hear them think."[13] But their

# Jimmy Hogan

play, their combination movements the next day was remarkable and placed the play of the Chelsea side in sharp relief. "From first to last, their football remained cogent and incisive, a triumph of socialism over individualism, for the ball was never held by one man, but transferred bewilderingly and immediately to another."[14]

Hogan indulged himself once the war was over. The return to normality opened the door for various opportunities to come his way. In June of 1946 Hogan accepted an invitation to attend a two-week coaching course in Rheims, north-east France as chief instructor for the French FA (FFF) as the French sought to replicate the FA's own course.[15] The *Burnley Express* reported that he declared the course "a most impressive experience." A cohort of seventy players had been gathered from the cities, regions and Algeria and were representative of all levels. It was his first experience of North African football, within a year he would be visiting plague-ridden Oran in Algeria to coach local youths there on behalf of the FFF. The French course was incredibly intensive, instruction each morning, notation in the afternoon, and an exam at the end of the course. The students were tested on the Laws of the Game, on positioning. The top pupil was Jean-Claude Samuel, the right half who had played against England in 1945. When he arrived back in an England still suffering from strict rationing the reporter let go a clue as to where his real interest lay. Yes, very interesting about the course but what was the food like? There was no milk, substitute coffee, but, said Hogan, saving the best to last "plenty of fruit, with delicious apricots and peaches at 1s 3d a pound."

Hogan had been expectant that Villa would renew their association with him, but the call never came. As a result, he was to take up a series of piecemeal roles starting in the July of 1946 when Harry Warren contacted him to see if he would assist in training the lads prior to the start of the first postwar season in the Football League, Hogan accepted. Hogan, who had first met Warren at the FA's Coaching Courses, was more than happy to oblige, taking up his post in the third week in August.[16] At the time Hogan had been in discussion with the owners of the *Daily Dispatch* newspaper who saw Hogan as being the perfect promotional vehicle for them and paid for him to conduct a nationwide tour.[17]

In the October he gave a speech at St Mary's Youth Club where in front of 200 people, including Cliff Britton, the prince of half-backs, and some of the Burnley players he explained that football "was a game of constructive and intelligent movement," he said. "I have no time for aimless and haphazard football," for he went on to say "the greatest mistake was to kick to a colleague who was 'marked'. I appeal to you all to play the game and stress the great need for good positional play. Wing play always provided greater dividends than down the middle play. Constructive wing play would always succeed over massed attack."[18] He demonstrated the art of heading, passing and shooting, and dwelt especially on ball control and body balance and backed this up with the statement that "to acquire perfect football poise was the greatest asset any player could hope to achieve."  He felt disappointed by the rejection by Villa and engaged in applying for any managerial jobs that were in the offing. In November the *Dundee Evening Telegraph* informed its readers that Hogan was in the running to become coach of Third Lanark but like his expectations regarding that Villa phone call, it came to nothing.[19]

# Jimmy Hogan

### Notes

1 ENSA was set up in 1939 to provide entertainment for the Armed Services during the War.
2 *Birmingham Daily Gazette*, 8 March 1940. He arrived on 9 March 1940.
3 *Sports Argus*, 9 March 1940.
4 *Coventry Evening Telegraph,* 18 April 1940.
5 Brian Glanville, *Football Memories* (Virgin Books, 1999), p. 98.
6 *Burnley Express*, 5 October 1940.
7 *Burnley Express*, 22 January 1941.
8 *Burnley Express*, 29 August 1942. He wasn't to return back to Blighty until 20 June 1945.
9 *Burnley Express*, 14 April 1943, speech given for the Burnley Rotarians.
10 In August he even went to the Orkneys, *Sunday Post*, 2 August 1944. In the same month it was reported that a Sergeant Major in the German Medical Corps had broken cover to surrender to British troops. "Don't shoot. I know Jimmy Hogan," he was reported to have said. *Liverpool Echo*, 14 August 1944.
11 *Liverpool Echo*, 2 August 1944.
12 *Daily Dispatch*, 20 November 1945.
13 *Soccer Nemesis*, 105.
14 *Ibid.*, 107.
15 *Burnley Express*, 29 June 1946.
16 *Lincolnshire Echo*, 15 July 1946. The period would be from 12-22 August 1946.
17 *Shipley Times & Express*, 18 September 1946.
18 *Burnley Express*, 5 October 1946.
19 Alongside Jimmy McMullan and John McMenemy. *Dundee Evening Telegraph*, 26 November 1946.

## SEVENTEEN

## 1947-1948
'There was resistance.'

There is a belief, widely shared amongst football historians, that the immediate postwar years represent the dark age of English football, that the famous defeats England suffered in the 1950s, to the United States, to the Hungarians and to the Swedes, were a result of an aversion to new ideas. Of this age, Bob Ferrier famously wrote " ... there was resistance to the very fact of having an England team manager, there was resistance to pre-match training sessions, there was resistance to the whole, new ambitious Football Association plan for a national coaching programme."[1] Brian Glanville, writing in 1955, felt that the problem was more social than structural, that the desire to get something for nothing became all-pervasive. There was "a new attitude among British footballers who, since the [Second] War, have been far less willing to work at the game ... than they were in the pre-war years."[2] Be that as it may, there were tiny shoots of green in the postwar game; they were there - you just had to look to find them.

Here and there one could see changes taking place, small changes at first that ushered in the shock of the new. Lawton's noisy complaint about his appearance fee compared to the size of the Wembley crowd during a wartime international was one.[3] Such an open comment, the fact that it was even reported, represented a deviation from what had gone before. It was a step toward an environment in which views previously wardrobed were now being openly discussed. A new generation was coming of age, and a generation who were not averse to trialling new approaches. The problem was not that there was no innovation. It was that what innovation existed was not gaining enough support to overcome the prevailing culture of reticence. That there were green shoots of innovation was as a result of a number of factors. The first that Chapman's WM was, by 1945, so long in the tooth that alternatives had to find favour. Secondly the postwar climate encouraged new thought and new approaches to everything in much the same way that changes were encouraged in the 1920s. In this matter, people, quite naturally, wanted a new world and to populate that world with new ideas and thought and old ways of doing things were gently being nudged out of the way. Thirdly, British people *were* responsive and aware of

## Jimmy Hogan

the challenge that was being posed by those outside of these islands. This had come about not only as a result of club tours of Britain after the war, by Dynamo Moscow and Norrköping being notable examples, but also as a result of players within the Armed Services seeing different ways of doing things in other parts of the world. But, perhaps, the most significant factor was the decision of the Football Association by offering professional footballers as Physical Training Instructors to support the war effort. This created a surfeit of early "coaches" within the British game in 1945 and in order to take up the slack of numbers being without work in Britain, the FA farmed these players out to Europe in those immediate postwar days.[4] One of those exports, famously, was George Raynor, arriving on the quayside in Gothenburg in 1946 and went on to become the finest coach we (never) had.

At this Hogan was finding piecemeal work where he could get it, and the feeling was that at the age of 64 it was likely that he had worked his last job. He spent the winter of 1946 and the early part of 1947 with Evelyn in Blackheath, South London where he stayed with Joseph and Frank. Evelyn had been ill for a time over Christmas and it was felt that rather than take the unnecessary journey up to Burnley that she should remain in South London until she was fit enough to travel north again. It was spring by the time she joined Jimmy at 119 Brunshaw Road but she then fell ill again in early March. She seemed to have recovered, relapsed and then died suddenly on the 24 March 1947. Like her step-mother, Evelyn had become a devout practitioner at St. Mary's, a church where her requiem mass was held that month. The effect of losing his wife of 35 years on the 64-year-old Hogan was, understandably, devastating. It seemed only right and proper that he should spend more time with his children and so Hogan went back to Blackheath to stay with his children, going into mourning for the best part of the summer and excluding himself from public life. He emerged from the other side, with typical resilience, by simply immersing himself in looking for more work. London seemed a better bet than Lancashire at that time and, through the grapevine, he heard that struggling Brentford were in need of a coach. The Brentford manager at the time was Harry Curtis. Secretary-manager since May 1926 and a Football League referee before this, Curtis had always deferred to an assistant coach when leading the side. In the 1920s he had brought Bob Kane with him from Gillingham and later appointed Jimmy Bain, his former centre-half, to sit alongside him. Curtis' real forte was knowing where his strength lay. He conducted exemplary business in the transfer market throughout his stay at Griffin Park, buying players to suit the tactical system that he worked out with the club coach.[5] And he had a good eye for who would make the best coach. Malcolm McDonald who had been a Celtic player in the 1930s and a first team regular was retained as a coach at the club, finally working under Jackie Gibbons. When Ron Greenwood was at Brentford he recalled McDonald saying to him "... if you want to do something and you've got the confidence, then do it. If you haven't, don't! It's your judgment that matters."[6] It was not just a load of hot air ether, Greenwood recalled seeing McDonald on more than one occasion trap the ball on the goal-line before selecting his pass to clear the danger, but the lesson about having that confidence and then quickly deciding on what action to take would play a key role in the make-up of the tactics employed by Greenwood at West Ham in the 1960s. McDonald would happily buy into the practices that Jimmy Hogan instituted when he worked at Brentford to such a degree that he was found to be still "religiously carrying out the coaching routine as laid down by [Hogan]" after Jimmy had left to join Celtic.[7] Another ex-Celtic player, George Paterson, was also retained by Curtis as youth team coach.

This system, of Curtis managing and the coaches coaching, had kept Brentford in the First Division prior to the War but things had moved on and in May 1946, the club was relegated and they now found themselves up against some of the biggest club sides in the country, the likes of Spurs, Sheffield Wednesday, West Brom and Newcastle all now fighting to get their place back in the First Division. Relegation from the First Division had signalled a series of wholesale changes at the club. Fourteen players left Griffin Park in the summer of 1947 and as much as £20,000 was spent on five new players. That investment, designed to secure an immediate challenge for the Second Division title, was seen to be a complete waste when in their first three matches they had not recorded a single point, had scored but one goal and sat at the foot of the table. Perhaps the purchase of the four players was uppermost in the mind of the programme editor at Griffin Park when he wrote: "The fees being asked for some players, not in the international class either, almost make one's hair stand on end, and although [Brentford] is prepared to buy," wrote "Busy Bee." "There has got to be wisdom behind further expenditure."[8] The club's problem was that now they had these new players there seemed no cohesion and little defensive shape. Brentford "[were] at the foot of the ... table without a point in their locker [and had] an adverse goal average of 1-16."[9]

On the 3 September they travelled to Luton Town, got thumped 3-0 and the same day Jimmy Hogan happily put pen to paper to become team coach. Signs at the club offered a stark warning as to the task in front of him. "The pitch ..." wrote Ron Greenwood years later, "was a notorious mud-heap ... there were times when the only visible grass was on the wings and along the goal-lines."[10] Hogan, unfazed, said "my methods will be the proper ones to get this team back to the First Division."[11] He remained guarded as to what methods would be employed but given his previous tactical musings you could be sure that the grass would soon disappear on those wings and accordingly, the club's fortunes rose, buoyed by a smart piece of work Curtis conducted in the transfer market. He did a straight swap when offering half-back Toulouse to Spurs for half-back Chisholm and from that moment on, the club started to exhibit a better defensive attitude. Where defeats were incurred they were done so by the odd goal and victories up to the middle of December saw the club raise themselves away from the bottom but one problem that was not solved was a lack of attacking bite. Brentford failed to score in sixteen League matches that season and their out and out striker, Jackie Gibbons, had come up with a grand total of four goals by the first day in 1947. This was a galling half-season total, especially since Gibbons had come from Bradford Park Avenue that summer on the back of scoring a goal every two games.

Perhaps Chisholm gave the side a bit more stability; they certainly scored more goals with him around but by and large it was a season that went mid-table nowhere for the Griffin Park side. And Hogan's impact in West London was hardly a profound one when the dust had settled.

# 1947-1948

## Notes

1 Bob Ferrier, *Soccer Partnership* (William Heinemann, 1960)
2 *Soccer Nemesis*, 119
3 England v Scotland, 168.
4 Even as late as 1950 the FA stated: "Since 1945 the demand for British coaches in foreign countries has grown rapidly, and the trickle has become a steady flow. Most of the requests for coaches are now handled by the FA and their records show that during the last five years at least a hundred coaches have gone out from this country to all parts of the world. At present at least fifty are working overseas. (*FA Yearbook*, 1950-1, p. 18.)
5 *News from the Hive*, 10 September 1947. "[Hogan] was given 'complete control of the playing side of the Club."
6 Ron Greenwood, *Yours Sincerely* (Collins, 1984), 122.
7 *Sunday Post*, 10 April 1949.
8 *News from the Hive*, 10 September 1947.
9 *Notes from the Hive*, programme notes Brentford FC, 10 September 1947 – with thanks to Mark Chapman.
10 *Yours Sincerely*, 123.
11 *Burnley Express*, 6 September 1947.

Jimmy Hogan

## EIGHTEEN

## 1948-1950
'People might scoff at the idea of an Englishman coming north to coach the Scots.'

Great football clubs with a glorious history have a tendency to be defined and restrained by that history in equal measure.[1] Such was the case with Glasgow Celtic Football Club in the years following the Second World War. They were and are a giant club within the game but that alone does not guarantee success in each season's Championship and whereas before the War they had the makings of a great side, the conflict had derailed their train and led to them experiencing a bleak period in the post war years. It hard to believe these days, but during 1947-48 the club were in such serious decline that it was likely, at one point, that they would be relegated from the top flight.

The problem that had brought this about was systematic. The club benefited from the favourable position of being the go-to club for a lot of the Glaswegian youth which obviated the need for an expensive transfer policy to be implemented. But it was a policy that was in serious need of overhaul. While Celtic pursued a no-transfer policy, that is not buying star players and existing on a diet of progressing young players through the ranks into the first team, opponents in the Scottish League had no such qualms bringing outsiders in to boost their club's chances in the race for silverware.[2] That situation was compounded further in the February of 1946 when the club's great inside-forward, Jimmy Delaney, left Glasgow to join Matt Busby's Manchester United.[3] As a result of the concerns Bob Kelly was elected as Chairman of the Board that spring armed with the responsibility to reverse the declining trend experienced by the club.

History would judge Kelly as a controversial figure but one who was headstrong and a canny operator, devoted to the fortunes of his club and one who understood the importance of the institution of Celtic Football Club within the Scottish game and at times used this when standing down the SFA. As such he was the perfect individual to set about challenging and dismantling that culture of self-sufficiency that was suffocating the club. Kelly's view was that new players must be brought in; indeed a new relationship with the outside footballing world must be forged if Celtic were to once again place themselves on an equal footing with their cross-town rivals and those of the great Edinburgh clubs. But the immediate transitional period would be a painful one before significant changes would be implemented. It would take a long journey for Kelly to rid Celtic of the institutional toxins that were afflicting the club. We can see that with the problems that assailed the club in 1946-47 season.

At the start of the 1947-48 season a defeat to Third Lanark led to an outpouring of public anger directed at the club management. Celtic's irate fans were clearly not going to silently hunker down to watch the club fall apart. A last match victory over Dundee[4] ensured survival[5] just above the relegation zone, and that was the moment when Kelly declared that enough was enough. In June 1948 he was responsible for two purchases that were both to have a positive long-term effect on his club and on the wider British game. During that summer he journeyed down to Brentford to meet up with Malcolm McDonald, George Paterson and Jimmy Hogan and convinced the latter that Hogan's proper calling was to help Celtic Football Club. Hogan accepted the offer without much ado.[6] However, the news that the club had picked an Englishman, regardless of his Irish Catholic background, to lead the training of the famous Glaswegian club did not go down too well with the Parkhead faithful. After a season of despair the arrival of Hogan seemed yet another step in the wrong direction; a sign that the proud traditions of the club were being betrayed by Kelly. Indeed it was almost incomprehensible that an Englishman could come north to teach and lecture the Scots about *their* game. The situation was bad enough for the club and Hogan to be forced to big up Hogan's Scottish affinities in the local press with Hogan issuing a statement that he was coming 'hame', that he considered himself a Scot by association with his ex-colleagues.[7] But Kelly, and Hogan, had supporters in the press and organised a campaign to win over the doubters. Jack Harkness, (a Wembley Wizard, no less) writing at that time for the *Sunday Post* expressed open support for the move in his influential column: "People might scoff at the idea of an Englishman coming north to coach the Scots," wrote Harkness, "But ponder on this. Recently in Paris, I saw a black man from French Africa[8] give an object lesson in inside-forward play to a Scottish international team.[9] The more Jimmy Hogan's we have amongst our teams, the less chance there'll be of that happening again."

At the time that contract was being signed the club's manager, the famous Jimmy McGrory, was in Ulster to invest the sale price of Delaney in securing three of Belfast Celtic's players.[10] Jones and Currie, centre-forward and centre-half, have by and large been lost to history[11] but it was the third person a quiet, shy, reticent Belfast man called Charles Patrick Tully that caught the imagination. An inside-left of supreme ability, Tully's place at

## 1948-1950

Paradise was assured thanks to a dazzling performance over Rangers in the Scottish League Cup[12] in one of his earliest games for the club. "If I say I was superb then I'm not exaggerating," wrote Tully later.[13] He mesmerised the foe, bedazzled the terrace faithful and, momentarily, kick-started a bizarre craze for Tully-inspired merchandise. Collectively, these factors catapulted the Irishman into a sphere of self-regard at which he felt untouchable. Not only was Hogan experienced in managing such big egos, having encountered Imre Schlosser in the 1910s and György Orth in 1925 but he welcomed the type of player Tully was because Tully made it very clear that he was not at Celtic Park to run countless laps around the pitch in order to improve his ball-skills.[14] It was only natural therefore that he would find purpose when working with Jimmy Hogan when training and the two quickly became compatible. Tully wanted the ball to train with, Hogan was more than happy to let him have it. From Hogan's point of view Tully's arrival was fantastic for a couple of reasons. Firstly, like Orth and Braun, Tully's skills helped convince the others of the benefits of Hogan's training activities. Secondly, because both Hogan and Tully were new to the club there was no sense of having to wean Tully off ideas that the previous coach had embedded in him. That still did not stop Tully from realising what he was letting himself in for when it came to being coached under Hogan: "… We got the surprise of our lives when [Hogan] turned up [as our new coach] … he promptly doubled our schedule. We got all the ball play we needed but we still had to do our programme of lapping and stamina building exercises. Suddenly all the slackness stopped. Jimmy Hogan was here for a purpose. … After the first day of his regime, Hogan called us all together, told us what he wanted and what he expected. It looked hard enough on paper, but brother was it murder at first."[15]

Some have argued that Hogan's arrival at the club came too late in his career; that his influence over the more established players was compromised by his frailties and his distaste for being the raging disciplinarian but whereas he was looked on with disdain by some of the senior pros, his influence and way of being with the younger players was profound. The religious devotion that Hogan had always professed to having, now became a key feature of his relationship with his new "lads". The loss of his mother and his wife compounded by the fact that he was now an elderly 65-year-old led to him adopting a series of strange acts. He "carried out a pre-match ritual [which] saw him perform a brief prayer over keeper Willie Miller's hands before he went around the dressing room and – irrespective of the player's religion – used his thumb to mark the sign of the cross on their forehead. Even at a club with Celtic's [religious affiliations] Jimmy's enthusiastic Catholicism was viewed as perhaps a little too ostentatious."[16] He also instituted a pre-match huddle with all the players in the centre of the changing room. It seemed to bemuse rather than inspire but such was the regard within which he was held added to the respect that used to be afforded to the old that the players did not challenge these new conventions. In light of this one would have offered a reasonable sum to have been a fly on the wall as Hogan first addressed the players the day after his introduction to all staff on the links at Uddingston Golf Course. Hogan "gave a speech interspersed with poetry and literary quotes which outlined his vision for the resurrection of this great club." Tommy Docherty, a trainee at the club in those years, explained that Hogan so believed that the players shared his belief in the faith that he was somewhat put out when the players did not follow him to Mass on Sundays, for Hogan had got it into his head that Celtic players must surely be Roman Catholics. However this informed of a deeper issue. Beyond his life at the club, Hogan lived a lonely life in Glasgow with only the game and his religious affiliation now giving him purpose. "Jimmy Hogan was ... in lodgings and we knew he was lonely, so we used to go to the cinema with him, but all we got was football, football, football."[17] But he was acquiring devotees all along the way, teaching the young players about the benefits of playing to a melodic rhythm and so they became more attached to him than distanced: "He used to say football was like a Viennese waltz, a rhapsody. 'One-two-three, one-two-three, pass-move-pass, pass-move-pass.' We were sat there, glued to our seats, because we were so keen to learn."[18]

It was little wonder that 55,270 would turn up on the first Saturday in expectation of the 1948-49 season but they were to go home disappointed when Motherwell claimed a 0-0 draw. There was clearly work to do and it was not helped with the amount of discord within the ranks. Tully and some of the young players were outspoken allies of Hogan,[19] but the other senior players seemed to spend more time sneering than practicing. "It's a bitter joke ... now," wrote Tommy Docherty, "but the established stars [at Celtic] would have nothing to do with [Hogan]. They ignored him. Classed him as some kind of theory-mad [loon]."[20] For those believers in the group, training suddenly became punctuated by phrases such as "keep the high balls low" and "keep the ball on the deck – it won't hurt the grass." There was a focus on technique, passing and movement. To Tully and the young apprentices, such as Docherty, the sound of the kicked ball seemed like a symphony compared to the monotone audio of feet constantly tapping on the cinder track. Practice in which the football played a central role gave purpose and reason to their training and would influence a number of them in their latter careers as coaches. Amongst those who would go on to coach was Jimmy Sirrel, later the high-regarded Notts County manager, who introduced a lively, attacking game with emphasis on wing play at Meadow Lane, tactics that were good enough to take County to the First Division and keep them there. The team appeared to have turned a corner, when Tully ran the show against Rangers in the League Cup, see above, he had already worked out a move with Hogan that he perfected after repeat practice sessions. This would see him put his foot on the ball, invite opponents to win possession off him and then use a side step to move into the space they had vacated.[21] It was a move that plays into the psychology of footballers who feel compelled to commit themselves when they otherwise have no need to. As a child I recall my late brother shouting out "don't commit" when he knew I might rashly make a challenge, so there were ways to counter it that even children could understand. However, by holding possession momentarily, Tully was allowing space to develop naturally in front of him and then he had the skill to go past players who moved toward him to so he was doubly effective in that regard but that simple technique of holding possession and delaying a forward pass, would devastate England when the Hungarians came to London.

It would take time for Hogan's knowledge to be fully inculcated into the way the team operated before the club improved. One example of this was Hogan working with Tully's skilful forward colleague Bobby Evans. Evans had been used in a makeshift forward position for some time before Hogan discussed with him the benefit of moving into the strategically vital role of half-back. It would prove the key transition for the team but it did not come soon enough for the public or the press. "No team has been more disappointing this season than Celtic," wrote the correspondent in the *Dundee Evening Telegraph*. "Great things were expected … but the blend isn't there and drastic changes are the order of the day at Celtic Park for tomorrow's match [with Dundee].[22] Hogan however was too old to be put off by supposed "slow-progress," he knew these things take time and spent the rest of the year consolidating his position as a "father" figure with the younger members of staff, taking them with him on another of his lecture tours as he brought prewar Germany to postwar Glasgow.[23] He gave a series of lectures on behalf of the Celtic Supporters' Association, one of

# Jimmy Hogan

them at St. Joseph's Hall[24] in front of Father McCabe saw him with six of the young staff at Celtic Park (Boden among them) going over his tried and trusted demonstrations. "Celtic," Hogan announced, "will be my last club," and he appeared good to his word when he signed up again for the club upon completion of his year's contract at Celtic.[25]

At the start of the following season, the first XI would be bolstered by the arrival of another young genius in the shape of Bobby Collins,[26] an outside right who had originally intended to play for Everton before the parties fell into dispute over contractual issues. Collins had been schooled by Hogan in the reserves during the 1948-49 season and made his debut in an August 1949 League Cup fixture against Rangers.[27] As debuts went it wasn't a bad way to start, the team exhibiting a confidence that brought thunderous applause from the green section on the terraces. Pat McAuley at left-half mesmerised his opposite number with a bewildering display of twists and dummies and Charlie Tully and outside left Haughney[28] delighted the crowd with their triangular pass and move game."[29] Perhaps these were not moves dictated by Hogan, but the freedom triggered by his training regimes that would otherwise have been denied to the players at other clubs was evidenced in their play that day.

1949-50 was not a successful season by any means but a fifth place finish in the League marked a steady improvement from the calamity that nearly descended the club before Hogan arrived. He would accompany the team on tour short tours, the first to the English West Country where they played Yeovil Town in a friendly in April 1950.[30] Hogan said, when interviewed: "Yeovil have a good team who play straight-forward football." Yeovil boasted two former Celts amongst their playing staff, Joe Rae and George Paterson, but Paterson was known to Hogan as a former staffer at Brentford and of him Hogan stated: "He always played football intelligently and was a gentleman on and off the field." He was informed by Bob Kelly at the end of that season that he would not be required the following year and so, as a final swansong that summer he journeyed with the first team on their short visit to Rome. Lazio were celebrating their 50th anniversary and Celtic had been invited out to play them and the 0-0 draw would be the last match in which Hogan coached Celtic Football Club. Perhaps it was a blessing that he was being let go because the friendly turned into a brawl that was anything but. Bobby Collins later said it was the most vicious game in which he ever played, and John McPhail and a Lazio player were both sent from the field. Hopefully the Papal audience that was granted to both players and officials helped soothed tempers with Hogan writing later: "We were a matter of only a few yards from the Pope. When the Celtic team was announced he looked at us directly and blessed us all."[31]

# 1948-1950

## Notes

1 Acknowledgement to Paul McQuade and Frank Rafters in this chapter.
2 Stanley Matthews played twice for Rangers during the War, helping them beat Partick Thistle 3-0 in the Glasgow Charity Cup final on 31 May 1941.
3 Request for a transfer was publicised on 28 January 1946 (*Dundee Evening Telegraph*); *Aberdeen Press & Journal*. Transfer confirmed 9 February 1946.
4 By the squeakiest of 3-2 victories on 17 April 1948.
5 Other results, it should be stated, did go their way, in the end; meaning that even if the game had been lost they would have retained their position in the First Division. But it showed clearly just how far the club had fallen.
6 27 June 1948.
7 See *Shamrock*, No. 5, p 32.
8 Harkness was referring to Larbi Ben Mbarek, the Moroccan who had first played for France in 1938. Pele, who seems to always have a good word to say about everyone, once said of him: "If I'm the King of Football, Barek is the God."
9 23 May 1948, match played in Paris. France won 3-0.
10 Purchases were confirmed on 28 June 1948.
11 Neither played a first team match for Celtic.
12 Celtic won 3-1 on 25 September 1948.
13 C. P. Tully, *Passed to You* (Stanley Paul, 1958), p. 24.
14 " ... One training day the younger players were wanting a ball out on to the field. Alex Dowdells (the Celtic trainer) refused them and shooed them off to track work. As a parting shot, Tommy Docherty ... shouted at Alex 'Yah! Bet you wouldn't do this if Tully were here.'" (*Passed to You*, 26).
15 *Ibid*.
16 http://www.thecelticwiki.com/page/Hogan,+Jimmy+-+Right+Man,+Wrong+Time
17 *Passed to You*, 22.
18 Quote attributed to Tommy Docherty, *Shamrock*, No. 5, p. 33.
19 A recruit, Alec Boden, would state: "By God, did Jimmy Hogan know football."
20 *Soccer from the Shoulder*, 16.
21 See quote from Johnny Paton, *Shamrock*, No. 5, p. 34.
22 11 February 1949.
23 He also attended Mossend Boys' Guild to present cup with McGrory on 25 November 1949 (*Motherwell Times*).
24 23 April 1949.
25 *Sunday Post*, 15 May 1949.
26 Signed 27 August 1948.
27 Celtic won 3-2. Haughney also made his debut that day.
28 Signed 29 January 1949.
29 http://www.thecelticwiki.com/page/1949-08-13%3A+Celtic+3-2+Rangers,+League+Cup
30 Yeovil won 2-0. *Taunton Courier*, 8 April 1950.
31 *Shamrock*, No. 5, 36.

Jimmy Hogan

# 1951-52

## NINETEEN

## 1951-52
'If only more clubs would dare to experiment with new ideas.'

Jackie Gibbons proved himself to be a suitable, although not a successful, replacement for Curtis. He had high aspirations for Brentford but despite clearly trying his damnedest to get the club back into the First Division never quite managed it. Nevertheless, in the three years that he was at the club he brought in a lot of big brains and was not awed by doing things others were reluctant to try. Off the field, Gibbons had convinced the Griffin Park hierarchy to employ some of the best minds in the game at the time. The quality of the coaching staff that Gibbons believed in was confirmed when Stan Cullis took Charles Reep to Molineux in 1951 and set about devising plans and a team that would be League Champions in the 1950s and challenge Busby's United prior to the Munich disaster.

Gibbons first met Reep during his wartime service in the RAF. Reep, who was a Wing Commander, had been a sportsman of some renown in his younger days but around 1933 his thinking was transformed when Charlie Jones, the Arsenal and Welsh international right-half, presented a lecture to Reep's Squadron at which he set out an overview of Chapman's tactics at Arsenal. Joy, later wrote of those tactics: "The switch from stern defence of their own goal to an eager, red-shirted forward crashing the ball home at the other sometimes took less than ten seconds. It was typically twentieth century: efficient, terse and cold-blooded. There were no frills or fancy work but it was breath-taking in its speed and boldness, and it won matches."[1] The impact on Reep was profound: footballers had always and always will self-reflect, Reep, however, became the first analyst to market himself as such and Gibbons saw the benefit in engaging Reep on that basis in the early part of 1951. At that point, Brentford were near the bottom of the Second Division and Gibbons was open-minded enough to seek Reep's view as to what the team was doing wrong. Reep clearly knew his onions because the fortunes of the club were reversed and Brentford were saved from relegation. The problem for Reep, as is the problem for Spen Whittaker and Sir Frederick Wall in this tale, is that when one historian starts to bad-mouth them, then all others follow like compliant cattle. Particularly scathing criticisms of Reep see him as the inventor of the "long ball," as if kicking the ball "long" is some sort of cardinal sin, but two things are significant in that debate. Firstly, there is nothing wrong

# Jimmy Hogan

with kicking the ball long as long as possession is retained when doing so. A couple of instances support this view. In the 1930s, Alex James kicked the ball long at Arsenal to Bastin or Hulme, revolutionised tactics in football forever and was widely, and rightly, considered an artist in baggy shorts. In the 1970s, Holland's total football team kicked the ball long when required, constructing both goals against Brazil in 1974 "semi-final" in that manner and you would be hard-pressed to find a critic of that team or of those two goals. Secondly, Reep did not necessarily promote the use of the long ball. What he did was record what happens to every possession on the field.[2] He felt, as Raynor and Hogan did, that the long ball can be hugely effective if applied with good reason because it converted defence quickly into attack which was a sure-fire way of creating an attacking opportunity because the opposition defence would not be readily organised. This is simple, basic stuff but for Brentford it returned dramatic dividends against Second Division opponents. In their last fourteen matches, the club they won nine and drew two and furthermore, the club's defence developed into a fine one, which was no doubt related to the fact that the game was being played more in the opposition's half than their own during that run. Reep would surely have built on this early success but because the RAF moved his posting north, Major Buckley was able to secure his services with the Wolves. He was not the only backroom figure at Brentford to make the move to Molineux that year. George Poyser, the youth team coach, was also snapped up by Wolves. That was the reason why Gibbons turned to Hogan to coach the youth team in the summer of 1951.

Gibbons would have happily engaged Hogan with the first team but there was that concern that his presence would have been disputed by the senior pros. Perhaps Gibbons had insight into what the senior professionals at the club would have made of having the old man teaching them how to control a pass and made his thoughts clear with the press at the time of the appointment. 'Brentford's officials realise that matured players are unlikely to benefit from [Hogan's] concentrated coaching but that it can apply the required finish to the malleable youngster."[3] It was not that the first XI did not need coaching, they clearly did and they also clearly had an appetite for the discussion of coaching theories. Two of their number would go on to have a massive say in the way British football developed over the next few decades and yet their relationship with Hogan seems not to have existed at all. Gibbons signed Ron Greenwood, a former team-mate of his, from Bradford Park Avenue and played him alongside Jimmy Hill. Hill would be a leading campaigner for the development of televised football, promoting the use of debate as to effective tactics as a result of his stint as resident analyst with the commercial channel ITV and the state broadcaster, the BBC. Greenwood would go on to coach West Ham United during their greatest spell of success and finally England following the departure of Don Revie. It's rather telling however that when Hill[4] and Greenwood,[5] a chief tactical architect of England's World Cup win, came to write their biographies neither made any mention of encountering or speaking with Jimmy Hogan whatsoever when he was working at Brentford. This is staggering in Greenwood's case, since he became absolutely convinced about the benefits of tactical and technical coaching and also, when he became first England manager in the late 1970s, tried unsuccessfully to institute the old MTK/Hungarian plan of fielding a club side at international level, a plan inextricably linked to Hogan from the 1910s: "It was while I was at Brentford … that my interest in coaching became a passion. … There would always be two quite separate groups of players, each in a different [train] compartment [when we travelled to away matches]. … In [ours] we talked football. Jimmy Hill and I were always in the latter, and we listened to Ted Gaskell, our goalkeeper, and Jackie Goodwin, our outside-right, talking with tremendous enthusiasm about the courses they had attended."[6]

As matters transpired, however, Hogan was placed away from the seniors, made the youth team coach where he encountered the likes of Terry Ledgerton, the outside left, whose performances inspired Hogan to say that he was "one of the brightest prospects I have dealt with in post-war football."[7]

Brentford's 1951-52 season was noteworthy for two events. In December, the *Yorkshire Post* mistakenly, or advertently, gave Hogan credit for Brentford's League position "another glorious tribute to his coaching work"[8] which, thanks to that, and Gibbons' guidance meant that Brentford had only conceded seventeen goals in twenty games. All was sweetness and light, the team were in the mix for promotion, but a defeat to Southampton led to Gibbons giving Greenwood the hair-dryer treatment in front of the rest of the players and the resulting fall-out pitched Greenwood and Jimmy Hill against the club's directors. Hill left for Fulham and Greenwood, much to Hill's surprise, stayed. From that one incident Gibbons' dreams of returning Brentford to higher pastures evaporated and the club have never recovered their First Division place. The second incident came a month earlier, in the November of 1951, when Brentford welcomed the touring Austrian national side, coached by the old *Wunderteam* star, Walter Nausch, in preparation of the match against England at Wembley.[9] Hogan and Nausch, respectively coach and captain of the 1930s side, shared pleasantries in the bright wintry sunshine, looking on as the current generation of Austrian footballers kicked the ball around and yet what they were seeing related back to their collective hey-day. For spraying passes about on the Griffin Park pitch was Ernst Ocwirk, a garage hand from Vienna and one of the finest creative half backs in the history of the game. His control of the ball was complete and he would saunter in that relaxed manner of his and then play a short pass or chip a long ball into the area for players to run onto. The second of these skills was in evidence the following day at Wembley when he controlled a pass on the edge of the defensive third, strolled a few steps to the right and then stroked over a simple twenty-yard lofted pass into the inside right position for the unmarked Melchior to run in and score with a first time shot against England. Compared to that artistry, some of the England players had acquired foreign "skills" alright but they were demonstrated in less aesthetic ways than those expressed by Ockwirk. Tottenham's Eddie Baily winning a penalty with a dive that consisted of a slight nudge on the leg and both arms being thrown to the skies as he dropped like a sack of spuds.

The international ended in a 2-2 draw and the *FA Yearbook* for 1952-53 opined about the Austrian style: "[they] are now playing a wonderful brand of football" and yet all that this "wonderful brand of football" amounted to was the bolt system of defence and a centre-half who had "a roaming mission like an attacking wing-half, and is often joined in the middle of the field by the centre-forward and wingmen as the attack's raiding party."[10] It was made to look good because of England's supposed deficiencies to cope with it, and of those suppositions a case in point was the idea that Billy Wright would be picked as an inside right to counter Ockwirk. Yet when making the cross for Melchior came over, Ockwirk was not being marked or harried at all by England's right half who should have been challenging for the ball. The writer went on "The Austrian type of centre-half is usually an astute ball player, able to join in a bout of close passing and yet ever ready to switch play by means of a long, low pass or a clever lob. Very often the close inter-passing is intended first to make the opposing side chase after the ball, after which a through pass is made to *a forward who slips through the defence almost unnoticed*" [my italics]. There were lessons within what the writer was writing that would come to haunt England in the November of 1953 and which we will come to later but they were lessons that the British had first perfected and, overtime, had forgotten. The writer went on:

> There is now a growing feeling that English football would be all the better and be more entertaining as a spectacle if only more clubs would dare to experiment with new ideas. There is really no dearth of ideas amongst managers and players, especially those who had had to cope with different styles on the Continent and in South America, but the sharp

competition in League football has so far discourages all but a few from trying them out.

You could argue that with his reliance on analysts like Reep and dedicated youth team coaches like Hogan that Gibbons was daring "to experiment with new ideas" but it wasn't getting him anywhere if the prevailing attitude of the influencers in Britain was to carry on doing what they had been doing and expecting a different result. The club were happy to sign Tommy Lawton when he became unhinged at Notts County. Yes, Lawton was a genius or as Greenwood wrote: "He was everybody's idea of what a centre-forward should be. He looked good and he was good"[11] but Lawton and the style of forward play that his qualities encouraged were out of keeping with the circuitous type of game that the Austrians and Hungarians were now playing and had been playing for some years. That was the paradox of the British game, they had excellent, clever players but playing in a way that was easy to read and easy to overcome. The Austrians, much in keeping with the tradition of Sindelar, saw the key position as being Ocwirk at centre-half not a focal point forward like Lawton, but they also saw the benefit of ingenuity when having an inside forward moving forward to run onto a pass opposite to where the British expected him to be. Perhaps the off-the-ball movement appeared foreign but both that concept and that of a centre-half drifting here and there and picking out a short pass or raking one to the wings was as much in keeping with Charlie Roberts in 1908 as it was with John Cameron's Spurs in 1901 and the game we used to play. The article in the *FA Yearbook* therefore disavows the belief that the English believed "themselves to be masters of the football universe. Arrogant and insular ...", as the current FIFA website, even to this day, continues to have it. The British, the players, the spectators, the administrators all knew there was something wrong but "sharp competition in the League football" was overriding all other concerns.[12]

Hogan helped in securing the signature of the James M'Kellar that month from Motherwell, calling in favours from Scottish friendships gained during his stay at Celtic Park but this and Ledgerton were merely highlights during another season of disappointment at Brentford. Money had been invested, players brought in, most notably Tommy Lawton for a club record fee, but there was nothing to show for all this talk of hope and expectation. A top ten finish was not enough to stave off the inevitable and in the summer, the decision was made to limit resources, start cutting the squad size and reduce the head-count, meaning that Hogan found his contract terminated by the Board in May 1952.[13] The club did their best to ensure that no aspersions be cast regarding Hogan. "Jackie Gibbons, the

Brentford manager, said that the directors decided that the wage bill was far too high and cuts had to be made in the size of the staff."[14] This being further confirmed on 17 May: "The directors were full of praise for Hogan … termination 'purely a measure of economy.' "[15] It was a form of public reference, a request from Hogan to save his good name being agreed by the club, an indication that he still felt well enough to continue working at the age of 69.

## 1951-52

### Notes

1 *Soccer Tactics*, 58-9.
2 Acknowledgement to Keith Lyons blog (Clyde Street) for that.
3 *Coventry Evening Telegraph*, 14 July 1951.
4 *The Jimmy Hill Story* (Hodder & Stoughton, 1988); *Striking for Soccer*, (Peter Davis, 1961.)
5 *Yours Sincerely*, (Willow Books, 1984.)
6 *Ibid.*, 127.
7 *Coventry Evening Telegraph*, 1 March 1952.
8 15 December 1951.
9 *Birmingham Daily Gazette*, 26 November 1951.
10 *FA Yearbook*, 1952-53, p. 5.
11 *Yours Sincerely*, 125.
12 *FA Yearbook*, 6.
13 *Northern Whig*, 6 May 1952. It was his decision to terminate the contract.
14 *Birmingham Daily Gazette*, 6 May 1952.
15 *Coventry Evening Telegraph*, 17 May 1952.

# Jimmy Hogan

## TWENTY

## 1952-1959

'You can see how we have learned his lessons.'

In 1952, Hogan entered a period of partial retirement in Burnley, sharing his stays between his sister, Kathleen, at Todmorden Road and Sarah and Fred's home on Burnshaw Road and demonstrated a sense of civic duty by providing presentations to students at Kathleen's school, St Mary's, at youth clubs and to local associations. His fame was perpetuated by the incongruity of his situation for having undertaken football's equivalent of the Grand Tour he was now living in a homely, Lancastrian town and the talks he gave were conducted against a backdrop of post-war austerity and presented to people who, in the main, had known no place but Burnley. His was a lonely figure in immaculate clothing, his only outlet was to talk about football and his career and think about his God.

The European continent could have been three oceans away for all that his audiences knew of the places Hogan had experienced and they were quite happy to forego his views on football if it meant getting an insight into something they had no experience of. But there was an unmistakable sense of reflection in what Hogan was saying; as if he was imprisoned by his past and had not been liberated by it. There was no future vision, just a reversion to things previously done. In February 1953, he gave a speech to the Burnley Young Conservatives about "scientific" football something he had been talking about for years but they would have been more inclined toward his description of Hungary and the Hungarian people he had known, whom he described as "polite" and "proud."[1] In the May, he gave a talk to the St Mary's Youth Club at which he issued his trusted patter: "The game is played on the grass, not in the air," he said.[2] He promoted the use of the space on the field. He called on clubs to use their wingers more, told them to avoid kicking the ball down the middle as if he was talking to a meeting of League chairmen rather than a group of his neighbours and local residents offering their support. That same year, at his sister's school, Hogan gave one of his old music hall "acts" that he had perfected since the 1920s. Kathleen was about to retire after 40 years at St Mary's[3] and he offered himself as a star turn for the children who had no doubt quizzed her on her famous brother. Jimmy Hogan turned up in his old Villa kit and demonstrated his ability to constantly hit a stationary object from a seemingly impossible distance. It was an act good enough to amaze his young audience to the extent that 50 years later one pupil remembered key elements of it. "He placed a bucket all the way at the end of St Mary's School Hall," recalled John Whittaker, "And he then chipped the ball into the bucket ten times out of ten from the other end of the hall. You see professional players these days not even able to control the ball, but Jimmy stamped his foot against the bouncing ball and made it roll back quietly to his foot with the top spin."[4] Reinvigorated by this, Hogan signed another contract with the *Daily Dispatch* to go on yet another lecture tour but like an entertainer or a reformed pop band playing to small crowds in old bingo halls it was hardly a rousing success. Hogan had once wowed a crowd of 2,500 people at Dresden's Exhibition Palace but on one occasion during the tour his sole achievement was convincing a cantankerous, old Welshman that skilful football could be entertaining. It seemed a poor way to bring the curtain down on an illustrious career. Brian Glanville was in attendance that night, and later wrote: "I had been lucky to catch up with Hogan not long before I left for Italy ... he had been giving coaching lessons in London schools, and I attended one of them. There was a scant evening audience of small boys and disgruntled adults. Hogan ... was ... irrepressibly lively and enthusiastic ... He kicked the ball against the same spot on the wall seven times in succession; then the audience finally applauded."[5] That the audience, out for an evening of light entertainment, were disgruntled possibly spoke more about them than Hogan for Britain was still struggling under the yoke of rations and having an old duffer kick a football about a wooden stage with dust sheets for decorations seemed pretty apt as the country stepped toward an uncertain future. And yet once again Hogan would be thrust into the national consciousness within months of that performance.

That autumn, Hogan returned to "big" football. In the September, he went to Stamford Bridge to see Villa play Chelsea and, after the game, met up with Eric Houghton, now Villa's manager but formerly one of the players within Hogan's 1930s team. They had a decent chat together but Hogan would not have been surprised to have heard that Villa appeared to be in the doldrums. Following Rinder's demise, Fred Normansell had considerably strengthened his position as Chairman and seemed to enjoy humiliating his manager. Normansell understood finance but Eric Houghton had played for Aston Villa and England before the War so you would have thought that the Chairman would have left the football side up to someone who knew what they were doing. But the truth was that rather than allow Houghton to boss the playing side and bring in his own men, Normansell got to select the coaches, one being Jimmy Easson, the acerbic ex-Scottish international, who replaced Hubert Bourne. Furthermore, Normansell felt it his responsibility to pick the team at one point inviting club captain Danny Blanchflower up to Normansell's office to help *him* decide who should be in Saturday's team. The whole thing smacked of that postwar hierarchical culture that blighted forward progress and would haunt Villa down the years. "What Villa needed at that time was someone to take the place by the throat and shake some life into it, a good dictator …" wrote Danny Blanchflower,[6] but Houghton was not allowed to be a dictator at all, he was just another of football's gentlemen and he was not being helped by Normansell's insistence on seeing him as an adjunct to the running of the club.

Hogan and Eric Houghton, however, had a strong mutual respect. Houghton later said of Hogan, "I have often blessed the day I met Jimmy Hogan, who taught me so much about the game and about myself," he said. "His methods were simple, 'the easier you make it, the better you will play it'." Hogan, possibly, privately, sympathised with Houghton's plight as manager because he had been there himself. Possibly, as a result of what was going on at the club, Houghton convinced Hogan to come aboard, thereby recruiting a personal ally and one that could easily be sold to Normansell. Perhaps that thought was in Hogan's mind when he sent a letter to the *Sports Argus* in Birmingham to report on the performance of the team against Chelsea for Hogan made sure that he did not criticise the way the club were playing football. "[Villa] always tried to do the right thing with the ball," Hogan wrote. "Moving into open spaces and exploiting the wing game. To me, the latter was the best feature."[7] The report also ensured that a further message was received loud and clear, that "Jimmy [although now 70 years of age] was out of billet at the moment and itching to get back in the game."

But the final decision to bring Hogan back rested with Normansell and that decision took place after the Villa v Army game that was held at Aldershot's ground on 14 October 1953. Normansell invited Hogan over to discuss the offer of youth team coach. Normansell wanted to ensure that Villa would not caught napping as the swing toward youth gathered pace amongst the biggest clubs. That summer, Whelan, Pegg and Edwards had led Manchester United to a stunning FA Youth Cup victory over a Wolves side, led by George Poyser. Normansell and Hogan met in that cosy boardroom they have there at Aldershot and decided over their tea and biscuits that Hogan could undertake the youth role and join Syd Dickinson and Joe Bradford[8] as one of the club scouts. The *Daily Herald*'s reporter spoke to Normansell after the Army fixture and he gave Hogan a ringing endorsement: "I have always considered Hogan to be one of the greatest

# Jimmy Hogan

coaches in the game,"[9] he said and so, on Friday, 16 October 1953, Jimmy Hogan re-joined Aston Villa.[10]

On 31 October, Hogan and Houghton, like a celebrity double act, attended the Morris Commercial Cars Amateur Boxing tournament and handed out prizes to the pugilists.[11] It made good copy and, no doubt, satisfied the corporate social responsibilities of the club but it seemed a strange way to use most qualified members of the Villa staff. The night before, Hogan started his youth coaching role not on a flat field of grass but on the car park tarmac behind the main stand under floodlights designed to ward off would be car thieves. The car park became a cacophony of noise whilst Hogan darted from group to group to oversee each of the different group activities taking place. It was an impossible task for anyone to work effectively in such an environment, least of all a 71-year-old who by rights, should have been managing a team of coaches. But Fred Normansell obviously knew better and the idea was comically played out.

If Villa were misunderstanding Hogan's coaching abilities and what miracles a coach could perform, others were not. A week earlier, England and a team representing FIFA had played out an amazing 4-4 draw at Wembley as the FA celebrated its 90th birthday. England's home record was saved by a late penalty-kick converted by their right-back, Alf Ramsey. The game may have ended in a draw but the performance of FIFA led Clifford Webb, writing in the *Daily Herald*, to refer to Hogan's input as being influential. The match had been played out on a slick wet surface and the England players were to be seen losing their footing on a number of occasions and yet this did not seemed to affect the FIFA players. Why? asked Webb. One reason was because of Hogan's old method of putting sticks in the ground and getting players to weave in and out when running with the ball which improved their balance and poise. Poise was not something that necessarily emanated from running laps around the pitch on training days. Webb told his readers that Hogan had taught players to undertake circuits with the ball as part of his work on the continent. Hogan had also instilled in players the understanding that they must have mastery over the ball to enable them to get out of tight spots in match situations. In the coming days, "The Ranger," Liverpool's anonymous football correspondent, recalled a conversation he had with Hogan during one of the prewar coaching courses at Carnegie. As he went through his repertoire a professional was heard to say "theatrical stuff."

"Maybe," said Hogan, "but mastery over the ball will get a defender out of a tight corner and enable a striker to score when he might otherwise not."[12]

Those party pieces should have been in keeping with what after all was a celebratory event but one professional Webb spoke to revealed a numbing mentality.

"If they try that in a Football League game they would be on the deck in no time."

"I'm afraid," wrote Webb, "it will take a long time for English football to shamble clear of its artisan outlook."[13]

Webb was not the only reporter to note the influence of Hogan that day, another stated that FIFA were "playing to their Hogan type pattern at Wembley."[14] But all this was but a precursor for the bigger game that was to be staged that November, a game that would have lasting implications for the way football was played in this country. Hungary, the reigning Olympic champions, would play England on 25 November in a much-anticipated match and one that would raise Hogan's stock as high as it has ever been held in Britain.

November 1953 was a very tiring month for Jimmy Hogan. As well as his full workload undertaking daily training sessions and scouting forays, in early November, he took charge of a new recruit to Villa Park by the name of Ken O. Roberts, who had made a very young start at Wrexham but had not been able to break through to the first team. The *Argus*'s reporter had stated that Roberts had faults "but nothing Hogan could not cure."[15] A week later Hogan was at Filbert Street, alongside Houghton, watching the Colts beat Leicester 5-3, casting his eye over another young star in the making, Peter McParland.[16] Then on the 21 November he was helping Easson and Roy Chapman present a series of three coaching films to a large audience of young lads at Sutton's Youth Club.[17] The Hungarian match, Hogan was interviewed by the national press. He told them that he had had to turn down an invitation to the Hungarian embassy to dine with the Hungarians post match because he was already pencilled in to train the lads at Villa that evening. On this point some confusion reigned as to what arrangements had been made. Hogan apparently felt miffed that he had not been invited as a guest of the Hungarians to the game to which Sebes said afterwards that they could not invite him since the FA had power over the arrangements. The second was that following the game Hogan felt he would have been invited back to the Embassy and then explained that he was attending a social event on behalf of Villa.[18] Hogan then gave a summary as to what he felt might transpire during the game:

> I'm thinking and hoping that England will win but they must play much better than they did against Ireland or there will be trouble. The British game is more open but if our passing is inaccurate and the Hungarians get

the ball they will dictate the play as a good ball-playing team can. On the other hand, accurate passing with our open game will have them guessing. I'm very glad Sewell is in the team. He's had far more experience than Quixall a good player who's not yet ready for international football. We play with a much harder ball than the Continentals. Theirs is not inflated so much – I'm inclined to agree with them on this point – and when they have to play with the harder English ball they always grumble about it. When these other fellows go on the field they play for the prestige of their country and they play the game of their lives. I wish our lads would give a little bit more of the same spirit. We take it a bit too lightly. But we're a nation of natural footballers. I've given a ball to an English lad of two or three years old and watched him put it down and kick it. I've done the same with a foreign lad and he's just used his hands to play with the ball. Intensive training and coaching, however, have made such an improvement that they are now better manipulators of the ball than we are. They probably yield to coaching better than English players do. I sincerely hope for the prestige of British football that we win. We taught the world football. And we still have the finest players in the world – individually. Whether we win or not depends on the open game, accurate passing and the will to play the game of our lives.[19]

Normansell agreed for Hogan to take a number of the youngsters to London with him to watch the match and so that morning, he travelled down from Villa Park with a small complement of the youth team players, one of whom included Peter McParland, but surprisingly, McParland makes no mention of the game in his autobiography. The game was played out in a fog like atmosphere at Wembley and Hungary, famously, won 6-3. England had, arguably, lost to "foreign" opposition before on English soil but the scale and manner of this defeat to Hungary was definitive. After the game, Sándor Barcs, President of the Hungarian Football Association, was interviewed by the British press. Norman Fox claimed that Barcs told them that "Jimmy Hogan taught us everything we know about football"[20] and a lot of writers have blindly accepted that as read but Barcs never said anything of the sort and it would have made no sense whatsoever if he had. What he actually said to the press was: "Jimmy Hogan taught us what we know of the best British football … you can see how we have learned his lessons."[21] In light of what happened that afternoon, Barcs comment makes sense whereas the comment attributed to him by Fox simply does not. This is because whereas the technical training of the Hungarians could, possibly, be traced to Hogan, the tactical manoeuvres in which the Hungarians played certainly could not. Hogan, who had last visited Hungary in the 1920s would not have been privy to the Hungarian tactical plans that had been formulated over the previous few years, so when he went to Wembley that day, and when he had had time to consider what he had seen before speaking to the press in Birmingham at New Street that evening, all would have been revelatory to him. On the platform at Birmingham, a *Daily Gazette* reporter asked him for his observations.[22] Hogan said: "Today I saw the Hungarians working out the moves I taught them. Always with men in position."[23] In truth Hogan did not have the foggiest idea as to what had happened, but to be fair to him the nature of the defeat that day has nigh on mystified most British writers and reviewers ever since and now I want to set out what I mean by that and this should give some idea as to the understanding that Hogan was as flummoxed by the Hungarian performance as were the Wembley crowd.

In the immediate aftermath of the game there were various proposals put forward by British writers which were aimed at instantly correcting the disparity that now clearly existed between British and Continental football. One thing that appeared to be the case was that Hungary seemed constantly to be having a man over whenever they attacked. And that led to the understanding that British players could replicate this if they were fitter and being able to get into position quicker. So the idea sprung up that what was required was more training or more physical exercise which is what Charlie Buchan stated in *Football Monthly*,[24] others stated that what was needed was for heads to roll; that Jesse Carver and George Raynor should now lead the national side.[25] Nearly two decades later, Marshall Cavendish's *Book of Football* felt that all that had happened was that Harry Johnston had ventured up-field to find Hidegkuti and the Hungarians had run into the opening he had vacated. Yet this analysis completely overlooked the plan Johnston had agreed with Walter Winterbottom to stay put following Raynor's discussion with Winterbottom in Vienna.[26] Later still, Jonathan Wilson remarked that Hungary's victory came about as a combination of tactics and technique.[27] What you notice therefore is that there's no coherent understanding as to why it went so wrong for England that afternoon and why Hungary won so heavily. Only one writer has ever really got to grips with the principle issue at play and that was Eric Batty writing in the tenth edition of the *International Football Book*. In that edition, Batty writes about "third man theory" which sounds like something out of a spy novel and, interestingly, there was a degree of ingenuity as to the formation of the concept and the way Batty felt it had been held close by several of the leading European coaches as recently as the mid-1970s. Gustav Sebes, President of the Hungarian Football Association, knew the importance of keeping trade secrets and there is clear evidence of this because in Sebes' notebook which sets out the formations for the Wembley fixture he makes a misleading references, for instance to Czibor being anchored to the left side of the field when, in practice, this was never the case. Once understood, most people might conflate third man theory with "running off the ball" but it was more than that. One thing it was not was the old Aston Villa Broome-Shell switch combination, that Hogan had had sight of in the 1930s. That was where one or the other would initiate an opening on the spur of the moment and allow the other to charge through into the space created.

Third man theory was explained to Batty by Dr Geza Kalocsai, one of the three coaches who worked under Sebes when Sebes was vice-president of the Hungarian Sports Association and the Magical Magyars were being formed into a national side. Kalocsai said "we needed a method of creating collectivity – making individual players think and move as a unit. What we called combinations were the result of this … the ordinary wall-pass … was easily spotted [because it was] in full view of the defender. [To develop this idea] Márton Bukovi [the second of Sebes' coaches[28]] "introduced" the third man to make a basic one-two-three, with the third man coming from behind and running into a position on the "blind side" of the defender."[29] A form of the idea had already been demonstrated by the Austrians at Wembley under Nausch and was obvious enough then to be identified by an FA observer the previous November. What the third man theory amounted to was "at exactly the right moment a player lays his inch-perfect pass and, apparently magically, a colleague drifts into the right position at just the right time."[30] Eric Batty, who wrote the article, went on: "Update this idea to the West Ham of [1968]. Left back John Charles passes up to left-winger John Sissons, Sissons moves inside with the ball (screened from the full-back) towards Geoff Hurst, taking the full-back with him. Once inside, Sissons plays the ball to Ron Boyce at inside right. Boyce puts the ball over the heads of the defenders to the left wing – where there is no Sissons, but Charles. Charles is the 'third man', the 'one put in from behind', not occasionally or accidentally, but as a matter of training or habit."[31]

Of course, there's nothing new under the sun, Cameron's Tottenham were demonstrating third man theory in 1901, it's just that in those days they called it combination football and if Spurs played like that, then Queens' Park had played like that and so had Everton, Cameron's former clubs, for Cameron had inured the understanding of such play from someone and somewhere else. However, because Hogan had never played at the level Cameron had, he did not take that tactical notion with him to the continent and so he did not understand what he had seen at Wembley. Another person who did not understand what he had seen was Alf Ramsey and I will demonstrate why I say that. The iceberg that sank England's ship that afternoon was not 4-2-4 or the way Hidegkuti played in a withdrawn

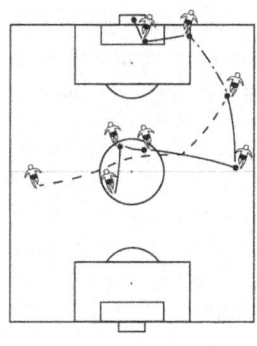

Fig. 9

role, it was the *manner* in which the defeat was conceived and nothing illustrated that more than Puskás' goal to make the score 3-1. That goal was "third man theory" in practice. The move looked like it was made up on the spur of the moment but was nothing of the sort. The move starts in the middle of the park and an inside forward passes it to Budai on the right wing who delays his pass as the third man, Czibor, gets into position. The delay between the first pass into the inside forward and Budai's to Czibor is pure subterfuge designed to attract the defence. Budai passes the ball down the right wing to Czibor, the *outside left* Czibor has worked his way, almost unnoticed, across the high defensive line, from one side of the field to the other and as he runs forward the person who keeps him onside is the England right back all the way over on the other side of the field, Alf Ramsey. Czibor now gets to the penalty area and messes up the inter-play with Puskas who has to produce a bit of improbable magic to beat Wright and clap the ball home. When it comes to that goal, Hogan's eye would not have been on the "men in position", as he called it, it would have been on the drag back from Puskás that put Billy Wright on his arse because that was all about technique and ball control. Third man theory therefore follows that when the ball is played out to Czibor in that position that one of the options is going to be a forward pass down the line behind the advanced defensive line. In essence, the Hungarians would not have given a monkeys as to whether the recipient was Budai or Puskás or Paloti or Elvis Presley. All that they wanted was to catch the advancing defence napping and have a player ready to move into the right wing space once Czibor received the ball in that position.

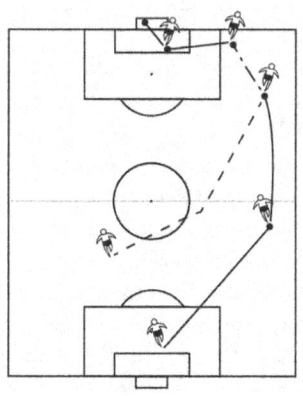

Fig. 10

Even the very best English coaches could not work it all out. Ramsey thought that the speed of movement of the Hungarians had nothing to do with the movement of the players but with their speed of transferring the ball as quickly as possible. He tried to imitate this speed of thought by using attacking wing-backs in Mexico and wide midfielders at Wembley to deliver the ball into the box as quickly as possible. He did it at Ipswich with Jimmy Leadbetter striking a pass from a withdrawn inside forward position for Crawford to run onto. Hurst's goal against Argentina in the quarter-final, his first in the 1966 Final, his goal against Belgium in 1970 also illustrate this thinking. Ramsey felt that typically precise wing play would play into the hands of the defence and so reverted against it. That's why Hurst's second goal in the 1966 Final sees Ball running like the clappers to a long ball down the right wing and cross the ball in at pace; he would not have been schooled by Ramsey to control the ball and work it into the area. Therefore there's no control when Ball reaches the ball at that speed and when the cross comes over Hurst was forced to retrieve the pass behind him and, in typical British style, twat it with all the power he could muster on the turn, which sent the ball flying so high above the keeper that it struck the cross bar and controversy has reigned ever since. Compare what Hurst did there with another World Cup Final goal and one for which there is no controversy whatsoever.

One would have thought that "third man" theory would have become ineffective and redundant as the game sped up in the 1970s but such a thought is wrong. In Munich in 1974, Schön, Hogan's ex-pupil, coached his West German side under the exact same principles as the Hungarians. In the 43rd minute of the Final, Hoeness passed to Grabowski out on the right wing. He then delays the forward pass and therefore invites three Dutch defenders to him. Bonhof, moving from the left side of midfield to the right wing, picks up Grabowski's pass and runs at the left side of the Dutch defence. He goes past Haan and smacks a pass across to Müller. Bonhof messes up the inter-play with Müller putting the ball behind Müller but Müller then turns on a six-pence and with three Dutch defenders converging on him, unlike Hurst, has the presence of mind to roll the ball to the far post past Jongbloed. It was a phenomenal goal and in the circumstances within which it was scored, the best I have ever seen. Third man theory therefore won the 1974 World Cup with a goal which was a carbon copy of Puskás' at Wembley. Third man theory was still effective because what Ramsey overlooked was that the delay in transferring the ball into space gave the attack the speed it needed to unhinge the defence and was simple subterfuge as the third man got into position. Hogan may not have understood or appreciated the philosophy behind that movement, but he certainly would have appreciated the weight of the forward pass and the finish from Puskás' just as he would have of Müller's finish. "Coaching this way is not easy," said Kalocsai. "It's far more difficult than coaching ball skills."

# 1952-1959

The Hungarian victory overwhelmed thinking thereafter. In football terms Britain had been sadistic before November 1953, there was a light-heartedness in their attitude to foreign players, that as they did not play as we did they could not be all that good. But ever since that match British football has displayed a remarkable masochism, absolutely accepting of the fact that the highest levels we cannot hope to compete with foreigners when it comes to professional football. That December, Charles Hewitt, the Millwall manager, actually signed an electrical engineer as player-coach purely on the basis that he, János Kedves, was a Hungarian. Suddenly there seemed nothing remotely insane about employing a 26-year-old foreigner to teach English professionals how to kick a football.[32]

In 1954, Scotland proclaimed a 4-2 loss to Hungary as some type of "victory" since it represented a better result than the whipping handed out to England. Jimmy Hogan was suddenly all the rage again. In the days following the game, the *Burnley Express*' correspondent, "Sportsman" wrote a short biography about Hogan in his column for those readers who were unaware as to Hogan's life story. The writer concluded: "Mr Hogan's methods ... emphasised ball control and the value of using the open space. He once told me that he was convinced that players in this country did not receive enough ball practice and meant correct control and when and how to part with it not merely 'shooting in' practice. And he could put into operation what he preached."[33] There were calls for Hogan to lead another national coaching scheme, this time for youngsters.[34] From his point of view the call was coming perhaps twenty years too late but he used his new-found fame to cash in where he could. The *Sport* newspaper contracted him to write a serialised autobiography which was published between January and February in 1954 and in between times, he continued to provide lectures.[35] In the January of 1954 he was invited to attend a small public meeting about the future of football at Stafford Borough Hall[36] alongside Freddie Mills and Freddie Steele. Apparently an increase in the amount of football on TV would save the national game, the audience were informed, although not by Hogan. But the respect afforded him at Villa Park was nevertheless depressing. Danny Blanchflower at Villa Park at the same time, saw Hogan's job as symptomatic of the wider ills the club was suffering from. Hogan had been brought in "to help Eric" according to Blanchflower: "but [Jimmy] spent most of his time in Eric's office dabbling away at a small typewriter answering the mail. It must have been frustrating for him because, despite his age, he was quite active and would have been a very good influence in the coaching of the younger players. I think he did this a bit but it wasn't enough for his liking or for the good of the youngsters."

# Jimmy Hogan

Whether Blanchflower was right or not in his analysis of the situation at Villa Park is hard to say. Hogan saw the arrival in the first team of Peter McParland and Roy Chapman in the January of 1954.[37] At first McParland struggled in the Villa side when he first placed in the outside left role. He was an extremely talented individual player but he was coming up short against seasoned right-sided pros. Hogan sat down with Houghton and considering matters in the round suggested placing McParland back in a less exposed position. It had worked with Bobby Evans at Celtic and was worth a try here because McParland, even at nineteen, was too good for reserve team football and he acknowledged the input from his mentor: "[Hogan] took me under his wing ... Whenever my confidence showed signs of flagging, he was there to boost me up again with a few words of advice. Jimmy was a great character ... he could do anything with a ball except make it talk. It was a real inspiration to the youngsters to watch him ... It was Jimmy's idea to switch me to left half to help me along a bit."[38]

Peter McParland, came to be a close friend of Hogan and for a good reason as well. As the confidence developed, McParland's career took flight: a Cup winner's medal, a *Boy's Own* World Cup memory and a wardrobe full of International caps in one of the greatest of Northern Ireland's teams. Hogan helped bring that along with his quiet words of encouragement and tactical tinkering. In addition to this the Board did acknowledge his contribution to assisting the balance sheet at the end of that season. One of the shareholders, a Mr Shaw, issued thanks to Fred Normansell for boldly bringing Hogan back to the club because thanks to his work in bringing on Roberts and McParland the club had probably saved themselves £50,000 in transfer fees.[39]

However, it was away from the club that Hogan's presence was still being felt. In May, England journeyed out to Budapest to play the Hungarians in a fixture designed to prepare England for the World Cup.[40] It was an ill-advised appointment, coming far too soon after the Wembley fiasco to serve any purpose whatsoever. Sándor Barcs had made good on his promise and invited Hogan out to Hungary to attend the game.[41] At the banquet following the game Hogan was interviewed by the British press. "We now have to start learning to play football all over again. The Hungarians play better football than ever I had dreamed possible."[42] Likewise, the Hungarian hierarchy were fulsome in their praise of the old coach with Sebes explaining that that the Hungarians owed a great deal to Hogan. While he was there, Hogan and the coaching staff of the Hungarian national team fell into discussion regarding the preparation of a coaching book, *Play Football the Hungarian Way*, that came to be published in a number of languages and which first saw light of day in the winter of 1954. Hogan wrote the introduction to the book but his part in the development of the 1953 and 1954 victories over England was somewhat illusory. Not that he saw it that way. In the introduction of the book he wrote of Orth and Braun and his days at MTK: "First I let them practise the correct treatment of the ball with each part of the foot and of the body. Then I taught them how they have to play tactically well thought-out and constructive football on the 'carpet' and these features are a characteristic of the modern Hungarian game."[43]

He may have laid the first bricks in the building of the great Magyar building but the ornate architecture was certainly the work of Mándi, Sebes, Bukovi and Csandi and owed as much to them as it did to the simple fact that, as a result of historical coincidence, six supreme footballers had reached their peak in one country at the same time. However for those six to be attracted to football it took football to be the primary, fundamental object of fascination and in *that regard* Hogan was immensely important. Just as he had done in Germany in the late 1920s so he was responsible for the Hungarian fixation on the MTK side of the Great War years for it was under him that the celebrated era of that great club was had.

But there was an ironic element to the publicity that when with introduction of that book to a British audience. On 16 December 1954, the *Yorkshire Post* gave oxygen to Hogan's views about the game upon publication of the book: "It boils down to three B's. Brains, ball control and balance. Trickery with the ball isn't [practiced] to make a show-boater," said Hogan. "... it is to help guide the footballer toward being subconscious when having possession of the ball. [Practice leads to an] automatic response to trap and control and know where other players were." Hogan explained that in order for players to reach this level of expertise over the ball it required six sessions per week each lasting two hours.[44] Yet on the same day the *Portsmouth Evening News* was highlighting that the lack of investment in proper training facilities was one of the reasons why British football was being held back. The correspondent reported that even at Villa Park, Hogan was to be seen overseeing a training session given on the concrete where the match-day cars could be parked. It might have helped inure confidence and control of the bouncing ball, but it was not an ideal foundation upon which to build Britain's footballing future.

That summer Hungary were to lose the 1954 World Cup Final to a West German side that was well worth their Gold-medal victory. Hogan made mileage out of stating that he had a hand in the development of the game in Hungary, Germany and Austria, whose side finished third, taking "modest" credit for the entire World Cup. The miracle of Berne they called the Final, a game which the West Germans "surprisingly" won 3-2, but the only miracle would have been if Hungary would have won because on the day, the West Germans demonstrated a far more constructive approach than their illustrious opponents. One incident in particular, over any other in that game, illustrated the gulf between the two teams in terms of their confidence, confidence borne of an approach to training and practice that resulted in "mastery over the ball [that] will get a defender out of a tight corner and enable a striker to score when he might otherwise not,"[45] as Hogan put it. During the second half of the World Cup Final in 1954, Kohlmeyer, the German player is seen to flick the ball with his heel over his head from his own penalty area and nod the ball nonchalantly on to a team mate. Remember the score was two-all at the time, and he was moving away from a congested penalty area.

Hogan stayed at Villa Park for the better part of his seventh decade. Even when he "retired" he scouted for the club. He became a voice-piece for the club, elevated by his association and close working relationship with Houghton. Prior to the 1956-57 season he was interviewed by the press. "Last season [Villa's] football was about the poorest ever served up by any team wearing the old claret and blue," wrote the *Hartlepool Daily Mail*'s correspondent. "Now, Jimmy Hogan ... considers their players (Jackie Sewell, Nigel Sims, and Jimmy Dugdale) as having made such headway that they well be on the road to the recapture of their former greatness."[46] He wasn't wrong. The club were two seasons away from a Cup run that was to provide their solitary piece of silverware for many a year. Hogan's impact on Villa's history cannot be gainsaid. Eric Houghton, later, wrote glowingly about his former boss and colleague:

> I have often blessed the day I met Jimmy Hogan, who taught me so much about the game and about myself.[47] His methods were simple. 'The easier you make it, the better you will play it,' he used to say. His method was to open out defences on the outside by using width in attack and making the ball do the work. I can hear him now, a stocky, ramrod-stiff, yet dignified man, pounding out his simple theories like: 'Remember, when passing or kicking the ball, it travels at least twice as fast as a man can run. Why bother to beat a man – unless you have to – when he can be beaten with an accurate pass? ... Defend in block and attack in block; either way, leave no gaps. Jimmy Hogan formulated what, to me, was the most successful Aston Villa team of my time, though we were robbed of our just rewards by the intervention of the Second World War, when I was convinced we were on the verge of enjoying a decade of success similar to the post-War [World War Two] periods enjoyed by Manchester United, Leeds United and Liverpool. But then, football is full of as many disappointments as pleasures. You must treat both the same.[48]

## 1952-1959

Houghton was let go by the club in the mid-winter of 1958 to be replaced by Hogan's pal, Joe Mercer. Hogan's work had continued in bringing on the likes of John Sleeuwenhoek, the centre-half, Norman Ashe, the winger and the inside forward, Alan Baker. All represented Villa in their quarter final displays in the 1959 and 1960 Youth Cup campaigns, and went on to gain honours for the England youth side while still below average age. Hogan finally retired, at the age of 76, from Aston Villa on 31 July 1959,[49] but would continue as a scout and the club would honour a commitment made right at the start of his second term there to pay him a pension for life.

# Jimmy Hogan

## Notes

1 *Burnley Express*, 28 February 1953.
2 *Burnley Express*, 23 May 1953.
3 Kathleen retired from teaching in August 1953 at the age of 61.
4 *Burnley Express*, 1 January 2017.
5 *Football Memories*, 97-8.
6 Danny Blanchflower, *The Double and Before*, (Nicholas Kaye, 1961), 67.
7 *Sports Argus*, 26 September 1953.
8 *Birmingham Daily Gazette*, 12 December 1953.
9 *Daily Herald*, 15 October 1953.
10 *Birmingham Daily Gazette*, 16 October 1953. It was wrongly reported that this was Hogan's 71st birthday.
11 *Birmingham Daily Gazette*, 31 October 1953.
12 *Liverpool Echo*, 28 November 1953. In the World Cup Final in 1954, Kohlmeyer, the German player is seen to flick the ball over his head from his own penalty area and nod the ball nonchalantly on to a team mate. The result of technical training and practice.
13 *Daily Herald*, 24 October 1953.
14 *Sport Argus*, 24 October 1953.
15 *Sports Argus*, 7 November 1953.
16 *Birmingham Daily Gazette*, 13 November 1953.
17 *Sports Argus*, 21 November 1953.
18 *Yorkshire Post*, 26 November 1953.
19 *Birmingham Daily Gazette*, 24 November 1953.
20 https://www.theguardian.com/football/2003/nov/22/sport.comment2 "We played football as Jimmy Hogan taught us," but I have never seen anything to confirm that statement was ever actually made. My feeling is that Wilson reinterpreted Fox's interpretation and just palmed it off as a fact.
21 *Birmingham Daily Gazette*, 26 November 1953.
22 He returned to Birmingham to see the Villa players play snooker at the Shirley Social Club.
23 *Birmingham Daily Gazette*, 26 November 1953.
24 *Charles Buchan's Football Monthly*, January 1954.
25 See further, Ashley Hyne, *George Raynor, the Greatest Coach England Never Had* (History Press, 2014).
26 Again, see *George Raynor*. That was the best proposal of the lot!
27 *Inverting the Pyramid*, p. 91.
28 The third was Janos Kalmar.
29 *International Football Book*, no. 10, (1968), p. 34.
30 *Ibid.*, p. 31.
31 *Ibid.*, p. 34.
32 *Lancashire Evening Post*, 21 December 1953.
33 *Burnley Express*, 28 November 1953.
34 *Yorkshire Evening Post*, 5 December 1953.
35 Appearing at Vicarage Road School in Birmingham that December. *Sports Argus*, 19 December 1953 and in January he appeared with his good friend Joe Mercer at the Livingstone Street Youth Centre, in Birkenhead. (*Liverpool Echo*, 14 January 1954).
36 *Birmingham Daily Gazette*, 15 January 1954.
37 *Birmingham Daily Gazette*, 21 January 1954.
38 Peter McParland, *Going for Goal* (Souvenir Press, 1960), p. 20.
39 *Birmingham Daily Gazette*, 7 August 1954.
40 Again, reference is made to George Raynor (see above) regarding the naïve tactics that were promoted by the English manager and national director of coaching prior to that game.

## 1952-1959

41 *Star Green 'Un*, 15 May 1954.
42 *Hartlepool Daily Mail*, 24 May 1954.
43 *Die ungarische fussballschule*, p. 7. Acknowledgement to Dr Andreas Hafer.
44 *Yorkshire Post*, 16 December 1954.
45 *Liverpool Echo*, 28 November 1953.
46 18 August 1956.
47 He had been in the Villa first team for seven years when Hogan arrived, and had already played several times for England.
48 *FA Yearbook*, 1978-79, p. 72.
49 *Aberdeen Evening News*, 29 July 1959.

Jimmy Hogan

## TWENTY-ONE

## 1960-1974
'The ball is intelligently kept on the floor.'

In the years before his death, Hogan had kept up public appearances which was a remarkable testament to his long-term physical health. He had just passed the age of 90 when he attended Burnley's home game against Cardiff in which Paul Fletcher grabbed a hat-trick[1] and although he had no need for respite in a care home, he did attend regular hospital check-ups. It was during this phase of his life that he met Paul Caine, a young local Burnley fan, who, at first, was confused as to who Hogan was. Hogan immediately introduced himself by saying: "I'm the famous football coach." The self-publicist to the very last.

Jimmy Hogan died at the end of January 1974 at the age of 91. Britain might have been the home of football but the house was in a right old mess. The same month Hogan died the FA and Football League got all pious as to whether football should be played on the Sabbath and yet in their next breath the Football League was asking TV companies to stump up more cash to broadcast football. Meanwhile, Alan Ball found himself £75 worse off for criticising referees, George Best, at the ripe old age of 26, announced he would never play for Manchester United again and Ajax Amsterdam beat AC Milan 6-0 in the second leg of their Super Cup tie. Of that victory, Leslie Vernon wrote in *Rothmans Football Yearbook, 1974-75* an article which had passing reference to Hogan's philosophy:

> ... Football ... has been going through a fascinating tactical revolution ... Ajax planted the sign-posts. They were the inventors and advocates of 'total football' – a term which implies fluency, vision, a desire to push forward eight or nine players at a time, and a need for a squad of excellent all-rounders. The ball is intelligently kept on the floor, one-twos are played around the box, and the players are encouraged to use their initiative. A minimum amount of regimentation with a fluid pattern, with everyone 'totally' involved in every facet of the action, has been the blue-print for the success which has made Ajax the leading club in Europe for three years.[2]

Since his death Hogan has become a figure of some interest in print media and on the internet. Unfortunately this interest has not been accompanied by a great deal of research into what he actually did. Writers have made a whole series of assumptions about Hogan based on bad evidence and that's been used to justify plonking Hogan on a throne

## Jimmy Hogan

without much ado. A decade ago, Jonathan Wilson wrote: "Hogan is regularly hailed as the father of Hungarian, Austrian and German football. What is trumpeted rather less is that he was also the grandfather of the Brazilian game."[3] But that is just nonsense borne of a struggle to give Hogan his due. I think you would be hard pressed to find anyone who would call him the "father of German football", for instance, when he coached in one part of the country 40 years after the game first took hold there. As for Austria, Hugo Meisl's role cannot be challenged and in Budapest he only got his start at one club because of the war and because Robertson had departed. As for Brazil, Wilson sees Hogan as having some Svengali-like influence over Dori Kürschner and yet the two only ever met in passing it would seem. That's not stopped some from making improbable leaps of faith, arguing that without Hogan there would have been no *Wunderteam* and no Magical Magyars. I don't see it like that.

It's true that you can't run unless you learn to walk first and you can't play highly skilled football unless you have first gained mastery over the ball, but Hogan was but a footnote in the tactical developments that went to create the Austrian side of the early 1930s and the Hungarians two decades later. That is because Hogan was much less concerned with the intracacies of tactical analysis than he was with the technical iterations of ball control. That may have had something to do with the fact that he played at a time when there was minimal outside influence on how a team should play. In his day the captain decided on the course of action to follow and when surveying Hogan's managerial career it is noticeable that apart from minor tinkering here and there he did not introduce any new ways of thinking. The most innovative ideas he came up with as a club coach was to suggest placing players in different positions, as he did with Peter McParland, or allowing the players to propose and suggest attacking ideas, as was the case with Jimmy Allen, Broome and Shell at the Villa. So one cannot just attribute the successes, or lack of success, of the great sides of the 1930s and 1950s to Hogan alone, he played a role in the development of them but that is all. So if that is accepted, how is it that Hogan is so highly-regarded? The one thing to note about Hogan is that he was all about control. He was self-assured and controlled his own dealings from an early age, something we can certainly see evidence of when he was boarding at St. Bede's and making a mark amongst all his school chums on the fields at Whalley Range and it was also a factor which had a role to play in his earliest contractual negotiations with Nelson Football Club when he first signed a professional contract. Although he was only nineteen years old he set out to the directors of that club what he felt he was owed. Hogan never needed intermediaries, securing himself one of the highest paid jobs anywhere in football when he went to Dresden in 1928.

Control was most importantly a feature of his dealings with the press. Hogan sustained a productive rapport with the print media, understanding earlier than most how he could use the media for his own ends. At one time this might mean securing a more favourable contract. Moving from Swindon to Bolton is a good case in point. At other times, using an alliance he had developed with influential editors, such as James Catton and Ivan Sharpe, he was quite vocal in calling for the professional clubs in England to embrace a culture of coaching. We could argue that he was sincere in what he was saying: that continental footballers were more skilled than their English counterparts because they saw virtue and value in being trained. But there was another implicit element at work within his musings because while the state of affairs in continental Europe was taking a turn for the worse, Hogan was busy, via his stream of letters and opinions, creating an environment in which he could operate back in the safety of England. You could argue that he single-handedly created an industry and a need within which he could be employed.

As a result of the way he conducted himself, Hogan became well paid, while he swanned around the great Lakes of the Swiss cantons, traipsed around the Left Bank in Paris and motored here and there in Saxony. But the money he earned though obviously welcomed served only to vindicate the decision he took when he left St Bede's. For at that momentous juncture he knew he had to show and prove to his mother that a career in football was the right choice. It was a way of trying to assuage the dispute with his mother over his choice of career. That is what his primary driver was. That's what inspired such a lengthy career, that's what saved him in Leipzig in 1926 at the "lecture". He had to keep pushing forward.

But what can we say of him as a coach? Was he really the "greatest teacher"?[4] Well, the first thing that can be said is that it helped Hogan immensely that he was not a naturally gifted footballer because that meant he had to learn how to play the game and how to train himself to be better. Secondly, the deficiencies that were constantly identified when he coached, in Vienna in 1912, in Leipzig in 1926, in Lausanne in 1933, at Fulham in 1934 and by Stanley Rous in the same year, were a reflection of his experience as a professional player when coaching consisted of the most rudimentary ideas. He coached from scratch. He had no mentor to train or guide him during his formal years and therefore we need to temper just how good a coach he was. When he did start coaching he was reliant upon the input from Hugo Meisl. Meisl knew his football alright, but like Hogan, he was not a coach and worked on a vague notion as to what the end product should resemble and yet both devised a scheme that was to signal the start of Hogan's career and a formal coaching structure in mainland Europe.

What saved Hogan as a coach was both his intellect and the acceptance of the Europeans he encountered to be taught the game. Raynor as we have seen, identified the second of these elements when speaking to Brian Glanville when he said "young British footballers learn by example not by tuition."[5] The Continentals wanted to be taught so that they could be released to play the game. But Hogan was also a smooth operator when networking and in his dealings with others across Europe with its polyglot of cultures and circumstances. He was, in the main, well thought of and well liked which helped him as he worked his way through the different cultures in Europe in the 1920s and 1930s, helped resolve those issues which cropped up about his coaching and helped smooth his way when working in England and Scotland too.

And so Hogan's influence grew and developed across Europe; was driven on by the transmigration of the Austrians and Hungarians after the First World War to various parts of the Continent, was promulgated by his relationship with the press and the advent of professionalism, which placed football on a business setting across the landmass, and finally found a home in British football where outside the mainstream, new thoughts and ideas were starting to spring up as clubs sought to challenge the dominance of Chapman's WM.

## Notes

1. 17 October 1972.
2. *Rothmans Football Yearbook*, 1974-75, p. 882.
3. *Inverting the Pyramid*, p. 107.
4. *Ibid.*, p. 27.
5. *Soccer Nemesis*, p. 117.

# Jimmy Hogan

# Appendix

# Appendix

## Extracts from *Practical Football Teaching*.

*Page 5.*

This book should not considered as a complete book on the game of football; it is simply a book about how to play the game, and should be considered a tool for players. My objective is to set out how best to play via practical and theoretical lessons. However, these lessons are completely worthless unless the player applies his mind to what he is doing when he is training. The small training sessions included in this book have been compiled by me and have been used by many football coaches in Europe.

In order to play football well, it is necessary to start at a young age when the body and limbs are supple. Many people do not start playing until it's too late, and that's why they're never going to be good players.

The main necessities for a footballer are: regular training with the ball, running (mainly short-distance training), jumping, dribbling and simple gymnastic exercises. All these exercises, if correctly executed, will aid in the development of the body and joints, and will help develop the characteristics required to play the game correctly.

The attraction of football around the world is clear evidence of its popularity. There is no game and no sport that can compare with it. Opponents of the game are either biased, have never seen football played properly, or have never played it themselves.

A player must be able to control the ball and not, as in many cases, the ball control the player. You can only learn to control the ball by continually practicing with the ball until you are able to master it. Undertaking gymnastics exercises, running and jumping and so on is a waste of time if you do not do enough proper training with the ball. Many footballers think that training is all about scoring and as a result never do any of the exercises that are really necessary, such as passing, heading, trapping, shooting and so on.

*Page 6.*

1. Striking the Ball.

There are a lot of players who cannot really kick the ball properly; they always strike the ball incorrectly toe-poking it and so on. In football, there is only one way to strike the ball and that is with the instep.

2. To keep the ball low (or to play the ball along the ground), strike the ball through the centre of the instep.

3. To chip the ball, to kick the ball high, strike the ball by placing the instep well under the ball, so that you elevate the ball.

Exercises.

Do not stand in front of the goal and just kick the ball with your right foot; this is pointless. You must learn to hit the ball on the run, on the volley and half volley with equal proficiency and with both feet.

4. Walk 20 or 30 yards with the ball, master it properly and then shoot into the goal.

b. Pass the ball between another player up to the edge of the penalty area and then shoot.

c. Have the players cross the ball from the right and left wing into the middle of the penalty area, strike the ball as it comes, and shoot. Or get the goalkeeper to throw the ball out to players outside the area and strike it immediately without hesitation or controlling the ball first.

2 Trapping the Ball.

Trapping the ball is very important and you have to have a lot of practice

*Page 7.*

5. Basic trapping. Throw or kick the ball towards each other and place the sole of your foot on it when the ball touches the ground. Players in the modern game have rarely enough time to do this but the exercise does teach them to understand this method of controlling the ball.

6. Trapping with the inside of the foot.

7. Trapping and playing at the same time with the inside of the foot.

8. Trapping and turning with the inside of the foot.

9. Trapping with the outside of the foot.

You have to learn to trap the ball in any position and with either foot; it requires constant practice.

*Page 8.*

3. Ball Control

A good footballer should not only be able to kick with his right and left foot, but he must also be able to kick the ball with the inside and outside of the foot. Many players can only kick the ball with the inside of the foot; therefore the game becomes unnecessarily difficult. During a game we often have to dribble with the ball and control it with the inside and outside

# Appendix

of the foot. When practicing ball control with the inside of the foot, it is very simple, on the other hand it is a real test for any player to control the ball with the outside of the foot.

*Exercises.*

10. Form a circle about 30 to 40 meters in circumference and run inside it by controlling the ball with the outside of the foot (first with the right foot and then with the left foot).

11/12 Dribble with the ball and control it with the outside and inside of both feet.

Dribble in a zigzag shape and control it with the outside of the foot.

The best practice for ball control and body control is to carry out the above exercises between posts that are placed 4 meters apart.

*Page 9.*

4. Heading.

The ability to head the ball is very important in football, but heading is quite futile if you are unable to place the ball where you want it to go. Always try to strike the ball with your forehead, which you have to take back and then bring to the front, if you want to get distance or speed on the header. If you want to bring the ball down to the feet, naturally the head must give direction to the ball.

13. The players form a circle, one goes into the middle. The players must try to head the ball to the man in the middle. The middle player is replaced.

14. An outside forward crosses the ball, and the rest of the players standing near the goal try to head the ball into the net, against two defenders and the goalkeeper.

15. The players stand one behind the other of 3 metres distance and head the ball backwards.

*Page 10.*

5. Extra Training.

For the goalkeeper

Players can perform these exercises from the center of the field in the direction of the goal until they enter the 16-meter space, then attempt a shot on goal to give the goalkeeper an opportunity to save, catch, divert the ball and clear.

16. Catching
17. Catching whilst running.
18. Punching the ball aside.

For the defenders.

In addition to the exercises mentioned, the defenders can strike the ball, one at a time (from one side of the field to the other), by taking the ball as it comes, on the volley, or the half volley and so on.

For the half backs.

In addition to the exercises mentioned above, the halves can form a circle and then practice controlling a moving ball by playing the ball first time to each other, first with the inside of the foot, then with the outside and the instep.

A player who has a little talent for the game and who practices these exercises enthusiastically and regularly will improve his game one hundred percent. I can almost guarantee that after a few months such a player will be able to control not only the ball but also his body.

6. Combination play.

Modern football is based on combination and this requires players being quick on the ball and holding the ball to attract the opponent. Then passing the ball and players do so in readiness to be able to receive the ball again. You should always keep an eye on your opponent, because it is sometimes necessary to control the ball immediately as soon as you get it regardless of whether it is played high or low to you. Many players

*Page 11.*

find the game difficult because they rely too much on dribbling and give up possession that way. Of course, there are occasions when dribbling seems expedient; but the real game is the combination game. If you want to play well, do not forget (in general) to go to the right with the ball and play it to the left or to the left and play to the right; this is the basis of the combination game.

*Exercises.*

19. A simple combination game with 2 players: run and play, first with the inside of the foot and then with the outside. b. The same exercise with 3, 4 or 5 players c. Combination with 2 or 3 players: walk to the left and play to the right, walk to the right and play to the left.

20. Add 3 players and change positions [see diagram].

# Appendix

*Page 12.*

21/22 These combinations can also be done between sticks in the ground, but only with 2 players at the same time.

7 Positional play.

In connection with the combination game you have to keep the ball always on the ground and do not always play high. Also, remember that pretty moves which do not result in a goal being scored are worthless. The aim of the game is to score, and we must try to do so by the shortest possible route. There are two possibilities:

a. the wing game or open game b. the midfield game or inside-game.

Personally, I prefer the wing game, but of course everything depends on how the opposing players play. For example, if the opposing players cover the outsides, then it is clear that the only real game is the midfield or inside game. The goalkeeper must work with the defenders, the halves must also provide assistance from time to time. The forwards must attack the opposing goal. The whole eleven must work together: the defenders support the halves, they support the forwards, and the inside right and inside left must always be willing to go back to help the halves and defence, if necessary.

8. The positions.

a. The goalkeeper.

This player has a great advantage because he is allowed to use his hands, but many goalkeepers are unnecessarily endangered by punching the ball instead of taking it with their hands. If the goalkeeper has time, he will try to gather the ball well but sometimes he will find that the best way is to divert the ball away from goal. One must never forget that it is better to have a corner

*Page 13.*

than to make a mistake and concede a goal. It is also necessary for the goalkeeper to work fully with his two defenders; he must always keep his eye on the ball.

a. The goalkeeper must try to make the narrow the angle for the player who cuts in to score.

b. The goalkeeper should run out when the opponent has managed to break through. The striker will have very little chance of success if the goalkeeper blocks sight of the goal.

c. The goalkeeper must also leave the goal (or try to do so) and challenge for the ball when a high cross or a ball comes toward the goal.

23. The goalkeeper may not need to catch a high shot on goal if the opponent is too close to him, but may divert the ball over the crossbar.

b. The defenders.

The defenders have to work together and support each other. Many defenders think they just need to stand near the gatekeeper and clear the ball; they have very little idea of posture and tactics. If the defender has time, he must try to control the ball well, just like a good half does. He has to let the goalkeeper decide when he is coming to meet the ball as well as mark his opponent.

What is very important for the defender, is the understanding between the defender and the outside forward, namely: if the outside forward attacks with the inside forward and the latter plays the ball to the outside forward, the defender must move toward the outside forward and the defensive half back must go to the inside forward, so both have to change automatically.

Therefore, it is clear that the defenders must be fast. You have to train a lot of short distance running.

In general, the defenders should take all freekicks in their half of the field and the halves must take care of the opponents.

The defenders should not be afraid to play the ball back to the goalkeeper when the situation is really dangerous. But this is often overdone.

The halves.

The halves have many obligations to perform: attack, defend, combine, assist, trap and shoot. Most important for the halves is to serveand support the forwards. Page 14 A thing you miss very often. It is also part of the right position game. How the halves have to play

In general, the halves have the duty to cover the opposing inside forwards, but ninety-five percent of our halves generally mark the opposing outside forwards and leave the centre-half to hold the three inside forwards. Sometimes it happens that the half has to mark the outside forward. If the opponents have a throw in, he must cover him. Then again there is a trap in which the ball goes from a free kick direct to the outside forward. In this case the half has to move toward him, but the other halves have to assist the half in doing so. The players have to change the game as much as possible. The marked half, for example, must not always pass up the right

# Appendix

wing or to the outside left.

How the halves have to attack.

The halves have to support their attackers in an oblique direction, but at the same time keep a close eye on the opposing players. If e.g. the right-half has to push ahead to attack the defender on the right wing; if the attack on the left side takes place, the left-half must go forward. The halves must also support each other. It is the duty of the half to risk a shot at the goal if they are in favorable positions.

The five forwards have a duty to attack the opposing goal and try to accomplish it by clever play. Random games, running games have little value. The halves must pay close attention to the opposing players and the centre-forward and play the ball to them, but also shoot themselves when the opportunity arises. If necessary, they should return to the defense and cover the opposing players when they throw in.

The players have to give the ball quickly and precisely rather than run with the ball to the foot of the corner flag, is not correct and does not correspond to the modern concept. Corner kicks and balls crossed into the area are not just kicked at the goal (for the goalkeeper), but a few metres in front of the goal. The outside forwards can change in the game by playing the ball to the inside left or right and sometimes even proceed inside, when opportunity arises.

The centre-forward plays a major role in modern football play. He has to spread the ball as best he can, keep his wing in motion, and be ready for a breakthrough or a goal. A brave man who thinks fast and can shoot and move well is suited to this post. The same with the outside forwards, they must be in the main in front, near the penalty area.

*Page 15.*

9 General

a. Running training for football players It is just as necessary for football players as it is for halves and must be exercised regularly: short runs of 30 metres, fast starts, several runs. b. Skipping It is one of the most beautiful exercises for footballers and can be done at home. Use an ordinary rope of 2.50 meters long and use daily (100 to 200 jumps). It's very easy. c. Hiking Short, sharp marches are great for football players and make for a great workout. d. Gymnastics exercises I hardly think it necessary to write about the exercises, as I'm sure all our players know more about it than me. I just want to say that one should choose simple exercises for training of the upper parts of the body and for the loosening of the hips. Playing football, jumping, hiking and running help influence the development of the lower parts of the body in an effective way.

Finally, the following should be emphasized: If a player wants to play football well, then he not only has to carry out all these exercises with great consideration, but he must also live like a sportsman. A glass of beer or a cigarette or cigar does not hurt much in itself, but continued drinking and smoking, combined with lack of sleep and appetite, are impossible things for a good player.

# Bibliography

## Bibliography

Norman Barrett, *World Soccer from A-Z* (Macmillan, 1973).
Erik Bergvall, *The Fifth Olympiad: the Official Report of the Olympic Games of Stockholm 1912*. Translated by Edward Adams-Ray. (Swedish Olympic Committee, 1913).
Henry Berry & Geoffrey Allman, *One Hundred Years at Deepdale* (Amblers, 1982).
Danny Blanchflower, *The Double and Before* (Nicholas Kaye, 1961).
Charles Buchan, *A Lifetime in Football* (Mainstream Publishing, 2010).
Márton Bukovi, & Jenö Csaknády, *Die ungarische Fußballschule* (Berlin, Sportverlag, 1955).
W. Capel-Kirby & Frederick W. Carter, *The Mighty Kick* (Jarrolds, 1933).
James Catton, *The Rise of the Leaguers* (Sporting Chronicle, 1897).
Herbert Chapman, *Herbert Chapman on Football*, (GCR Books, 2010).
Winston Churchill & Martin Gilbert, *The World Crisis 1911-1918* (Penguin Classics, 2007).
F. N. S. Creek, *Association Football* (J.M. Dent, 1947).
Tommy Docherty, *Soccer from the Shoulder* (Stanley Paul, 1960).
Bob Ferrier, *Soccer Partnership* (William Heinemann, 1960).
*The Football Association Coaching Manual* (Evans Brothers, 1950).
*FA Yearbook*, 1950-1, 1952-53 & 1978-79.
Norman Fox, *Prophet or Traitor: The Jimmy Hogan Story* (Parrs Wood Press, 2003).
Alfred Gibson, *Association Football and the Men Who Made It* (Caxton, 1906).
Brian Glanville, *The Footballers' Companion* (Billing and Sons, 1962).
Brian Glanville, *Football Memories* (Virgin Books, 1999).
Brian Glanville, *Soccer Nemesis* (Secker & Warburg, 1955).
Geoffrey Green, *The History of the Football Association* (Naldrett, 1953).
Ron Greenwood, *Yours Sincerely* (Collins, 1984).
Uli Hesse, *Tor!* (WSC Books, 2013).
Jimmy Hill, *The Jimmy Hill Story* (Hodder & Stoughton, 1998).
Jimmy Hill, *Striking for Soccer* (Peter Davis, 1961).
Jimmy Hogan, *Praktische Fussball-Lehre*, (Wilhelm Andreas Leipzig, 1929).
Rev. R. K. G. Hunt, *First Steps to Association Football*, (Arthur Pearson, 1924).
Ashley Hyne, *George Raynor, the Greatest Coach England Never Had* (History Press, 2014).
David Jack, *Soccer 1934* (Putnam, 1934).
Brian James, *England v Scotland* (Pelham, 1970).
Gordon Jeffrey, *European International Football* (Evans, 1963).
W. M. Johnston, *The Football League: the Competitions of Season 1937-38* (Association of Football Statisticians, 1984).
Bernard Joy, *Forward Arsenal* (Phoenix House, 1952).
Bernard Joy, *Soccer Tactics* (Phoenix House, 1962).
Eberhard Kolb, *The Weimar Republic* (Routledge, 1990).

# Jimmy Hogan

Clive Leatherdale, *The Book of Football*, (Desert Island Books, 1996).
Ed Lee & Ray Simpson, *Burnley: a Complete Record* (Breedon Books Sport, 1991).
William Limpert, *Official Report of 1936 Olympic Games* (Organisationskomitee fur die XI. Olympiade Berlin, 1936).
Peter McParland, *Going for Goal* (Souvenir Press, 1960).
Simon Marland, *Bolton Wanderers: the Complete Record* (DB Publishing, 2011).
Charles Marriott & Charles Alcock, *Association Football* (Routledge, London, 1903).
Willy Meisl, *Soccer Revolution* (Sportsmans Book Club, 1956).
Peter Morris, *Aston Villa* (Naldrett, 1960).
Jimmy Murphy, *United, Matt and Me* (Souvenir Press, 1968).
Ernest Needham, *Association Football*, (Soccer Books, 2003).
Otto Nerz & Carl Koppehel, *Der Kampf um den Ball* (Prismen Verlag, 1933).
László Rejto, *Kilenc Klub Krónikája* (Budapest, 1969).
*Rothmans Football Yearbook*, 1974-75.
Stanley Rous, *Football Worlds* (Faber & Faber, 1978).
Peter Salzmann, *Fussballheimat Dresden - Geschichte und Geschichten zwischen Abpfiff und Anstoß* (Sächsisches Druck- und Verlagshaus GmbH (1995).
Helmut Schön, *Fussball* (Ullstein, 1978).
Helmut Schön, *Immer am Ball* (List Verlag, 1970).
Gustáv Sebes, *A Magyar Labdarúgás* (Budapest, 1955).
Montague Shearman, *Athletics and Football* (Longmans, Green, 1894).
T. Stratton Smith, *International Football Book No. 10* (Souvenir Press, 1968).
Charles Tully, *Passed to You* (Stanley Paul, 1958).
Dennis Turner, *Fulham: the Complete Record* (Breedon Books, 1984).
Martin Tyler, *Cup Final Extra* (Hamlyn, 1981).
Nick Walsh, *Dixie Dean* (TBS, 1977).
James Walvin, *The People's Game* (Mainstream Publishing, 1994). 2nd revised edition.
Andrew Ward & Rogan P. Taylor, *Kicking and Screaming* (Robson Books, 1998).
R. J. Whitty *et al*, *Association Football* (Caxton, 1960).
A. N. Wilson, *Hitler* (Harper Press, 2012).
Jonathan Wilson, *Inverting the Pyramid*, (Orion, 2009).
Percy Young, *Bolton Wanderers* (Stanley Paul, 1961).

## Index

| | |
|---|---|
| III Kerületi TVE | 77 |
| | |
| Abegglen, Max | 91, 95, 97n |
| Abeles, Dr Ignaz | 50 |
| AC Milan | 229 |
| Ajax | 229 |
| Alcock, Charles | 16, 23n |
| Aldershot Town | 213 |
| Allen, Jimmy | 131, 165, 171, 174, 176, 230 |
| Allen, Sam | 33 |
| Allison, George | 155, 177, 180n |
| Ampleforth College | 23n |
| Amsterdam | 141 |
| Anfield | 81, 141 |
| Appleyard, Bill | 31 |
| Archduke Franz Ferdinand | 61 |
| Argentina, national football team | 220 |
| Arsenal FC | 17, 25-27, 35n, 38, 53, 99, 127, 129-30, 137n, 140, 147-8, 155, 161, 166, 170, 174, 177, 180n, 203-4 |
| Ashcroft, Jimmy | 26 |
| Ashe, Norman | 225 |
| Ashton Gate | 23n |
| Aston Villa FC | vii, 5, 74, 132, 165-6, 167, 170-177, 179n, 212, 214, 218, 224-225 |
| Athersmith, Charlie | 5 |
| Austria | 42, 48, 61, 67, 76, 81, 83, 99, 143 |
| Austrian football, style | 60 |
| Austria, national football team | 47, 49, 54-56, 87-88, 154, 157, 167, 205-207, 230 |
| Austrian Football Association | 47, 53, 62-63, 78, 82-83 |
| Austrian Olympic squad | 50, 53-55, 59-60, 76, 167 |
| Austrian Red Cross | 63, 67, 79n |
| | |
| Bailey, Eddie | 206 |
| Bain, Jimmy | 190 |
| Baker, Alan | 225 |
| Ball, Alan | 220, 229 |
| Ballina | 1 |
| Barcs, Sándor | 216, 222 |
| Barrett, Norman | 73 |
| Barson, Frank | 179n |
| Basle (Basel) | 85-86, 89-92 |
| Bassett, William (Billy) | 20-21, 108 |
| Bastin, Cliff | 129, 204 |
| Batty, Eric | 217-218 |
| Baverstock, Herbert | 37 |
| Belfast Celtic | 196 |
| Belgium | 39, 81, 220 |

245

| | |
|---|---|
| Belgium, national football team | 220 |
| Bell, "Bunny" | 174 |
| Bell, Mark | 28, 35n |
| Berckel, Nol van | 43 |
| Berkessy, Elemér | 129-131, 135, 137n |
| Berne (Bern) | 63, 85, 88, 90-92, 95, 96n, 128, 223 |
| Berry, W. A. | 67, 78 |
| Best, George | 229 |
| Biddlestone, Fred | 166 |
| Birmingham | 170-173, 178, 183, 213, 217, 226n |
| Blackburn, Lancashire | 4 |
| Blackburn Etrurians | 7 |
| Blackburn Rovers FC | 11n, 24n, 25, 28, 44, 72, 79n, 163n |
| Blackpool | 44 |
| Blackpool FC | 11n, 85, 150 |
| Blanchflower, Danny | 213, 221-222 |
| Bloomer, Steve | 5, 19, 21, 23n, 59, 65n |
| Blythe family | 63, 65n, 67, 83 |
| Boden, Alec | 200, 201n |
| Boer War | 25, 37-38 |
| Bologna | 88 |
| Bolton, Lancashire | 4, 46n |
| Bolton Wanderers FC | 6, 19, 34, 35n, 37-41, 44, 56, 59, 82, 85, 90, 95, 96n, 100-01, 105n, 114, 124n, 170, 231 |
| Bonhof, Rainer | 220 |
| Borbás, Gáspár | 55-56 |
| Bourne, Hubert | 213 |
| Bouvy, Nico | 38, 42, 55 |
| Boyce, Ron | 218 |
| Boyle, Tommy | 141, 143 |
| Bradford | 1, 10 |
| Bradford City FC | 37, 79n, 85 |
| Bradford, Joe | 213 |
| Bradford Park Avenue | 192, 204 |
| Bradshaw, Harry | 11n, 18, 25-33, 35n, 38, 41, 53 |
| Brammer, Dave | 35n |
| Braun, József | 74-76, 95, 100-101, 103, 118, 197, 223 |
| Braunsteiner, Karl | 57n |
| Brazil | 91, 204, 230 |
| Brearley, John | 59 |
| Brentford FC | 150, 152, 177, 180n, 190, 196, 200, 203-204, 207-208 |
| Bristol City FC | 23n |
| British Expeditionary Force | 183 |
| Britton, Cliff | 186 |
| Broome, Frank | 171-5, 218, 230 |
| Brühl | 85 |
| Brüll, Arpad | 67-68, 71-75, 79n |
| Bryn Central | 9 |
| BSC Old Boys | 85 |
| Buchan, Charles | 23, 96n, 132, 217, 226n |
| Buckley, Frank | 21, 204 |

| | |
|---|---|
| Budapest | 48, 67-68, 71, 73-78, 83, 89-90, 95, 96n, 99-100, 102, 104, 109, 111, 120, 161, 222, 230 |
| Bukovi, Márton | 218, 223 |
| Bullock, Norman | 21, 23n, 25, 131, 147, 174, 180n |
| Bunyan, Charlie | 81 |
| Burgess, Herbert | 76 |
| Burnden Park | 34, 37, 40, 44 |
| Burnley Belvedere FC | 6-7, 30 |
| Burnley Express | 30 |
| Burnley FC | 3, 7, 9, 11n, 18-19, 21-22, 24n, 25, 28-29, 35n, 114-115, 141, 143-44, 145n, 148, 153, 170, 186, 229 |
| Burnley, Lancashire | 3-4, 6, 61, 78, 81, 138n, 167, 184, 190, 211 |
| Burnley School League | 142 |
| Burnley Young Conservatives | 211 |
| Bury FC | 147 |
| Busby Babes | 135 |
| Busby, Matt | 135-136, 195-196, 203 |
| | |
| Caine, Paul | 229 |
| Callaghan, Ernie | 176 |
| Cameron, John | 4, 49, 57n, 71-72, 207, 218 |
| Cardiff City | 229 |
| Carnegie Physical Training College | 160 |
| Carter, Raich | 135 |
| Carver, Jesse | 217 |
| Cate, Caesar ten | 55 |
| Catton, J. A. H. | 33, 35n, 81, 96n, 231 |
| Celtic Park | 197, 199-200, 207 |
| Celtic Supporters' Association | 199 |
| Central German FA | 104, 109, 111, 124n |
| Chadwick, Edward | 38, 43-44, 55 |
| Chapman, Herbert | 17, 26, 99, 119, 127, 129, 131-32, 134, 137n, 144, 147, 149, 152, 189, 203, 232 |
| Chapman, Roy | 215, 222 |
| Charles, Alf | 145n |
| Charles, John | 218 |
| Chelsea | 154, 159 |
| Chelsea FC | 33, 38, 46n, 69, 72, 128, 132, 149, 185-86, 212-13 |
| Cheshire County League | 128 |
| Chesterfield FC | 22, 24n, 34 |
| Cheyne, Alex | 128 |
| Chisholm, Jack | 192 |
| Churchill, Winston | 59, 61 |
| Cimera, Robert | 55, 57n |
| Civil Service FC | 57n |
| Cliftonville | 72 |
| Clitheroe | xii, 23n, 79 |
| Clitheroe Central | 9, 11n, 23n |
| Coles, Fred | 38 |
| Collins, Bobby | 200 |
| Colombes | 128, 135 |

| | |
|---|---|
| Concordia Delft | 46n |
| Constantine, Learie | 145n |
| Corinthians | 159 |
| County Ground | 33 |
| Cove-Smith, Dr Ronald | 161 |
| Craven Cottage | 28, 37, 41, 46n, 148, 150, 152, 185 |
| Crawford, Jimmy | 18 |
| Crawford, Ray | 220 |
| Creek, F. N. S. | 149, 159, 161 |
| Cruyff, Johan | 163n |
| Cullin, Mary | 3, 10n |
| Cullis, Stan | 203 |
| Cummings, George | 166, 175-176 |
| Curtis, Harry | 190, 192, 203 |
| Czibor, Zoltán | 217-219 |
| | |
| Dalrymple, Robert | 31 |
| Dean, Dixie | 132 |
| Dean, John | 148-149, 153-154 |
| Delaney, Jimmy | 195 |
| Delfour, "Momo" | 135 |
| Den Haag ADO | 43 |
| Derby County FC | 5, 19, 28, 35 |
| Deutscher FC Prag | 53-54, 57n |
| Diagne, Raoul | 129-130, 137n |
| Dick, Johnny | 30, 53-54 |
| Dickenson, Norman | 114 |
| Dickinson, Syd | 213 |
| Dirsztay, Baron Gedeon | 67, 72-73 |
| Docherty, Tommy | 198-199, 201n |
| Doig, Ned | 5 |
| Dordrecht FC | 38-42, 44, 46n, 47, 50, 55, 110, 144 |
| Dowdells, Alex | 201n |
| Drake, Ted | 166 |
| Dresden | 80n, 104, 109-110, 112-113, 117-120, 123, 125n, 128, 212, 231 |
| Duckworth, Teddy | 30, 85, 90-91, 95, 139 |
| Dugdale, Jimmy | 224 |
| Duncan, Scott | 178 |
| Dundee FC | 28, 196, 199 |
| Dunn, Jimmy | 16 |
| Dusseldorf | 175 |
| Dutch Football Association | 39, 43 |
| Dutch national football team | 38-39, 43-44, 46n, 55, 88, 97, 140, 204, 220 |
| Dynamo Moscow | 185, 190 |
| | |
| Easson, Jimmy | 212-213, 215 |
| Edelston, Joe | 149, 154 |
| Edinburgh | 196 |
| Edwards, Duncan | 213 |
| Eintracht Frankfurt | 86 |

| | |
|---|---|
| Egypt national football team | 95 |
| England | 100, 106, 112-114, 117, 123-124, 128, 130, 132, 140-141, 144, 148, 151-152, 154, 167, 169, 171, 173-174, 186, 231-232 |
| England national football team | 72, 87, 109, 115, 121-123, 127, 129, 133-134, 137, 143, 167, 175-176, 180n, 186, 189, 193n, 199, 205-206, 212, 214-219, 221-223, 225, 227n |
| England national rugby team | 161 |
| English, Jack | 178 |
| ENSA | 183, 185, 188n |
| Evans, Bobby | 199, 222 |
| Everton FC | 4, 33, 37-38, 46n, 49, 57n, 70, 81, 123, 132, 200, 218 |
| | |
| FA Cup | 8, 13, 19, 23n, 31, 35n, 36n |
| Fässler, Paul | 88-89, 97n |
| FC Aarau | 89, 90, 96n |
| FC Basel | 97n |
| FC Bern | 89, 90, 97n, 139 |
| FC Biel | 89 |
| FC Blue Stars Zürich | 86, 90 |
| FC Luzern | 86, 88 |
| FC Nordstern Basel | 86, 90, 94 |
| FIFA | 214-215 |
| Feldmann, Gyula | 75, 77 |
| Ferencváros | 55, 68, 71-75, 77, 79n, 101, 105n, 129 |
| Ferrier, Bob | 189 |
| Filbert Street | 215 |
| First Vienna FC | 57n, 61, 137n |
| First World War | ix, xi, 31, 63, 65n, 78, 83, 87, 99, 107, 127, 223, 232 |
| Fischera, Adolf | 47 |
| FK Austria | 50, 153 |
| Flamengo | 91 |
| Fleming, Harold | 33, 36n |
| Fletcher, Paul | 229 |
| Fogl, Károly | 77 |
| Football Association (FA) | 28, 37-38, 62, 82-83, 96n, 101, 142-143, 154, 157-159, 168, 176, 183, 186, 189-190, 214-215, 229 |
| Football League | 3, 13, 25, 28-29, 31, 35n, 36n, 39, 52, 81, 101, 137n, 145n, 147, 166, 168, 176, 183, 186, 190, 215, 229 |
| Football National War Fund | 82-83 |
| Footballer's Battalion | 63 |
| Fox, Norman | 10, 29, 82, 96n, 109, 112, 124n, 128, 132, 135, 137n, 180n, 216, 226n |
| France | ix, 76, 127, 136, 139, 178, 183-184, 186 |
| France, national football team | 92, 135, 138n, 201n |
| French Air Force | 183 |
| French Football Association | 186 |
| Frontz, Antal | 99 |
| Fryer, Jack | 28, 35n |
| Fulham FC | 22, 28-32, 35n, 36n, 37, 41, 43, 46n, 84, 130, 144, 147-155, 156n, 160, 165, 167, 172, 205, 231 |

| | |
|---|---|
| Fulham Rotary Club | 152 |
| Fylde | 44 |
| | |
| Gallacher, Hughie | 132 |
| Gannon, Barney | 72, 79n |
| Garbutt, William | 31 |
| Gaskell, Arthur | 85 |
| Gaskell, Ted | 205 |
| Geneva | 85, 91-92 |
| German Football Association | 107-8 |
| German Olympic team | 54-55, 59 |
| Germany | 127, 132, 142-143 |
| Germany, national football team | 134, 220-224 |
| Gibbons, Jackie | 191-192, 203-207 |
| Gillingham FC | 190 |
| Ging, József | 77 |
| Glanville, Brian | 46n, 53, 189, 212, 232 |
| Glasgow Celtic | 14, 191, 194-200, 201n, 222 |
| Glasgow Rangers | 27, 33, 35n, 49, 68-69, 197, 199-200, 201n |
| Goldie, Willie | 28-29, 35n |
| Goodwin, Jackie | 205 |
| Gothenberg | 190 |
| Grabowski, Jürgen | 220 |
| Graham, Len | 158 |
| Graubart, Bernhard | 57n |
| Grasshoppers | 85 |
| Great Britain Olympic team | 54, 87 |
| Great Harwood FC | 7 |
| Great War see under First World War | |
| Green, Geoffrey | 38, 82 |
| Greenwood, Ron | 68, 71, 191, 204-205, 207 |
| Grey, Sir Edward | 61 |
| Griffin Park | 190-192, 203, 206 |
| Grimsdell, Arthur | 159 |
| Guthrie, Jimmy | 181n |
| Guttman, Bela | 95 |
| | |
| Haan, Arie | 220 |
| Haarlem HFC | 38, 42 |
| Hädicke, Johannes | 104, 109, 116-117, 120 |
| Hamburg | 90, 116 |
| Hamburger SV | 114 |
| Hamilton, Robert C. | 29, 31, 35n |
| Hampden Park | 140 |
| Handley, George | 85 |
| Hardman, Harold | 57n |
| Harkness, Jack | 196, 201n |
| Haughney, Mike | 200, 201n |
| Haworth, Bob | 28 |
| Haycock, Fred | 180n |
| Heart of Midlothian (Hearts) | 28, 79n |

| | |
|---|---|
| Heck, C. | 42 |
| Hewitt, Charles | 221 |
| Heywood FC | 8 |
| Hidegkuti, Nándor | 217-219 |
| Hiden, Rodolphe | 136 |
| Highbury | 129, 132, 140, 144 |
| Hill, Jack | 141, 143 |
| Hill, Jimmy | 204-205 |
| Hill, Raymond H. | 171 |
| Hilton, Harold | 44-45 |
| Hodgson, John | 101-2 |
| Hoeness, Dieter | 220 |
| Hogan family | 2-3, 10n, 78, 156n, 184, 190 |
| Hogan, Cornelius | 11n |
| Hogan, Evelyn (née Coates) | 34, 40, 44, 50, 59-62, 78, 85, 95, 99, 156n, 184, 190 |
| Hogan, Frank | 95, 144 |
| Hogan, Joseph | 50, 59, 95, 128, 139, 144, 145n, 185 |
| Hogan, Mary | 59, 95, 128, 177 |
| Hogan, Margaret (née O'Donnall) 1, 179n | |
| Holland see under Netherlands | |
| Holmes, Bob | 23n, 72-73, 79n |
| Honved | 68 |
| Houghton, Eric | 175, 212-215, 224 |
| Howcroft, J. T. | 9, 39-41, 46n, 47 |
| Huddersfield Town | 147 |
| Hughes, Billy | 37, 57n |
| Hulme, Joe | 204 |
| Hungária FC | 71, 104 |
| Hungarian Football Association | 74, 216 |
| Hungarian Olympic team | 53-56 |
| Hungary | 67, 76, 81, 83, 99, 143, 211 |
| Hungary national football team | 68, 71-72, 85, 95, 189, 199, 205, 207, 215-222 |
| Hunt, K. R. G. | 87, 159 |
| Hunter, Billy | 37, 44, 95 |
| Hurst, Geoff | 218, 220 |
| Hussak, Ludwig | 54-55, 57n |
| | |
| ILK | 74 |
| Ipswich Town | 176, 220 |
| Irving, Dan | 82 |
| Italy | 31, 74-76, 144, 148, 185, 212 |
| Italy national football team | 71, 88, 92, 114, 169 |
| Italian Olympic team | 55 |
| Iverson, Bob | 171, 176 |
| | |
| Jack, David | 85, 90, 100-101, 119, 127, 134, 140 |
| Jackson, Alec | 16 |
| Jackson, Archie | 35n |
| Jackson, Jimmy | 26-27 |
| Jeny, Rudolf | 95, 103 |
| Jobey, George | 21, 178 |

| | |
|---|---|
| James, Alex | 16, 99, 129, 204 |
| Johnston, Harry | 217 |
| Jones, Charlie | 203 |
| Jones, T. G. | 70 |
| Jongbloed, Jan | 220 |
| Jordan, Auguste | 136, 149 |
| Joy, Bernard | 14-15, 26, 203 |
| | |
| Kainberger, Edouard | 167, 169 |
| Kalocsai, Dr Géza | 218 |
| Kane, Bob | 190 |
| Kedves, János | 221 |
| Kelly, Bob | 148, 195, 200 |
| Kennedy, Fred | 128-129 |
| Kerr, Albert | 178 |
| Kertész, Vilmos | 73-74, 77, 89-90 |
| Key, George | 69 |
| Kirwan, Jack | 57n |
| Klein, A. | 42 |
| Klein, C. | 42 |
| Kleve | 43, 46n |
| Kohlmayer, Werner | 224, 226n |
| Kohut, Vilmos | 101 |
| Konrád, Jenö | 76, 104 |
| Konrád, Kálmán | 69, 73, 76-77, 104 |
| Koopman, F. | 42 |
| Koopman, H. | 42 |
| Kunz, Ernst | 167 |
| Kurpiel, Ladislaus | 57n |
| Kürschner, Dori | 86, 90-91, 94, 131, 230 |
| | |
| Lamb, Sammy | 85 |
| Lambert, Jack | 148 |
| Lancashire | xii, 1, 22, 25, 30, 50, 114, 190 |
| Lancashire Amateur League | 7 |
| Lancashire FA | 8 |
| Langley, Ambrose | 147 |
| Lausanne | 89, 95, 105n, 136, 139, 231 |
| Lausanne-Sports | 90, 95, 136, 139, 141, 143, 160, 231 |
| Lawrence, Jimmy | 57n, 122 |
| Lawton, Tommy | 189, 207 |
| Lazio | 200 |
| Leadbetter, Jimmy | 220 |
| Ledgerton, Terry | 205, 207 |
| Leeds | 160, 167 |
| Leeds City | 147 |
| Leeds United | 31, 38, 149, 166, 224 |
| Leicester City | 176, 215 |
| Leipzig | 231 |
| Lewis, Reg | 155, 177 |
| Lévy, Jean-Bernard | 127-129, 134-136 |

| | |
|---|---|
| Lincoln City FC | 22 |
| Liverpool | 4, 59, 62, 81, 96n, 226n |
| Liverpool FC | 19, 28, 35n, 68, 81, 141, 145n, 214, 224 |
| London | 13, 26, 28, 30, 35n, 61, 69, 72, 79n, 83, 94, 96n, 127, 129-130, 137n, 140, 143, 149, 153, 155, 157, 184, 190, 192, 199, 212, 216 |
| London Casuals | 57n |
| Lotsy, Dirk | 38, 42 |
| Lotsy, Karel | 55 |
| Luton Town | 191 |
| Lutjens, Guus | 43 |
| McAuley, Pat | 200 |
| McCracken, Billy | 57n |
| MacDonald, Billy | 19 |
| MacDonald, Malcolm | 191, 196 |
| McEwan, Marshall | 39 |
| McGrory, Jimmy | 196, 201n |
| McIntyre, James | 147-148, 152 |
| M'Kellar, James | 207 |
| McMenemy, John | 188n |
| McMullan, Jimmy | 16, 165-166, 176, 179n |
| McParland, Peter | 74, 215-216, 222, 230 |
| McPhail, John | 200 |
| McWilliam, Peter | 57n |
| Madden, John | 14 |
| "Magical Magyars" | 68, 230 |
| Magnall, Ernest | 6 |
| Maine Road | 141 |
| Major, Ernest | 161 |
| Makant, Angus | 44 |
| Manchester | 4 |
| Manchester Central FC | 23n |
| Manchester City FC | 5, 8, 141, 165 |
| Manchester United | 94, 196, 203, 213, 224, 229 |
| Mándi, Gyula | 95 |
| Mandl, Franz | 169 |
| Manor Ground | 27 |
| Mansfield Town | 128 |
| Manuel, M. | 139 |
| Martin, Jackie | 173-174, 180n |
| Massie, Alex | 171, 175-176 |
| Matthews, Ernie | 174 |
| Matthews, Stanley | 201n |
| MAV Gepgyar | 77 |
| Mayer, Gueleve | 145n |
| Mbarek, Larbi ben | 201n |
| Meadow Lane | 199 |
| Mears, Gus | 69 |
| Meisl, Hugo | 32, 47-53, 59-61, 71, 76, 97n, 129, 140, 143, 159, 180n, 230-231 |

| | |
|---|---|
| Meisl, Willy | 48-49, 51, 60, 72-73, 76, 91 |
| Melchior, Ernst | 206 |
| Mercer, Joe | 225, 226n |
| Meredith, Billy | 5, 8, 21, 23n |
| Merz, Robert | 5-55, 57n |
| Middlesbrough FC | 49 |
| Middleton, Bob | 79n |
| Miller, Willy | 198 |
| Mills, Freddie | 221 |
| Millwall FC | 221 |
| Molineux | 203-204 |
| Molnár, György | 89 |
| Montpellier | 138n |
| Morris, Peter | 165-166 |
| Morrison, Willie | 28 |
| Morton, Alan | 16 |
| Morton, Harry | 166 |
| Motherwell FC | 198, 207 |
| MTK FC | 67-69, 71-78, 79n, 90, 99-100, 205, 223 |
| Müller, Alois | 54-55, 57n |
| Müller, Gerd | 220 |
| Murphy, Jimmy | 135-136, 180n |
| Murray, Bill | 135 |
| | |
| Nausch, Walter | 144, 205, 218 |
| Needham, Ernest | 17, 19, 21, 69 |
| Nelson FC | 8-9, 21-22, 24n, 230 |
| Nelson, Lancashire | 1 |
| Nemes, Sándor | 77 |
| Nerz, Otto | 142, 167 |
| Netherlands (Holland) | 81, 87, 143 |
| Neubauer, Leopold | 57n |
| Neuchâtel | 91 |
| Newcastle United | 26-27, 31, 37, 46n, 49, 57n, 191 |
| Newton, Frank | 147-148, 153-154 |
| Nîmes, football club | 128 |
| Noll, Otto | 57n |
| Norddeutscher FV | 59 |
| Normansell, Fred | 177, 212-216, 222 |
| Norris, Sir Henry | 147 |
| Norrköpping | 190 |
| Northern Ireland football team | 222 |
| Northwich Victoria | 128 |
| Norwegian Olympic team | 55 |
| Norwich City | 150, 152 |
| Notts County | 39, 45, 46n, 154, 199, 207 |
| Nürnberg FC | 73 |
| | |
| Oberhauser, August | 94, 97n |
| Ocwirk, Ernst | 99, 206-207 |
| O'Donnall family | 1 |

| | |
|---|---|
| O'Donnell, Frank | 176 |
| Oldham Athletic | 31 |
| Old Trafford | 70 |
| Oran, Algeria | 186 |
| Orkney Islands | 188n |
| Orth, György | 73-77, 89, 95, 197, 223 |
| Oympic Games | 47, 54, 85-87, 90, 93, 95, 139, 168-169 |
| | |
| Pache, Robert | 139 |
| Parc de Princes | 129 |
| Paris | 91, 128, 135, 139, 184, 196 |
| Partick Thistle | 201n |
| Pataki, Mahály | 55 |
| Paterson, George | 191, 196, 200 |
| Pegg, David | 213 |
| Pele | 201n |
| Pentland, Fred | 59 |
| Peru, national football team | 168-169 |
| Phoenix, Arthur | 128 |
| Pisa | 74 |
| Plattko, Ferenc | 89 |
| Platzer, Peter | 138n |
| Plymouth Argyle FC | 85, 150 |
| Pollitz, Aron | 94 |
| Port Vale FC | 27 |
| Portsmouth FC | 134-135, 165, 181n |
| Poyser, George | 204 |
| Pozzo, Vittorio | 70, 169 |
| Prague | 14, 30, 48 |
| Preston, Lancashire | 4 |
| Preston North End FC | 19, 23n, 25, 27, 72, 99 |
| Prince Albert Victor | 35n |
| Pulver, Hans | 88, 94, 97n |
| Puskás, Ferenc | 68, 163n, 219-220 |
| Pym, Dick | 90 |
| | |
| Queen's Park | 13-14 |
| Quick Nijmegen | 43 |
| Quixall, Albert | 216 |
| | |
| Racing Club de Paris | 127-129, 130, 134-139 |
| Rae, Joe | 200 |
| Ramsey, Alf | 218-220 |
| Ramseyer, Rudolf | 88-89, 94, 97n |
| Rapid Vienna | 88 |
| Rappan, Karl | 93, 131, 139 |
| Råsunda stadium | 54 |
| Ranson, Harry | 72 |
| Raynor, George | 23n, 25, 31, 60, 77, 131, 173, 190, 204, 217, 226n |
| Reading FC | 30, 148, 153 |
| Reep, Charles | 203-204, 207 |

| | |
|---|---|
| Revie, Don | 205 |
| Reynolds, William | 87 |
| Rheims | 186 |
| Rinder, Fred | 168-170, 175-177, 212 |
| Roberts, Charlie | 21, 23n, 70, 207 |
| Roberts, Ken O. | 215 |
| Robertson, Jacky Tait | 68-69, 71-72, 77 |
| Robinson, Billy | 37 |
| Rochdale | 44 |
| Rochdale Town | 9, 11n, 21 |
| Roker Park | 138n |
| Rome | 200 |
| Ross, Harry | 28 |
| Ross, Nick | 19 |
| Rous, Stanley | 143, 154, 159-161, 179n, 183, 231 |
| Rowe, Arthur | 15 |
| Royal Air Force | 183, 203 |
| Rudolfshügel | 77 |
| Ruhleben POW Camp | 63 |
| Rumbold, Karl | 55 |
| | |
| St Bede's College, Manchester | 4-6, 10n, 230-231 |
| St Bernard's FC | 28 |
| St Gallen | 85 |
| Samuel, Jean-Claude | 186 |
| Sands, Percy | 26-27 |
| Sarajevo | 61, 72 |
| Sárosi, György | 71-72 |
| SC Wacker Wien | 134 |
| Schaffer, Alfred | 73, 75, 77 |
| Schlosser, Imre | 73-75, 77, 79n, 197 |
| Schön, Helmut | 160, 220 |
| Scotland, national football team | 68, 127, 149, 221 |
| Scottish Football Association | 99, 195 |
| Sebes, Gusztáv | 215, 217, 222 |
| Second World War | 73, 195, 224 |
| Serbia | 61 |
| Servette FC | 85, 95, 139 |
| Settle, Jimmy | 57n |
| Sewell, Jackie | 216, 224 |
| Sexton, Dave | 94 |
| Sharp, Jimmy | 28 |
| Sharp, John | 57n |
| Sharpe, Ivan | 101, 117, 122, 231 |
| Shearman, Montague | 27 |
| Sheffield United FC | 19, 23n, 71, 154 |
| Sheffield Wednesday | 191 |
| Shell, Frank | 171-173, 218, 230 |
| Shepherd, Albert | 37, 46n |
| Shires, Edward | 68 |
| Simmeringer SC | 57n |

Sims, Nigel 224
Sindelar, Matthias 121, 136n, 153, 173, 207
Sirrel, Jimmy 199
Sissons, John 218
Skene, Leslie 31
Sleeuwenhoek, John 225
Smith, Bert 87, 90, 96n
Smith, Joe 44
Southampton FC 145n, 205
Southern League 49
Spanish national football team 85
Sparta Prague 104
Sportplatz Spitalacker 97n
Sports Club Rapid 57n
Staal, Tonny 38
Stamford Bridge 69, 129, 132-133, 148-149, 212
Starling, Ronnie 176-177, 180n
Steele, Freddie 221
Stephenson, Clem 21
Stienmetz, Klement 169
Stockhill, Reg 130, 137n
Stockholm 47, 53
Stockport County FC 7, 147, 171
Stoneyhurst College 23n, 79n
Street, Ernie 72
Studnicka, Johann 57n
Stuttard, Jack 28
Stuttgart 175
Sudell, Major William 19
Sunderland AFC 5, 135, 148
Sunderman, ___ 42
SV Amateure Wien 103
Swatosh, Jakob 57n
Sweden 54, 94
Sweden, national football team 189
Swindon Town FC 33, 34, 36n
Swiss Football Association 88
Swiss Olympic team 86, 90, 94
Switzerland 84-85, 90-91, 96n, 99, 139, 143
Switzerland national football team 30, 68, 86-89, 93-95
Syrvet, André 95, 139
Szabó, Peter 77
Szegedi, Peter 76, 80n

Tandler, Johann 103
Tassin, André 129-130
Taylor, Rogan 68
Tekusch, Karl 57n
Third Lanark AC 28, 187, 196
Thorpe, Jimmy 135
Tilson, Fred 165

| | |
|---|---|
| Titkos, Pál | 71 |
| Threlfall, Fred | 31 |
| Törekvés | 76, 90 |
| Tottenham Hotspur (Spurs) | 15, 32, 37, 49, 53, 57n, 71, 191, 206-207, 218 |
| Toulouse, Cyril | 192 |
| Townley, William | 85, 90-91, 94, 97n |
| Traneberg | 55 |
| Tully, Charles | 196-200 |
| Tunbridge Wells | 151 |
| Turf Moor | 3, 6-8, 18, 25, 29, 35n, 153 |
| | |
| Újpest FC | 71 |
| USA national football team | 189 |
| Urania Genève Sport | 89 |
| Uruguay national football team | 94 |
| | |
| VAC Budapest | 75 |
| Vasas SC | 74 |
| Vaughan, Cardinal Herbert | 4 |
| Veitch, Colin | 57n |
| Vernon, Leslie | 229 |
| Vienna | 32, 47-53, 56, 59-61, 67, 72, 76-77, 83-86, 88, 90, 95, 96n, 128, 132-134, 136, 160, 167-168, 217, 231 |
| Villa Park | 28, 166, 170, 176, 183, 215-216, 221-223 |
| Villanueva, Alejandro | 168 |
| Vizard, Ted | 44, 90 |
| | |
| WAC Austria | 136 |
| Wacker München | 73 |
| Wales, national football team | 135, 203 |
| Walker, Gordon | 62, 96n |
| Walker's Tobacco Company | 81, 84, 96n |
| Wall, Sir Frederick | 63, 82-84, 132, 142-143, 157, 203 |
| Wallace, Jock | 33 |
| Wardrope, Willie | 28, 30, 35n |
| Warren, Harry | 186 |
| Watford FC | 31 |
| Webb, Clifford | 214-215 |
| Weber, Albert | 54 |
| Weber, Franz | 57n |
| Wembley | 165, 189, 205-206, 215-218, 220 |
| West Bromwich Albion | 20, 135, 165, 191 |
| West Ham United | 94, 191, 205, 218 |
| Wharton, Arthur | 10n |
| Whelan, Billy | 213 |
| Wislaw Krakow | 135 |
| White, Jack | 38 |
| Whittaker, John | 212 |
| Whittaker, Spence (Spen) | 18, 21-22, 203 |
| Whittaker, Tom | 129, 159 |

| | |
|---|---|
| Wiener AC | 57n, 84, 96n |
| Wiener AF | 57n |
| Wiener Amateur SV | 57n, 60 |
| Wiener Sport Club | 57n |
| Willing, Referee | 55 |
| Wilson, A. N. | 141 |
| Wilson, Andy | 128 |
| Wilson, Jonathan | 49, 57n, 96n, 217, 226n, 230 |
| Wilson, Stanley | 161 |
| Winterbottom, Walter | 162, 217 |
| Wolverhampton Wanderers | 159, 204 |
| Woodward, Vivien | 57n |
| Woolwich Arsenal, see under Arsenal FC | |
| World Cup | 99, 143, 148, 223, 226n |
| Worthing | 183-184 |
| Wrexham AFC | 215 |
| Wright, Billy | 206, 219 |
| *Wunderteam* | 63, 68, 84, 132, 140, 173, 205, 230 |
| | |
| Yeovil Town | 200 |
| York | 23n |
| Young Boys FC | 84-85, 87-89, 96n, 97n |
| Young, Percy | 37 |
| | |
| Zwaluwen VV | 39 |
| Zsák, Károly | 77 |
| Zsengellér, Gyula | 71 |
| Zürich | 85, 91, 143 |

www.ingramcontent.com/pod-product-compliance
Lightning Source LLC
Chambersburg PA
CBHW070420010526
44118CB00014B/1840